The Parent-School Board Feuds

The Parent-School Board Feuds

Essential Steps by Parents to Improve Schools

Gerard Giordano

ROWMAN & LITTLEFIELD
Lanham • Boulder • New York • London

Published by Rowman & Littlefield
An imprint of The Rowman & Littlefield Publishing Group, Inc.
4501 Forbes Boulevard, Suite 200, Lanham, Maryland 20706
www.rowman.com

86-90 Paul Street, London EC2A 4NE, United Kingdom

Copyright © 2025 by Gerard Giordano

All rights reserved. No part of this book may be reproduced in any form or by any electronic or mechanical means, including information storage and retrieval systems, without written permission from the publisher, except by a reviewer who may quote passages in a review.

British Library Cataloguing in Publication Information Available

Library of Congress Cataloging-in-Publication Data Available

ISBN 9781475874020 (cloth) | ISBN 9781475874037 (pbk.) | ISBN 9781475874044 (epub)

Parents inspired this book. Their courage, enthusiasm, and absolute commitment to their children has transformed education. This book is dedicated to them.

Contents

Preface: Who Started the Feuds?   ix
Acknowledgments   xiii

1	The School Library Feuds	1
2	The School Masking Feuds	11
3	The Parenting Feuds	23
4	The Teachers Union Feuds	33
5	The Testing Feuds	43
6	The Web Filter Feuds	57
7	The School AI Feuds	69
8	The School Bus Feuds	79
9	The Student Safety Feuds	91
10	The School Funding Feuds	101
11	The School Athletics Feuds	111
12	The Social-Emotional Learning Feuds	123

References   135
Index   183
About the Author   189

Preface
Who Started the Feuds?

[Although I was] in a public place . . . [at] an open [school board] meeting . . . and invited to be there [I was arrested].—Parent Jon Tigge, 2023

An Ohio woman sued after a school board president told her to "zip it."—The Wall Street Journal Editorial Board, 2022

[School boards should] put the interests of their community before their own political agendas.—Fight for Schools Director Ian Prior, 2022

Parents know the needs of their children best.—School Board Candidate Tanya Hardaker, 2022

Parents wanted information about their children. They could gather it easily when their children were at neighborhood playgrounds, athletic fields, or places of worship. After all, they personally could observe them in these situations.

Parents could not observe their children when they were at school. They had to go through teachers and school boards for information.

The teachers were eager to provide information about students. They summarized it on report cards. They embellished it with details during parent-teacher conferences.

The school boards were equally eager to share information about students. They provided district-wide data on websites, in media reports, and at public meetings.

The parents expected that they would be informed about school board decisions affecting their children. During the COVID-19 pandemic, they learned about an extraordinary decision: the school boards planned to replace face-to-face classes with online classes.

Many parents were terrified of the deadly virus. They did not want their children to contract it. They assumed their children would be protected if they stayed at home and took online classes. They were pleased with this plan.

Not all parents were pleased with the pandemic plan. Some were critical. They worried their children would struggle during online classes because they did not have the optimal technology or Internet access. Those parents who worked away from their homes worried about the practicality of securing supervision and the expense of arranging childcare.

The enthusiastic and the critical parents had different reactions to online classes. However, both groups acknowledged that these classes would have a major benefit: they would give them an unprecedented opportunity to observe their children during school days. They could observe firsthand the instruction their children received, the testing they completed, and the classroom learning materials on which they relied.

Some of the parents were pleased by their observations. They were especially pleased by lessons focused on gender, race, ethnicity, sexual orientation, and religion. They believed these lessons were bolstering their children's social and emotional growth.

Other parents observed the same lessons but reacted quite differently. They questioned whether those lessons were appropriate. They objected to the lessons themselves, the learning materials connected to them, and the tests that measured student achievement. They wanted resolutions for these problems.

The parents eventually sent their children back into face-to-face classes. Some were still upset by the issues that they had detected during the school closures. However, they identified other issues and complained about them. They had complaints about athletics, libraries, immunizations, technology, discipline, student safety, school bus transportation, charter school funding, and social-emotional learning.

The disgruntled parents wished to make fundamental changes to the schools. But other parents wished to keep schools mostly as they had been. Unable to agree, they asked their local school boards to step in and settle the disputes.

Many school boards declined the offer. They did not wish to get too closely involved with either faction of feuding parents. They tried to persuade them to compromise.

Some school boards took a different tack. They were eager to get involved in the feuds. They selected parents with whom they agreed, empowered them, and acted on their recommendations. They were pleased when the empowered parents became ebullient.

The disempowered parents had a different reaction. They were disappointed. They asked the school boards to reconsider their recommendations. When they were ignored by the school boards, they tried to get their attention:

they wrote newspaper editorials, posted online comments, staged rallies, and interrupted their meetings.

The disempowered parents were no match for the school boards. They resolved to find allies. They contacted journalists, politicians, businesspeople, and the leaders of professional associations. With their support, they became much more formidable.

FEATURES

This book focuses on parents. It chronicles the scholastic feuds they had with each other, local school boards, and state school boards. It examines their extraordinary accomplishments during these feuds.

The chapters in this book are presented in a special format: they rely on the case method. They pair a noneducational problem with an educational one. They then challenge readers to consider whether the solution to one problem reveals the solution to the other.

SERIES

The Parent-School Board Feuds is part of a series. Earlier books in the series included *Parents and Textbooks, Parents and School Tech, Parents and School Violence,* and *Parents and Marginalized Students.* These books were published by Rowman and Littlefield Education.

AUDIENCE

This book is for a general audience. It will engage parents and school board members. It also will engage teachers, school administrators, educational professionals, and college students from a wide range of academic disciplines.

Acknowledgments

This book is part of a series about the impact that parents have had on education. I could not have written it without the advice of my remarkable editor Tom Koerner. Tom's advice has been gentle but persistent . . . and always insightful.

Chapter 1

The School Library Feuds

[The attempts to ban books during] the last two years have been exhausting, frightening, outrage inducing.

—Director of the *American Library Association's Office for Intellectual Freedom* Deborah Caldwell-Stone, 2023

Shelves have been left barren . . . because of . . . [repressive] school library regulations.

—Journalist Nirvi Shah, 2023

Those who might cheer specific edits . . . should consider how the power to rewrite books might be used in the hands of those who do not share their values.

—*PEN America* CEO Suzanne Nossel, 2023

The important issues . . . impacting . . . education . . . [do not include] the books in my library.

—High School Media Specialist Ginger Brengle, 2023

> National security leaders allowed foreign aeronautical balloons to pass through American airspace. They believed that they posed little risk to the nation. However, they had to deal with critics, who demanded that they shoot them down.
>
> School librarians acquired books about socially marginalized groups. They believed that they posed little risk to students. However, they had to deal with critics, who demanded that they remove them from their shelves.

AERIAL SURVEILLANCE

US national security leaders were committed to protecting Americans. They had an annual budget of more than 800 billion dollars for this mission. They spent a good deal of this money gathering data about potential weaknesses and threats.

The national security leaders gathered vast amounts of data. They conducted aerial surveillance of the entire country to ensure that the military infrastructure was sound and secure. They also arranged for aerial surveillance of other countries. They wished to determine if those countries were planning actions that would damage the United States.

In earlier eras, the national security leaders had used balloons to conduct aerial surveillance. However, they later replaced the balloons with special spy aircraft, spy satellites, and spy drones. They used these devices for communication eavesdropping, radar monitoring, high-resolution photography, and chemical detection.

The national security leaders had confidence in their aerospace and aeronautical spy technology. However, they never doubted that the leaders of hostile nations had equally sophisticated technology. They wished to detect their devices, discover how they operated, and block them.

The national security leaders had advanced equipment to detect aircraft, drones, and satellites. They then used this technology to disable or obstruct the devices that posed threats.

The national security devoted hardly any time to tracking spy balloons. After all, they did not have spy balloons in their equipment arsenal. They doubted that other countries had them in their arsenals.

The national security leaders had no reason to believe that their policy on balloon monitoring would ever be challenged. However, they changed their minds in the winter of 2023.

Members of the public had detected a large high-altitude object sailing over Montana. With the aid of telescopes, they could discern that it was a balloon with a large piece of equipment tethered to it. They captured images and posted them online.

Tens of thousands of people were intrigued by the object. They speculated that it was a Chinese spy balloon. They were sure that it posed a threat. They wanted national security leaders to shoot it down.

The national security leaders played down the threat from the balloon over Montana. However, they could not reassure skeptical Montanans, persons who had viewed online images, and journalists. Alarmist editorialists at the *Wall Street Journal* asked the question that their readers were asking: Why hadn't the balloon been shot down as soon as it had been detected?

The national security leaders met with elected officials in the White House and Congress. After those meetings, they announced that they would be dealing differently with the Montana balloon.

The national security leaders explained that they had a new plan of action. They intended to shoot down the Montana balloon. However, they would wait until it had left American airspace. They explained that they wished to avoid any collateral damage from falling debris.

The national security leaders added a caveat. They had a new policy for dealing with all foreign balloons. They would require that their sponsors obtain permission to send them through American airspace. They would shoot down any balloons that did not have permission.

Enthusiasts

US national security leaders had not detected any problems from foreign balloons. For this reason, they had ignored them. However, they reconsidered this policy because of the publicity surrounding an alleged Chinese spy balloon.

The national security leaders announced that they had been using a case-by-case approach to assess threats from foreign balloons. However, they were ready to replace that approach with a zero-tolerance approach. They hoped that elected officials in the White House and Congress would be pleased by this announcement.

The elected officials were pleased. They were even more pleased after the military began to shoot down balloons and gather the debris for forensic analysis. They later admitted that all the balloons they shot down had "benign purposes." Nonetheless, they insisted that the new balloon protocols were appropriate, useful, and long overdue.

Skeptics

The national security leaders wondered how journalists were responding to their new policy. They worried about those journalists who had been fanning the public's emotions with their alarmist reporting.

The alarmist journalists were still upset. They were convinced that the national security leaders, who earlier had been cavalier about intruding international balloons, had now become cavalier about shooting them down.

The Wall Street Journal's editorial writers had been scornful of the original policy. In an editorial entitled *Biden and the Chinese Spy Balloon*, they attached a byline asking: Why did he wait so long to order the airspace intruder shot down?

These editorialists were equally scornful of the "shoot down" policy. In an editorial entitled *Mystery Invasion Object of the Week*, they mocked the new policy as an effort to suppress public furor rather than raise national security.

SCHOLASTIC SURVEILLANCE

School boards ensured that school libraries were stocked. However, they rarely became involved in this task. They delegated it to educational administrators.

Like the school boards, the educational administrators delegated the task. They assigned it to their school librarians. They provided them with funds and told them to use their professional expertise to purchase suitable materials.

The school librarians used their funds to acquire printed magazines, books, and reference materials. They made sure that they had shelves on which to display these resources and desks at which students could examine them.

The school librarians also purchased digital materials. They acquired e-books, e-magazines, and subscriptions to digital sites. They then acquired computerized devices on which students could read these resources.

The school librarians had to decide how to allocate their funds between printed and digital reading materials. They knew that their students overwhelmingly preferred digital materials. However, they wanted to surround them with printed materials as well.

The school librarians hoped their students would examine the printed books, become intrigued, and then borrow them. They tried to lure them with books that were literary award winners, critics' favorites, or video-game spinoffs. They eventually had to admit that they had only been somewhat effective with these strategies.

The school librarians had another strategy with which to make printed materials more enticing to their students. They picked books that would appeal to their social concerns, emotional insecurities, and school-related fears.

The school librarians were sure that many students feared that they could become marginalized because of race, ethnicity, religion, economic status, or gender. They acquired books that portrayed characters who had been marginalized and who were trying to deal with it.

The school librarians had hoped that students would be enticed by books about marginalized youths. However, they were disappointed when students still showed little interest in them.

As an example, a librarian at a Westport Connecticut high school acquired three novels about characters exploring gender identity. This librarian reported that one of these books, *This Book Is Gay*, had been checked out five times over a several-year period. The other two books, *Gender Queer* and *Flamer*, had been checked out a single time each.

The students at the Westport Connecticut school did not seem to be paying a great deal of attention to the books in their library. Neither did their parents. The parents had been invited to examine the library's books and to request reviews of any that they felt were inappropriate. During a 20-year span, only once had a parent requested a review.

School librarians across the country had experiences that were like those of the Westport librarian. After acquiring books about socially marginalized characters, they conceded that their students showed little interest in them. However, they eventually did detect a change—not among the students but among their parents.

More and more parents were becoming interested in library books. In fact, some of them were becoming irate about them. They confronted the school librarians about those books that featured marginalized groups. They scolded them for acquiring, displaying, and circulating them.

The irate parents told the school librarians to remove the objectionable books from their shelves. They were pleased with those who cooperated. They were furious with those who were defiant.

The defiant librarians explained that they had been professionally trained to select books that would interest and benefit students. They believed that books about marginalized groups had these characteristics. They intended to retain those books, display them, and make them available to students.

Some parents had confidence in the defiant librarians. Others were unhappy with them. Those who were unhappy met with their local school boards. They asked them to get directly involved with the school libraries.

Some school boards acquiesced to the unhappy parents. They reviewed the librarians' policies for acquiring books. However, many of them then took the side of their librarians.

The parents who wished to regulate the school libraries were unhappy when they did not get support from their local school boards. However, they did not give up. They asked their state boards of education for their support.

In Florida, the State Board of Education was responsible for 69 school districts. It comprised members who were aware of the turmoil that parents had raised about the school libraries in many of those districts. They were not surprised when some of these parents came to them.

The unhappy parents presented their concerns to the Florida State Board of Education. They gave its members details about their feuds with the school librarians. They also gave them details about their feuding with the principals, superintendents, and local school boards members who had supported the librarians.

The state board members assured the parents that they would protect their right to stay informed about the books being acquired, displayed, and circulated at school. They also intended to protect their right to request a review of any book to see if it was appropriate. They enacted a new rule to ensure that school districts respected those rights.

The school librarians followed the new State Board of Education rule. They then scheduled district reviews of books that parents challenged. They pledged to take those books off their shelves if the district reviews found them inappropriate. They intended to keep them on their shelves if the district reviews found them appropriate.

Enthusiasts

School librarians had felt the pressure from parents to remove books that contained damaging misinformation. Many of them had succumbed to that pressure. After they had removed the books, they wondered how parents were responding.

Many parents supported book bans. For example, some progressive-minded parents had objected to books that featured derogatory pictorial images of racial minority groups. They zeroed in on Theodor Geisel, who had written and illustrated the widely popular Dr. Seuss books. They contended that his books contained racial stereotypes that made them unsuitable for young readers. They wanted to bar them from library shelves.

Progressive-minded parents spoke out against the popular books that Roald Dahl had written for children. They highlighted some of the crude and derogatory language in them. They urged school librarians to remove these books and replace them with less offensive versions.

Conservative-minded parents also wanted to ban books. For example, they objected to books in which the characters practiced LGBTQ lifestyles. They urged school librarians to replace them with books depicting characters with heterosexual lifestyles.

The parental factions could not agree on the books that should be restricted. However, they both claimed to be highly principled. The members of one faction explained that they were restricting books to promote inclusion. The members of the other rejoined that they were restricting them to promote parental rights.

Skeptics

The school librarians had been pressured to seek parents' advice when they acquired books about socially marginalized groups. Some of them obtained and then followed their advice.

The school librarians wondered about the impact of their new policy on leaders in the community, business, and government. They also wondered about its impact on the journalists who influenced these key groups.

Many progressive journalists were upset with the librarians. They were convinced that they had acceded to book bans. They protested the damage they were causing. They encouraged like-minded readers and viewers to join their protest.

Although the school librarians were not surprised when progressive journalists expressed skepticism about placing restrictions on books, they were surprised when conservative journalists also expressed skepticism. However, they discovered that the conservative journalists had their own reasons for being skeptical.

The conservative journalists had examined the way that school librarians had implemented parent-centered book policies. They detected ulterior motives for their actions.

The school librarians had removed books to which parents had objected. However, they also had removed books that had not drawn any parental objections. They may have hoped that the removal of these additional books would create a media ruckus.

QUESTIONS ABOUT SUDDENLY CONTENTIOUS ISSUES

This section focuses on the preceding two cases. The first case involved the leaders at national security agencies.

The national security leaders were concerned about aerial surveillance by hostile nations. They monitored the skies for their aircraft, drones, and spy satellites. Convinced that these devices could pose safety threats, they did not allow them to pass through American airspace without permission.

Members of the public had shown high interest in spy drones, spy satellites, and piloted spy crafts. They felt better after they were assured that they were being protected from them.

The national security leaders were aware that foreign balloons sometimes approached American airspace. However, they were convinced that these balloons, which were launched by hobbyists and businesspeople, did not pose safety threats. They allowed them to enter the nation's airspace, pass through it, and depart.

Members of the public historically had shown no interest in foreign aerial balloons. However, they changed their minds after an incident in the northwest. Montanans observed an unusually large balloon sailing over their state. They began to track it.

The Montanans posted online images of the object they were tracking. They hypothesized that it could be a Chinese spy balloon. They recommended that the military shoot it down.

Scores of journalists were captivated by the aerial balloon over Montana. They agreed that it could be a Chinese spy device. They repeated the public chant to shoot it down. When they detected hesitation by national security leaders, they chanted even louder.

The national security leaders were surprised by the media storm surrounding the Montana balloon. They were even more surprised when they received an order to investigate all foreign balloons, determine if they had approval to enter the nation's airspace, and shoot down any that did not have approval.

While the first case in this chapter focused on national security leaders, the next case focused on school librarians. The librarians acquired books, displayed them, and made them available to students.

The librarians hoped that students would be excited about the information in printed books. They faced a challenge because most students preferred the digital information they could access on laptops and cellphones.

The librarians acquired printed books that they believed would entice their students. They selected works that dealt with the challenges that children and young adults faced. For example, they acquired books about socially marginalized groups.

Some parents browsed through the books that the librarians were acquiring, displaying, and loaning to students. They did not always approve of them. They advised the librarians to remove those to which they objected.

The parents were pleased when the librarians followed their advice. They were disgruntled when they refused.

The disgruntled parents wanted to put pressure on the librarians. They looked for allies. They asked principals, superintendents, and school board members for their support. Some went outside the schools and asked journalists and elected officials for their support.

The school librarians were not intimidated by the confrontational parents. However, they were shocked by the turmoil that they created. They decided to copy their strategy and look for supporters outside the schools. They were able to find journalists and elected officials who took their side in the feud.

The following questions will assist you if you are going through this book on your own. They provide opportunities like those you would have in a college classroom where the professor is using the case method. They also will help you if you are in an actual college classroom with a professor who is using this approach.

Question 1: Why Did Security Leaders Allow Foreign Balloons to Pass through American Airspace?

National security leaders monitored and protected American airspace. Convinced that foreign aeronautical balloons posed little danger, they allowed them to pass through undisturbed.

How did different groups respond to the security leaders? Focus on two groups: journalists and elected officials.

Did the journalists have low confidence, moderate confidence, or high confidence in the way that the national security leaders were behaving? How did the elected officials feel? Explain the basis for your answers.

When answering these questions, as well as those that follow, you can rely on the information in this chapter. You also might rely on some of the sources identified in the references at the rear of the book. If you are reading this chapter with colleagues, you are encouraged to converse with them about the best way to answer the questions.

Question 2: Why Did Security Leaders Later Forbid Foreign Balloons to Pass through American Airspace?

National security leaders were publicly censured for underestimating the threat from foreign balloons. They began to shoot down any in American airspace.

How did different groups respond to the security leaders? Focus on two groups: journalists and elected officials.

Did the journalists have low confidence, moderate confidence, or high confidence in the way that the national security leaders were behaving? How did the elected officials feel? Explain the basis for your answers.

Question 3: Why Did School Librarians Circulate Books about Socially Marginalized Groups?

School librarians circulated books to students. Convinced that books about socially marginalized groups would motivate them to read, they regularly circulated them.

How did different groups respond to the school librarians? Focus on two groups: journalists and parents.

Did the journalists have low confidence, moderate confidence, or high confidence in the way that the school librarians were behaving? How did parents feel? Explain the basis for your answers.

Question 4: Why Did School Librarians Stop Circulating Books about Socially Marginalized Groups?

School librarians were publicly censured for underestimating the threat from books about socially marginalized groups. Some removed them from their shelves.

How did different groups respond to the school librarians? Focus on two groups: journalists and parents.

Did the journalists have low confidence, moderate confidence, or high confidence in the way that the school librarians were behaving? How did parents feel? Explain the basis for your answers.

SUMMARY

National security leaders allowed foreign aeronautical balloons to pass through American airspace. They believed the balloons, which had been launched by hobbyists and businesspeople, posed little danger. They were surprised when they were depicted as hostile crafts that should be shot down.

School librarians displayed and circulated books about socially marginalized groups. They believed the books which dealt with issues like those that young people were confronting posed little danger. They were surprised when they were depicted as damaging misinformation that should be banned from schools.

Chapter 2

The School Masking Feuds

[We recommend] universal indoor masking by all students (age 2 and older).

—Centers for Disease Control and Prevention (CDC), 2022

[Researchers are making a plausible] case against masks at school.

—Medical Scientists Margery Smelkinson,
Leslie Bienen, & Jeanne Noble, 2022

[The school board's facemask policy] was not based on science or reason, but instead some combination of the political leanings, emotions, irrational fears and psychological anxieties.

—Parental Lawsuit against a Florida School Board, 2023

[Florida has banned mandatory masking at school because parents] know what is best for their children.

—Florida Commissioner of Education
Richard Corcoran, 2021

Florida withholds money from school districts [that don't comply with its ban against mandatory masking].

—Journalist Sarah Mervosh, 2021

My decision [on whether to comply with the Florida ban against mandatory masking won't] be influenced by a threat.

—Florida Superintendent Alberto Carvalho, 2021

The FDA respected the professional training and expertise of audiologists. They gave them exclusive authority to prescribe hearing aids. However, they were challenged by consumers who wished to acquire hearing aids on their own.

The CDC respected the professional training and expertise of the medical researchers on their staff. They gave them exclusive authority to craft school facemask policies. However, they were challenged by parents who wished to craft these policies on their own.

HEARING AIDS

Elected officials were responsible for national and state healthcare policies. However, they expected medical professionals to provide the actual care. They typically collaborated with them before they enacted policies. They also collaborated with patients who received the care and the businesspeople who funded it.

The elected officials occasionally gave directives to healthcare professionals, businesspeople, and patients. For example, they required them to follow the policies and practices of the US Food and Drug Administration (FDA).

The FDA had for more than a century played a critical role in public health. It monitored and regulated all aspects of food and drugs.

The FDA had additional responsibilities. It monitored and regulated medical devices, including those that promoted auditory health. Aware that audiologists handled most patients with auditory health issues, they consulted them about ways to protect healthy hearing and cure hearing problems.

The audiologists were eager to assist the FDA. They reported that the Americans were suffering from an unprecedented hearing epidemic. They judged that this problem should have been anticipated because citizens were living longer, and their hearing was declining as they aged. They advised the FDA that this problem could be solved with hearing aids.

Mental health professionals agreed with the audiologists. They explained that aging Americans needed to socialize. They worried that those who were hard of hearing could stop socializing and then become isolated, depressed, and even suicidal. However, they predicted that those with access to hearing aids would be able to maintain their personal dignity, preserve their social status, and avoid the troublesome psychological correlates of hearing loss.

The FDA leaders listened to the reports from the audiologists and the mental health professionals. They were impressed. However, they noted that hearing aids, although beneficial, were extremely expensive. They asked the businesspeople who manufactured them why they were so costly.

The manufacturers noted that the hearing aids were frequently characterized as simple amplification devices. They disagreed.

The manufacturers pointed out that hearing aids truly were sophisticated computers that processed spoken sound to make it more easily understood. They explained that some of them could sort through the multiple voices in a crowded room and isolate those of interest to the hearing aid's wearer.

The manufacturers pointed to additional advanced features of modern hearing aids. For example, they noted that they had Bluetooth connectivity that enabled wearers to link to electronic devices, such as smartphones, computers, and televisions. They claimed that the prices they charged for their hearing aids were modest when one considered the extensive research required to engineer these advanced features.

The manufacturers viewed hearing aids as sophisticated assistive technology for hard-of-hearing patients. They insisted that only highly trained audiologists could diagnose a patient's hearing problem, determine whether hearing aids would solve that problem, select the optimal style of hearing aid, and then program that hearing aid so that it complemented the hearing profile of that patient. They were pleased that the audiologists concurred with this recommendation. They were even more pleased after the FDA leaders concurred.

The FDA leaders had established a policy in which audiologists prescribed and programmed hearing aids. They admitted that this policy was expensive. However, they believed it was in the best interest of those American citizens with limited auditory acuity.

Many citizens tacitly agreed with the FDA leaders. They visited audiologists to see if they would benefit from hearing aids. They followed their advice and expressed gratitude for the care they provided.

Some citizens were suspicious of the FDA leaders. They questioned whether they were looking out for their financial interests. They noted that the citizens of other countries had a choice of consulting with audiologists or simply purchasing over-the-counter (OTC) hearing aids on their own. They noted that they could purchase the OTC devices that audiologists were recommending or vastly cheaper models.

The FDA listened to recommendations from the proponents of OTC hearing aids. They admitted that those recommendations would affect the hearing aid market and lower the cost of some devices. They also predicted that they would help some individuals but harm others. They then decided to retain their ban on OTC sales.

Enthusiasts

The FDA leaders felt pressure to continue their decades-long ban on OTC hearing aids. They were sensitive to the pressure from the audiologists and hearing aid manufacturers. However, they were also concerned about members of the public.

After they kept their ban in place, the FDA leaders realized that some members of the public were supportive. They listened gratefully as these citizens insisted that the ban advanced the hearing health of Americans.

The pro-ban citizens had confidence in the FDA. They believed it had relied on research to scientifically validate the ban. They identified elected officials who shared their confidence. However, they searched for still more pro-ban allies. They went to journalists for assistance.

The journalists worked for national media companies with massive audiences. Many of them were eager to defend the ban. They profusely praised it. They also praised the elected officials, FDA leaders, and medical professionals who endorsed the ban. They depicted their adversaries as unsophisticated political activists who did not comprehend the need for medical professionals to make decisions about access to hearing aids.

Skeptics

Not all citizens approved of the FDA's ban on hearing aid sales. Some of them disapproved for practical reasons. They worried that people who could not afford audiologist-prescribed hearing aids would go without aids. They were especially concerned about socially isolated elderly people going without aids.

The anti-ban citizens predicted that people who could not afford audiologist-prescribed hearing aids would purchase sound amplifiers instead. They noted they could purchase an inexpensive pair of air buds and then transform their smartphones into a primitive sound amplifier. They feared they then would set the amplification too high and cause even greater damage to their ears.

Some anti-ban citizens questioned whether the FDA's leaders had been biased when reviewing research data about the benefits and risks of OTC hearing aids. They noted that qualified medical authorities in other countries had reviewed these data but recommended OTC sales. They cited the European Association of Hearing Aid Professionals as a prominent example. They added that even in the United States, the American Academy of Audiology had given a qualified endorsement for OTC hearing aid sales.

The anti-ban citizens met with FDA leaders. However, they had been unable to change their minds. They realized that they would need allies to put greater pressure on them. They persuaded scores of journalists to take their side. They also recruited some elected officials. They were excited after they then persuaded the FDA leaders to remove their ban.

SCHOOL FACEMASKS

School boards expected their educational administrators to prioritize students' physical and mental health. They directed them to follow the advice of state medical professionals when they crafted their health policies. They assumed that they would then implement those policies with the collaboration of school nurses, educational psychologists, coaches, teachers, and parents.

The school boards had rarely mandated health practices on their own. However, they recognized that they might have to become more directive in 2022 when the entire nation was dealing with the dangerous COVID-19 pandemic. They felt pressure to make changes that would keep students from contracting this virus.

The school boards did become more directive. They informed the parents in their districts that they would be closing their children's schools, suspending face-to-face instruction, and substituting online instruction.

Many parents were dismayed. They explained to the school boards that they had jobs that would prevent them from supervising their children at home. Moreover, they could not afford a suitable sitter. They pleaded with them to reconsider their plan and keep schools open.

The school boards responded that they were following orders from their state boards of education, their state departments of education, and the Centers for Disease Control and Prevention (CDC). They reminded the parents that the CDC had the authority to take charge and craft a national school safety policy.

The CDC leaders assured the public that they were taking charge. They explained that they had directed the medical researchers on their staff to formulate a national policy that would help the schools handle the viral threat. They reported that these researchers viewed school closure as an important element in that policy. They promised that they would recommend that schools reopen after their researchers determined that the threat had diminished and that face-to-face instruction was safe.

The CDC leaders kept their eyes on the school boards. They wanted to see how they were responding to their call for temporary school lockdowns.

The school boards kept more than 50 million students from face-to-face instruction in 2022. They noted that most of them kept them away for half of that school year but that some kept them away for the full year or even longer.

The CDC leaders realized that their policy would fail without strong support. They detected this type of support from medical professionals, elected officials, and some parents during the first month of school closures. They hoped that they would continue to detect it during subsequent months.

The CDC leaders had enormous confidence in school closures. However, they carefully monitored the public to see if they shared their confidence. They soon became convinced that the public's confidence was slipping month by month. Even more disturbing, they realized that parents and elected officials were among those who had lost confidence.

The CDC leaders were convinced that the school closures had reduced cases of COVID-19 among schoolchildren. Nonetheless, they realized that they did not have the political and public support they would need to maintain the closures.

The CDC leaders worried that elected officials and parents would force them to send children back to school for face-to-face instruction. They decided to compromise with them.

The CDC leaders announced they had consulted with their medical researchers about ending the lockdowns. They had been assured by them that children could return to school. However, they also had been assured that all children, even those as young as two years old, should wear facemasks at school.

Enthusiasts

School boards had complied with the orders to close schools. However, they felt pressure to reopen them and resume face-to-face instruction. They were particularly sensitive to the pressure from the parents.

Some school boards agreed with the parents who had insisted that the schools should reopen. They took steps to open them expeditiously.

Some school boards had wished to delay the reopening of the schools. They still reopened them to relieve the pressure that parents were exerting on them. However, they made it clear that they would follow the CDC adjuration and require universal face masking at all the recently opened schools.

After the school boards had prescribed face masks, they realized that some parents were extremely supportive. They listened to these parents insist that masks were essential.

The pro-masking parents had confidence in the CDC. They believed it had relied on research to scientifically validate the value of face masks. They identified elected officials who shared their confidence. They were pleased when these officials directed their state offices of education and state boards of education to require facemasks for the students at all schools.

Some pro-masking parents had to deal with state offices of education and state boards of education that were skeptical about the benefits of mandatory school masking. They calculated that they needed additional allies to keep the mandates in effect. They went to journalists for assistance.

The journalists worked for national media organizations with massive audiences. They were eager to defend pro-masking policies. They profusely praised them. They also praised the parents, elected officials, CDC leaders, and medical professionals who endorsed mandatory school facemasks.

Skeptics

Not all parents approved of mandatory masking at school. Some of them had practical concerns. They worried that masks could interfere directly with breathing and indirectly with learning. They were especially concerned about the masks' impact on the health and education of preschoolers, kindergartners, and early elementary school students.

Some parents questioned whether the CDC leaders had been biased when reviewing research data about masking for schoolchildren. They noted that qualified medical authorities in other countries had reviewed these data and not recommend mandatory masking. They cited the World Health Organization and the European Centre for Disease Prevention and Control as prominent examples.

The parents who did not support mandatory facemasks went back to their school boards. However, they became frustrated when those boards displayed little sympathy for them. They realized that they needed allies. In Florida, they asked state officials and the Florida Board of Education to take their side. They were excited after both groups took their side and pledged to ban mandatory face masking at school.

QUESTIONS ABOUT HEALTH RESTRICTIONS

This section focuses on the preceding two cases. The first case involved leaders at the FDA.

FDA leaders were concerned about all aspects of American citizens' health, including their auditory acuity. They monitored the types of hearing problems they were experiencing, their symptoms, their prevalence, and their causes. They then recommended treatments for them.

The FDA leaders collected data that revealed the diverse causes for hearing problems. As examples, they were able to identify problems resulting from trauma, disease, genetics, and aging.

The FDA leaders recognized the complexity of hearing problems. Nonetheless, they still believed that they could devise policies to reduce the severity of those problems or even cure them.

Audiologists took the lead in the efforts to help individuals with hearing problems. They wished to meet with individuals to assess their problems.

Hard-of-hearing patients were impressed by the audiologists' diagnostic skills. They also were impressed by their therapeutic treatments, which frequently entailed hearing aids.

The patients viewed the hearing aids as devices that amplified and clarified sound. They generally approved of them. However, they did have one major reservation—their costs.

The patients had been given opportunities to purchase hearing aids. However, they would have to pay thousands of dollars for them. They were confused.

The patients did not understand why the prices for hearing aids were so different than those for other health devices, such as reading glasses. They recounted that they could go to retail stores and purchase reading glasses OTC for less than 10 dollars.

The patients explained that they could have paid optometrists hundreds of dollars to prescribe and order reading glasses. However, they had avoided this expense by using trial and error to locate suitable pairs. They wished to purchase hearing aids in the same fashion.

The FDA leaders told individuals who were hard of hearing that the pricing for hearing aids was not comparable to that for reading glasses. They pointed out that the hearing aid prices reflected the manufacturers' massive investments in research and testing.

The FDA leaders characterized hearing aids as sophisticated medical devices. They did not believe that they could be sold OTC. They insisted that they should be prescribed by highly trained audiologists.

The FDA leaders explained why the audiologists were needed. They said that they had to diagnose hearing problems and confirm that hearing aids would solve those problems. They added that they then had to decide which hearing aids would be optimal and how they should be programmed. For all these reasons, they were not ready to approve OTC hearing aids.

Journalists were captivated by the tussle among consumers, audiologists, and hearing aid manufacturers. Some of them were extremely sympathetic to the consumers. They were intrigued by the consumers' accusation that manufacturers and audiologists were colluding to protect their self-interests.

The journalists supported the consumers who wished to purchase hearing aids without prescriptions from drug stores, department stores, and online retailers. They believed that the ensuing competition would lower the cost of hearing aids.

The FDA leaders were caught off guard by the media turmoil that enveloped hearing aids. They judged that the simplest and quickest way to suppress it would be to remove their ban on OTC hearing aids. However, they were not sure how this change would affect the nation's auditory health.

While the first case in this chapter concerned FDA leaders, the next case focused on leaders at the Centers for Disease Control and Prevention (CDC). The CDC leaders had directed their medical researchers to develop policies that would limit the spread of COVID-19 through the nation's schools.

The CDC leaders followed the advice from their researchers. They directed school boards to keep students at home and provide them with remote instruction. They then observed the impact.

The CDC leaders were pleased after more than 50 million students stayed away from schools. They noted that some stayed away for months while others stayed away for more than a year.

The CDC leaders were under pressure to identify when it would be safe for students to return to school. They also had to specify how they would keep students safe after they returned. They again followed their researchers' advice.

The CDC leaders eventually determined that the schools should reopen. They directed the school boards to inform students to return. They also were to inform them that they should wear face masks at their schools.

The CDC leaders believed parents would be excited about their children returning to classrooms and resuming face-to-face instruction. Nonetheless, they wondered how they would respond to the masking policy.

The CDC leaders began to calculate the number of parents who were skeptical about the effectiveness of masks. They were shocked by the size of the group. They also were shocked by the number of politicians and journalists who sided with the skeptical parents.

The CDC leaders listened as skeptical parents requested permission to choose whether their children would wear masks at school. However, the leaders refused to modify their mandatory masking order.

The CDC leaders were distressed by the resistance to mandatory masking. However, they were pleased when many parents, journalists, and elected officials declared that they were pro-masking. They hoped that the pro-masking groups would attract as much attention as the skeptics were attracting.

The following questions will assist you if you are going through this book on your own. They provide opportunities like those you would have in a college classroom where the professor is using the case method. They also will help you if you are in an actual college classroom with a professor who is using this approach.

Question 1: Why Did the FDA Ban OTC Hearing Aids?

FDA leaders were responsible for the auditory health of American consumers. Convinced that hard-of-hearing consumers needed to consult audiologists before purchasing hearing aids, they banned OTC purchases.

How did different groups respond to the FDA leaders? Focus on two groups: hard-of-hearing consumers and journalists.

Did the hard-of-hearing consumers have low confidence, moderate confidence, or high confidence in the way that the FDA leaders were behaving? How did the journalists feel? Explain the basis for your answers.

When answering these questions, as well as those that follow, you can rely on the information in this chapter. You also might rely on some of the sources that are identified in the references at the rear of the book. If you are reading this chapter with colleagues, you are encouraged to converse with them about the best ways to answer questions.

Question 2: Why Did the FDA Remove the Ban on OTC Hearing Aids?

FDA leaders discovered that hard-of-hearing consumers in other countries were purchasing OTC hearing aids and benefiting from them. Persuaded by this discovery, they removed their ban on OTC hearing aids.

How did different groups respond to the FDA leaders? Focus on two groups: hard-of-hearing consumers and journalists.

Did the hard-of-hearing consumers have low confidence, moderate confidence, or high confidence in the way the FDA leaders were behaving? How did the journalists feel? Explain the basis for your answers.

Question 3: Why did the CDC Ban Parent-Crafted School Masking Policies?

CDC leaders were responsible for protecting schoolchildren from COVID-19. Convinced that the medical researchers on their staff had the training and expertise to craft health masking policies for the schools, they banned parent-crafted policies.

How did different groups respond to the CDC leaders? Focus on two groups: parents and journalists.

Did the parents have low confidence, moderate confidence, or high confidence in the way the CDC leaders were behaving? How did the journalists feel? Explain the basis for your answers.

Question 4: Why did the CDC Refuse to Remove the Ban on Parent-Crafted School Masking Policies?

CDC leaders discovered that parents in other countries were crafting masking policies and were keeping their children healthy. Unpersuaded by this discovery, they refused to remove the ban on parent-crafted masking policies.

How did different groups respond to the CDC leaders? Focus on two groups: parents and journalists.

Did the parents have low confidence, moderate confidence, or high confidence in the way the CDC leaders were behaving? How did the journalists feel? Explain the basis for your answers.

SUMMARY

The FDA maintained that audiologists had the expertise and training to prescribe hearing aids. They gave them exclusive authority. However, they upset those hard-of-hearing consumers who wished to make OTC purchases.

The CDC maintained that the medical researchers on their staff had the training and expertise to craft school facemask policies. They gave them exclusive authority. However, they upset those parents who wished to devise policies.

Chapter 3

The Parenting Feuds

[Students' gender preferences] aren't political issues . . . [but] human rights issues.
     —Pennsylvania School Board Member Abby Deardorff, 2023

[A Massachusetts school] implemented a policy requiring . . . staff to actively hide information [about students' gender preferences] from parents.
     —US District Judge Mark Mastroianni, 2022

[A mother is suing a] school district in California over their "parental secrecy" policy.
     —Journalist Amy Nelson, 2023

[Parents have the right to know] what's going on in the school with their children . . . [and] that [right] is being denied.
     —Attorney Rick Claybrook, 2023

[How schools handle gender preference is moving from the] classroom to the courtroom.
     —Attorney Wendy Patrick, 2023

> Airline managers crafted explicit passenger boarding policies. They directed their gate agents to follow them. However, they later allowed them to relax the policies for some passengers, such as those with nut allergies. They were surprised by the turmoil that ensued.
>
> School boards crafted explicit parental communication policies. They directed their educational staff to follow these policies when dealing with sensitive information about students. However, they later allowed them to relax the policies for certain students, such as those who wished to change the pronouns by which they were addressed. They were surprised by the turmoil that ensued.

AIRLINE BOARDING

Airline managers expected their gate agents to board passengers efficiently. They stressed the importance of the flights departing on time.

The airline managers had to select an approach for boarding passengers. They realized that first-class travelers had paid more for their tickets and expected to be treated with deference. They intended to reward them with special meals, complimentary cocktails, and oversized seats. However, they did not stop there.

The airline managers also intended to offer special boarding and deplaning privileges to first-class ticket holders. They explained that they would be able to board before the other passengers and then deplane before them as well. They instructed the gate agents to follow this policy.

The gate agents were ready to implement the boarding policy. However, they soon realized that they had to make some exceptions. For example, they had to deal with passengers in wheelchairs. If they did not board them early, they worried they would disrupt the entire boarding process and cause a late departure.

The gate agents used their discretion to provide wheelchair-bound patients with priority boarding. However, they repeatedly had to use their discretion. For example, they had to make decisions about boarding passengers who were relying on walkers, canes, crutches, or the physical support of traveling companions.

The gate agents had to use their discretion for boarding families traveling with extremely young children. They had to use it for service members and veterans. They had to use it for individuals with helper animals. They had to use it for people who disclosed that they had hard-to-detect psychological or medical problems.

The gate agents even had to decide how they would handle passengers who had peanut allergies. They listened as these passengers argued that they needed to board early so that they could wipe down their entire seating areas to remove any minute peanut particles.

The airline managers had developed precise boarding policies. Nonetheless, they realized that their gate agents were using discretion. Some of them were uncomfortable with this situation. They insisted that the gate agents strictly follow their boarding policies.

The airline managers who wanted to strictly regulate passenger boarding still intended to show deference to flyers who had purchased expensive first-class tickets. They therefore instructed the gate agents to allow priority boarding for only one other group: individuals who would so disrupt boarding processes that they would prevent on-time departures.

The airline managers worried that some passengers would be miffed by their strict boarding policies. They therefore came up with one more group that they would allow to board early: passengers who paid a special fee. They typically set this fee between 10 and 30 dollars.

Enthusiasts

The airline managers were pleased with their boarding policy. They provided early boarding to passengers who paid for expensive tickets. They adapted that policy to include passengers who paid a supplementary fee.

The airline managers believed that boarding fees would generate money, expedite the boarding process, and please passengers. They were eager to see how passengers were responding.

Some passengers were willing to pay modest fees for early access. They worried that they might be unable to find overhead suitcase storage if they boarded later. They paid the fees for peace of mind and security.

Skeptics

Passengers carefully reviewed the strict boarding policies. Some of them were disgruntled.

The disgruntled passengers explained why they were reluctant to pay special boarding fees. For example, they complained about American Airlines, which would charge a nine-dollar fee on some flights but a fee eight times higher on others.

The disgruntled passengers noted that flyers in wheelchairs had no difficulty making convincing case for priority boarding without payment of special fees. However, they argued that flyers with not-easily-detected psychological or medical problems had greater difficulty making their cases to the gate agents.

The disgruntled passengers noted that passengers who were in wheelchairs were able to board early without paying special fees. However, they questioned whether some of their mobility restrictions were genuine. They had observed individuals request wheelchairs for boarding but then show no impairment after they were aboard. One witty skeptic referred to these suddenly ambulatory individuals as "miracle" flyers.

The disgruntled passengers were convinced that clever flyers had strategies with which they were circumventing the early boarding policies. They concluded that the policies themselves were ineffective, exploitative, and arbitrary.

PARENTING

School boards directed administrators and teachers to discipline their students. They assured them they had this authority because they were acting in loco parentis—in place of the parents.

The administrators and teachers needed behavioral codes to discipline students. They then could monitor whether students were following those codes. They could compliment those who were following them and chastise those who were not.

The administrators and teachers had to designate the behavioral code on which they would rely. They could choose a lax, moderate, or severe behavioral code. Some chose one that was extremely severe. They published this code and stated that they would show zero tolerance for students who violated it. They typically expelled the guilty students.

Some parents were distraught about zero-tolerance behavioral codes. Parents of children with disabilities were especially upset. They maintained that their children, who frequently found it difficult to control their behaviors, should have been treated with leniency. They scolded the school staff for failing to act in loco parentis.

The school staff rejoined that zero-tolerance policies were not effective unless they were implemented without exceptions. They insisted that they were acting with the support of many parents.

The school staff realized that zero tolerance was a problematic behavioral issue. They doubted that they could implement it without offending some parents. However, this was not the only problematic behavioral issue with which they were dealing. They had to deal with the misbehavior of students who were sent to counselors.

When they met with students, school counselors encouraged them to discuss extremely personal information. They explained that they could be completely honest because counselors were required to keep these discussions confidential. At the same time, they made it clear that counselors were legally bound to disclose any plans by students to cause serious harm to themselves or others.

School administrators realized that some parents were upset about the confidentiality assurances. They listened to complaints that counselors who withheld information from parents were not acting in loco parentis.

Parents noted that school counselors could have legitimate reasons for keeping student information confidential. Even parents who were irked by confidentiality assurances conceded that counselors could not gain students' trust without these assurances. They reluctantly gave their approval.

The disgruntled parents reluctantly gave their approval to the counselors who were providing confidentiality assurances to students. However, they were not going to give approval to other school groups that were providing these assurances to students.

The disgruntled parents identified administrators and teachers who had been dealing with students who questioned their gender identities and who wished to change the pronouns by which they were addressed at school. They had discovered that the administrators and teachers had approved the changes and implemented them, but then kept this information from the students' parents.

The school administrators and teachers admitted that they had been using changed student pronouns even when the parents were likely to object. They explained that they had kept this information confidential to keep parents from inflicting emotional or physical harm.

Enthusiasts

Some students had changed their pronouns at school and concealed these changes from their parents. They were pleased by the confidentiality assurances they had received from school staff. They felt emotionally secure, socially protected, and personally fulfilled.

Students who had concealed pronoun changes hoped their parents would not discover these changes. They were anxious about how their parents would react if they did find out.

Some parents surprised their children. They supported them. They also supported the way that their school boards had acted. They were joined by parents who had not been directly involved but who believed that the boards were right to have acted quickly and confidentially.

The supportive parents realized that some school boards were in precarious situations. They therefore looked for allies to strengthen them. They went outside the schools to find them.

The supportive parents turned to journalists. They asked them to publicize the courageous actions that the school boards had taken to protect vulnerable students. They also contacted elected officials and asked them to take steps to protect student-centered school boards. They became excited as many journalists and elected officials joined them.

Skeptics

Parents did discover that their children had changed their pronouns at school and then kept this information from them. Some of them were disgruntled.

The disgruntled parents scolded their children. They also scolded school boards and school staff. They were disappointed with them for concealing substantive information about their children. They also were disappointed with them for secretly altering their disclosure practices.

The disgruntled parents did not think that the school boards and school staff had acted in the spirit of in loco parentis. They accused them of replacing parents' values with their own values.

The disgruntled parents looked for journalists to help them. They found many who were eager to air their grievances.

The disgruntled parents then turned to like-minded state officials for help. They pleaded with them to ensure that school boards were posting student information disclosure policies and then following them. They were pleased when they attracted ardent advocates. They were even more pleased when these advocates enacted parent-empowering legislation. They highlighted their success in Alabama, Arkansas, Florida, Indiana, Iowa, Kentucky, Montana, North Dakota, Tennessee, and Utah.

QUESTIONS ABOUT HIGHLY EDITORIALIZED GROUPS

This section focuses on the preceding two cases. The first case involved airline managers.

Airline managers hoped to design optimal boarding policies for their flights. They realized that optimal policies would reduce departure delays. They noted that they also would reduce passenger complaints.

The airline managers made sure that their boarding policies explicitly identified the order in which passengers entered planes. For example, they allowed passengers with expensive first-class seats to enter before those with less expensive main-cabin seats.

The airline managers directed their gate agents to assiduously follow the published boarding policies. However, they did not anticipate the difficulties that they inadvertently had created.

The gate agents received requests from people who wished to board before the first-class ticket holders. For example, they received them from people confined to wheelchairs.

The gate agents gave priority boarding to the passengers in wheelchairs. They then had to decide how they would treat people who were ambulatory but who required walkers, canes, therapy animals, or emotional support animals. They had to decide how they would handle people with a wide range of disabilities, including those who had hard-to-detect psychological problems and complex medical problems.

The gate agents had to decide how they would deal with people who did not have ailments or disabilities but who still required additional time to board planes and occupy their seats. For example, they had to consider when to board slow-moving senior travelers. They also had to consider when to board adults with young children in carriages, strollers, or car seats.

The gate agents received requests for early boarding from military travelers. They noted that they came from active-duty personnel in uniform, active-duty personnel out of uniform, and veterans. They had to decide if all, some, or none of these travelers should board early.

The airline managers realized that the gate agents faced many situations that they had not anticipated. They therefore allowed them to use their discretion. They made it clear that they were to show empathy for all passengers, allow some of them to board early, still expedite the boarding process, and try to avoid offending those passengers who had paid for first-class seats or those who had paid for priority boarding.

Journalists were captivated by the boarding practices at airports. Many of them traveled regularly by air and had personally witnessed the confusion that accompanied them.

The journalists were generally respectful of early boarding by military personnel, individuals with limited mobility, and families with young children. However, they playfully satirized some of the other early boarding groups. For example, they questioned whether people with emotional support animals or those with peanut allergies genuinely required priority boarding.

While the first case in this chapter concerned airline managers, the next case focused on school boards. The school boards enacted student information disclosure policies. They expected their educational administrators, teachers, and professional staff to follow them.

The school boards wanted their disclosure policies to be clear, comprehensive, and legal. They typically specified that school staff should alert parents to substantive information about their children. However, they stipulated that the information gathered by school psychologists, school counselors, and mental health workers would be revealed only if it entailed a plan to cause serious harm.

The school staff sometimes were unsure whether to disclose sensitive information about students. For example, they had to make decisions about students who were questioning their gender identities.

Some students had decided to change the pronouns by which they were addressed at school. They asked the staff to respect their decision. Moreover, they did not want them to reveal this information to their parents. They explained that they were fearful of the reactions of disapproving parents.

Some school boards amended their student information disclosure policies. They still intended to keep most psychologist-gathered and counselor-gathered information confidential. However, they also intended to keep information about student-requested pronoun preferences confidential. They then did not share these amended policies with parents.

Parents did find out that their children had requested to change their pronouns at school. They were surprised by their children and the school staff. They were surprised that their children had made the requests. They were surprised that school staff had approved the requests, implemented changes, and failed to inform parents.

The parents were confused and upset. They demanded that the schools develop clear policies on student information disclosure. They also demanded that they follow those policies.

Journalists were captivated by the dispute over student information disclosure policies. Some of them took the side of school boards. They publicized the courageous decisions that they had made to protect vulnerable students.

Some journalists took the side of the parents. They publicized their heroic efforts to force the school boards to articulate student information disclosure policies and then follow them.

Elected officials became involved in the dispute between the parents and the school boards. They revealed the same division as the journalists: some defended the boards while others defended the disgruntled parents.

The following questions will assist you if you are going through this book on your own. They provide opportunities like those you would have in a college classroom where the professor is using the case method. They also will help you if you are in an actual college classroom with a professor who is using this approach.

Question 1: Why Did Airline Managers Strictly Enforce Boarding Policies?

Airline managers directed their gate agents to strictly follow their published boarding policies. They believed this practice would speed up the boarding process and please passengers.

How did different groups respond to the airline managers? Focus on two groups: passengers and journalists.

Did the passengers have low confidence, moderate confidence, or high confidence in the way that the airline managers were behaving? How did journalists feel? Explain the basis for your answers.

When answering these questions, as well as those that follow, you can rely on the information in this chapter. You also might rely on some of the sources that are identified in the references at the rear of the book. If you are reading this chapter with colleagues, you are encouraged to converse with them about the best way to answer the questions.

Question 2: Why Did Airline Managers Relax Boarding Policies?

Airline managers discovered that the gate agents sometimes did not comply with boarding policies. For example, they learned that they had made exceptions for passengers with a wide range of problems, including peanut allergies. They approved of their behavior, contending that it was in the best interest of passengers.

How did different groups respond to the airline managers? Focus on two groups: passengers and journalists.

Did the passengers have low confidence, moderate confidence, or high confidence in the way that the airline managers were behaving? How did journalists feel? Explain the basis for your answers.

Question 3: Why Did School Boards Strictly Enforce Student Information Disclosure Policies?

School boards directed school staff to strictly enforce their published student information disclosure policies. They believed this practice would benefit students and please parents.

How did different groups respond to the school boards? Focus on two groups: parents and journalists.

Did the parents have low confidence, moderate confidence, or high confidence in the way that the school boards were behaving? How did journalists feel? Explain the basis for your answers.

Question 4: Why Did Some School Boards Relax Student Information Disclosure Policies?

School boards discovered that staff sometimes did not comply with student information disclosure policies. For example, they learned that they had made exceptions for students who changed the pronouns by which they were addressed. They approved of the staff's behavior, contending that it was in the best interest of the students.

How did different groups respond to the school boards? Focus on two groups: parents and journalists.

Did the parents have low confidence, moderate confidence, or high confidence in the way that the school boards were behaving? How did journalists feel? Explain the basis for your answers.

SUMMARY

Airline managers expected their gate agents to follow published protocols when boarding passengers. However, they later allowed them to make exceptions for certain passengers, such as those with nut allergies. They seemed shocked by the commotion they created.

School boards expected their educational staff to inform parents of sensitive information about their children. However, they later allowed them to make exceptions for certain children, such as those who wished to change the pronouns by which they were addressed. They seemed shocked by the commotion they created.

Chapter 4

The Teachers Union Feuds

The Chicago Teachers Union (CTU) has become a political colossus.
—*Wall Street Journal* Editorial Board, 2023b

CTU is on the mayoral ballot in the name of [the candidate it endorses].
—*Wall Street Journal* Editorial Board, 2023c

[CTU is] taking teachers' money to fund [the candidate it endorses].
—Unsuccessful Chicago Mayoral Candidate Ja'Mal Green, 2022

How do you send a child to the principal [at a CTU-staffed school where] the principal is on strike?
—*Wall Street Journal* Editorial Board, 2023a

[CTU] retains an effective veto over school reform.
—*Wall Street Journal* Editorial Board, 2023d

Families that can get their children out [of CTU-staffed schools] are leaving in droves.
—*Wall Street Journal* Editorial Board, 2022a

> DC's elected officials encouraged commuters to rely on the municipal bus and rail systems. However, they were aware that they sometimes did not pay fares. Under pressure from the press, they deliberated about the changes they should make.
>
> Chicago's elected officials encouraged unionized teachers to staff their schools. However, they were aware that these teachers sometimes engaged in disruptive strikes. Under pressure from the press, they deliberated about the changes they should make.

DC'S COMMUTERS

Elected officials in the District of Columbia acknowledged that commuters were frustrated by the area's massive traffic problems. They also acknowledged that they had been facing those problems for decades.

The DC elected officials had certainly attempted to solve the traffic problems. They had copied strategies that had been helpful in other cities. As an example, they had encouraged commuters to abandon their cars and rely on the district's two main mass transportation systems: its buses (Metrobus) and rapid transportation railways (Metro).

The DC officials realized that their mass transportation systems were far from ideal. They had repeatedly promised to expand, renovate, and improve them. However, they had struggled to find the money.

The DC officials renewed their improvement pledges during the early months of the pandemic. However, they were more optimistic this time. They had received unusually generous federal funding for 2019. They were ready to allocate some of this funding to their municipal buses and the Metro.

The DC officials intended to make the buses and Metro more efficient, safe, and comfortable. They had predicted that they then would attract more commuters.

The DC officials made improvements and then assessed their impact. During their 2021 assessment, they examined the figures for bus and Metro passengers for the previous year. They could not help but be disappointed and confused by the data. Instead of seeing more passengers, they saw fewer.

The DC officials were disappointed because the number of bus and Metro passengers had declined. They also were disappointed because the number of fares they collected had declined. They wondered how the Washington Metropolitan Area Transit Authority (WMATA) managers would deal with the revenue shortfall.

The managers explained that they would have to reduce spending in response to this decline. They cut back both bus and Metro services. They noted that they could not predict when they would have the funds to restore those services.

The WMATA managers were unable to restore services for 2022. However, they were optimistic that commuters and fares would increase during 2023. They predicted that they then could restore all services. They even hoped to add some new bus routes and new Metro stations.

The DC elected officials paid close attention to the number of commuters using the buses and Metro. They were disappointed that they still lagged the pre-pandemic figures. They asked the WMATA managers for an explanation.

The managers believed that the transportation figures for riders were deceptive. They explained that they did not include those bus riders who rushed by drivers without paying fares or those Metro riders who hopped over the station turnstiles without paying fares.

The managers noted that bus and subway workers witnessed many fare evaders. They contended that they could hardly be expected to confront them. They also contended that local police officers were too preoccupied with dangerous criminals to help with fare evaders. They urged the elected officials to solve this problem.

The elected officials needed a solution for fare evading. They were under pressure from the understaffed WMATA managers. They also were under pressure from commuters who paid their fares but were irked by those traveling for free. They even were under pressure from journalists who decried the high number of fare evaders.

Not all journalists were upset by the fare evaders. Some characterized the evaders as residents struggling financially to recover from the pandemic and save enough money for fares. They urged elected officials to permit them to ride free.

Although some journalists had a sympathetic view of the fare evaders, others had a different view. Politically conservative journalists depicted fare evaders as residents who were taking advantage of DC's flawed progressive policies. They penned censorious editorials with titles such as "In D.C., the Bus Fare Is Merely a Polite Suggestion".

The elected officials felt pressure to deal with fare evasion. They devised a clever plan. They would run their bus system without collecting any fares at all. They would depend completely on local tax revenue and federally supplied funds. They announced that they would commence this plan in July 2023.

The elected officials had decided that they did not need fares to run their buses. However, they did need them for the Metro. They considered a hybrid plan for the Metro.

The elected officials proposed to provide DC residents with monthly one-hundred-dollar Metro vouchers. They intended to hold them responsible only for the fares that exceeded the voucher amount. However, they eventually rejected this plan as too complicated and expensive.

The officials needed a simple and inexpensive plan for dealing with the Metro's fare evaders. They came up with a three-phase plan in 2022.

The officials had already initiated the first phase of their plan. They had posted warning signs throughout the Metro. They had printed on them: *Remember to pay your fare before riding—If you don't pay your fare, Metro Transit Police could fine you.*

The officials resolved to keep the warning signs in place. However, they were ready to begin the next phases of their plan.

The officials increased the number of Metro Transit Officers. They directed the new hires to look for individuals skipping fares. They told them to stop them and fine them.

The officials moved on to phase three of their plan. They removed some of the gates over which fare evaders had been leaping. They then replaced them with taller gates. They hoped that these new gates would stop all but the most athletic evaders.

Enthusiasts

The elected officials needed to gather information about how commuters had reacted to their bus and Metro plans. They commissioned surveys and scheduled public meetings.

DC's commuters were generally supportive of the decision to eliminate bus fares. They assumed elected officials had enough federal money and local taxes to compensate for the lost fares and keep the buses running.

The commuters who had been riding buses for free were pleased. They would continue to ride for free. However, they now did not have to worry about fines or harassment.

The commuters who had been paying for their bus fares also were pleased. They would be saving money.

DC's commuters reacted quite differently to the decision to retain Metro fares. Those who had been riding the Metro for free worried that they would receive citations for fare evasion. However, they later relaxed after they discovered that the chances of being given citations were low.

Commuters who had been paying for Metro fares were disappointed. They had hoped that they would be treated the same as bus riders. They instead had to continue paying fares.

Many journalists were pleased with the elected officials. They admired the restrained plan that they had implemented. They conceded that this plan had not deterred fare evading on the Metro. However, they believed that it might have appeased critics.

Skeptics

DC's elected officials were curious about how commuters reacted to their plans for bus and Metro fares. They were just as curious about journalists.

Journalists had distinct perspectives on the plans for dealing with bus and Metro fares. Some of them had been extremely critical of the fare evasion problem. They doubted that this problem had been solved.

The critical journalists cited statements by paid-fare commuters who had witnessed evaders hopping gingerly over turnstiles. They recounted how they had cheered when subway police occasionally stopped evaders, arrested them, or sprayed them with caustic chemicals. They also recounted the high estimates of the fare revenue that was being lost.

The elected officials worried that the reports from critical journalists would create problems. For example, they worried they would affect the federal transportation funds they received. They were relieved when they did not.

The officials worried that the reports from critical journalists could damage their reelection chances. They were relieved when polls revealed that they were not having any impact on their prospects.

DC voters showed little interest in the journalists who worked at conservative media sites such as *Fox News*, *The Wall Street Journal* (*WSJ*), and *The American Conservative*. They dismissed their reporting as mean-spirited, inaccurate, and unfair. They were more interested in the local journalists who had praised the efforts of their elected officials.

CHICAGO'S UNIONIZED TEACHERS

Elected officials relished positive publicity. They looked for ways to attract it. They relied heavily on ads. They referred to the ads that they commissioned as paid media.

Elected officials valued earned media even more than paid media. They inspired earned media when journalists reported about them and their initiatives.

The elected officials hired public relations consultants to guide their media efforts. They asked them to identify paid media opportunities that would impact voters. They also asked them to identify newspapers, online sites, radio programs, and television programs that would generate earned media coverage for them.

The elected officials hoped that their media efforts would attract the attention of numerous groups. Nonetheless, they were especially eager to attract parents' attention. Aware that the parents consistently identified education as their top concern, they tried to persuade educational journalists to inform them about their educational achievements.

Politically conservative elected officials were not naive when they were dealing with journalists. They realized that they could have marked biases. They assumed that those journalists who shared their political views would have the highest likelihood of getting them earned media attention. They were greatly impressed by the journalists at the *WSJ*.

The *WSJ* journalists had several educational initiatives they featured. For example, they regularly published reports about the positive impact that for-profit schools were having on education. Within those reports, they encouraged parents to entrust their children to the teachers at these schools.

The *WSJ* journalists drew an unflattering contrast between the teachers at the for-profit schools and those at unionized public schools. Although they disparaged all unionized teachers, they reserved their special scorn for CTU teachers.

The *WSJ* journalists characterized CTU teachers as lazy, unprofessional, self-centered, and ineffective. They alleged that they were responsible for "a rolling scandal of incompetence interspersed with rising union demands and walkouts to extort politicians." They repeatedly branded them as the worst teachers in the nation.

The *WSJ* journalists exhorted Chicago parents to "wake up" to the student damage that CTU teachers were causing. They encouraged them to join the "thousands of students and their families . . . leaving Chicago schools."

The elected officials in Chicago realized that the *WSJ* journalists had blamed them for allowing the CTU to exercise "an effective veto over school reform." Although they were offended by these journalists, they wondered about their impact on local parents.

Enthusiasts

Chicago's elected officials hoped to attract positive earned media and avoid negative earned media. They realized that the *WSJ*'s anti-teacher diatribes were prime examples of negative earned media. They worried that they could harm the CTU and its teachers. They also realized they could harm incumbent politicians and their prospects for staying in office.

Lori Lightfoot was Chicago's 56th mayor. She had been elected in 2019. She had surprised most political analysts, who believed a candidate could not win the mayoral race without CTU's endorsement. She won without that endorsement.

The *WSJ* journalists were not pleased with Lightfoot. They attacked her mercilessly throughout her four-year tenure as mayor. They attacked the CTU with equal ferocity.

Lightfoot wished to run as a Democrat for a second mayoral term in 2023. However, she first had to win the Democratic primary election. She would have to face several candidates, including Brandon Johnson, who had CTU's backing.

The *WSJ* journalists disapproved of both Lightfoot and Johnson. Nonetheless, they focused on Lightfoot during the primary election.

The *WSJ* journalists were ready to celebrate after the primary votes were tallied. They reported that Lightfoot had lost. They believed that they had contributed to her defeat.

Skeptics

The *WSJ* journalists realized that Chicagoans had voted historically for CTU-backed mayoral candidates. They told them to abandon this practice. They explained that they should reject Brandon Johnson, who was the CTU-backed candidate for the 2023 election. They predicted that he would cause irreparable harm to the city, its residents, and the schools.

The WSJ journalists were miffed when Chicagoans listened to the CTU instead of them. They warned them to prepare for declining urban safety, declining business opportunities, and declining public school enrollments.

Mayor Johnson and his politically progressive associates gave little attention to the *WSJ* journalists. However, they did wonder how much attention their constituents were giving to them.

The mayor and his associates had worried that the *WSJ* journalists might influence the attitudes of the city's many progressive voters. They were relieved after they discovered that they were having no discernible effect.

The voters respected the reporters from Chicago more than those from New York. They ignored the New Yorkers' mean-spirited caricatures of their city, elected officials, public schools, teachers, and unions.

QUESTIONS ABOUT JOURNALISTIC CARICATURES

This section focuses on the preceding two cases. The first case involved elected officials in the District of Columbia.

DC's elected officials were concerned about the many commuters who drove their personal vehicles. They encouraged them to rely on the district's two main mass transportation systems: its buses (Metrobus) and rapid transportation railways (Metro).

Chapter 4

The officials hoped that the increased use of Metro and Metrobus would reduce traffic congestion, pollution, and road wear. They also hoped that this use would generate positive publicity for them, enhance their political standing, and increase their reelection prospects.

The officials searched out journalists who were making positive comments about the Metro, Metrobus, and their riders. They classified their comments as earned positive media. They valued this earned media, which was free and influential.

The officials also identified journalists making negative comments about the Metro, Metrobus, and the commuters who used them. They noted that many focused on the riders who did not pay fares. They worried that this negative earned media could jeopardize the city's federal transportation funding. They also worried that it could damage their prospects for reelection. They decided to assess the impact of the negative earned media before they made any changes.

The first case in this chapter concerned elected officials in the District of Columbia. The next case focused on elected officials in Chicago.

The Chicago officials were responsible for hundreds of public schools and thousands of students. They encouraged CTU instructors to staff their schools and educate their students.

The Chicago officials kept a close eye on parents' educational views. They realized that the parents wanted their children to succeed academically. They promised that their children would do well if they kept them in CTU-staffed schools. They made a special plea to parents on the verge of sending their children to private schools.

The officials worried because CTU-staffed schools had decreasing enrollments. They noted that they had been losing students for decades. They noted that they also had been losing the federal, state, and local per-student revenue linked to those students. Because they had fewer students and less money, the officials had scaled back plans to purchase school technology, renovate buildings, and hire critically needed personnel.

The officials wished to halt the declining school enrollments. They were sure this would benefit students, themselves, and many political incumbents.

The officials beamed when journalists praised CTU-staffed schools. They classified their comments as positive earned media. They tried to cultivate additional positive earned media from them.

The officials cringed when journalists criticized CTU-staffed schools. They classified their comments as negative earned media. They did their best to repudiate their comments.

The officials noted that many critical journalists focused on the city's failure to prevent CTU strikes. They tried to assess their educational impact on enrollments. They also tried to assess their political impact on elections.

The following questions will assist you if you are going through this book alone. They provide opportunities like those you would have in a college classroom with a professor using the case method. They also will help you if you truly are in acollege classroom with a professor using this approach.

Question 1: How Did DC's Elected Officials Deal with Transportation Problems?

Elected officials in the District of Columbia realized that automotive commuters were facing complex transportation problems. They encouraged them to use the municipal bus and rail systems.

How did different groups respond to the elected officials? Focus on two groups: DC's residents and journalists.

Did DC's residents have low confidence, moderate confidence, or high confidence in the way that their elected officials were behaving? How did the journalists feel? Explain the basis for your answers.

When answering these questions, and those that follow, you can rely on the information in this chapter. You also might rely on some of the sources identified in the references at the rear of the book. If you are reading this chapter with colleagues, you are encouraged to converse with them about the best way to answer the questions.

Question 2: How Did DC's Elected Officials Deal with Fare Evaders on the Bus and Rail Systems?

Elected officials in the District of Columbia noted that the commuters who used the municipal bus and rail systems did not always pay their fares. Concerned about the evaders on the bus system, they eliminated bus fares. Although they were concerned about the evaders on the rail system as well, they made minimal efforts to dissuade them.

How did different groups respond to the elected officials? Focus on two groups: DC's residents and journalists.

Did DC's residents have low confidence, moderate confidence, or high confidence in the way that their elected officials were behaving? How did the journalists feel? Explain the basis for your answers.

Question 3: How Did Chicago's Elected Officials Deal with Public School Staffing Problems?

Chicago's elected officials realized that their public schools had complex staffing problems. They encouraged CTU instructors to staff them.

How did different groups respond to the elected officials? Focus on two groups: Chicagoans and journalists.

Did Chicagoans have low confidence, moderate confidence, or high confidence in the way that their elected officials were behaving? How did the journalists feel? Explain the basis for your answers.

Question 4: How Did Chicago's Elected Officials in Chicago Deal with CTU's Labor Disruptions?

Chicago's elected officials noted that CTU instructors sometimes participated in disruptive labor strikes. Although they were concerned about this behavior, they made minimal efforts to change it.

How did different groups respond to the elected officials? Focus on two groups: Chicagoans and journalists.

Did Chicagoans have low confidence, moderate confidence, or high confidence in the way that their elected officials were behaving? How did the journalists feel? Explain the basis for your answers.

SUMMARY

DC's elected officials encouraged residents to use the municipal rail and bus systems. However, they were aware that they sometimes did not pay their fares. Under pressure from the press, they deliberated about how to respond.

Chicago's elected officials encouraged unionized teachers to work in their public schools. However, they were aware that they sometimes participated in labor strikes. Under pressure from the press, they deliberated about how to respond.

Chapter 5

The Testing Feuds

Most K-12 parents say [the] first year of [the COVID-19] pandemic had a negative effect on their children's education.

—*Pew Research Center* Analysts Dana Braga & Kim Parker, 2022

The Covid-19 pandemic . . . caused historic learning setbacks . . . according to . . . a national test.

—Associated Press, 2022

[Post-pandemic test scores] reveal the damage from school closures.

—*Wall Street Journal* Editorial Board, 2022a

[Post-pandemic test scores are the result of] long-standing and systemic shortcomings of our education system.

—Los Angeles Unified School District Superintendent Alberto Carvalho, 2022

[Post-pandemic test scores are the result of] school shootings, violence, . . . classroom disruptions, . . . teacher and staff vacancies, absenteeism, cyberbullying, and students' use of mental health services.

—National Center for Education Statistics Commissioner Peggy Carr, 2022

[Post-pandemic test scores are the result of the] move away from academic standards . . . [and] school discipline, along with a rising emphasis on "social-emotional learning."

—*New York Post* Editorial Board, 2023

University administrators relied on the Law School Admissions Test (LSAT) to admit students. They also relied on it to rank law schools. However, they worried that this test was hurting minority students. They therefore turned to different approaches to admitting students and ranking programs.

Public school administrators relied on standardized tests to assess students, teachers, and schools. However, they worried that the post-pandemic test scores had declined, especially among some minority groups. They therefore advocated different approaches to assessment.

TESTING COLLEGE STUDENTS

Consumers could choose from a wide assortment of products during the 1930s. They had to decide which products were most effective. Some relied on manufacturers' recommendations. Others relied on advice from friends and relatives.

A group of researchers sympathized with the consumers. They were ready to help them. They purchased household products, tested them, and then compared their effectiveness. They then ranked the products according to their results. They made this information available in a publication entitled *Consumer Reports*.

The staff at *US News & World Report* were impressed by *Consumer Reports*. They noted that millions of consumers had purchased it for decades. They wished to duplicate that success. However, they were not going to rank household products; they were going to rank colleges and universities.

The magazine's staff did not have access to the information they would need to rank colleges and universities. They had to request it from the administrators at those institutions.

The magazine's staff tried to convince the administrators to supply the requested data. They told them that a high institutional ranking would generate a trove of positive publicity. They were excited when the administrators agreed to supply the needed information.

The magazine's staff began to publish annual college rankings. They attracted a large audience. They assumed that parents were using the rankings to make decisions about the institutions to which they would send their children.

The magazine's staff wished to expand their rankings' scope in 1987. They decided to rank law schools. They once again requested data from university administrators.

University administrators deliberated carefully about whether to cooperate with the *US News* staff on law school rankings. In the end, they cooperated for the same reason that they had cooperated with them on undergraduate academic program rankings. They valued the opportunity to get free, positive publicity.

The university administrators had to supply the magazine's staff with data about their facilities, faculty, and funding. They also had to supply them with their students' scores on the Law School Admission Test (LSAT).

The administrators submitted the data that the magazine's staff had requested. They then waited patiently for the rankings.

Some administrators were confused by the ranks assigned to their law schools. They had not seen the formula that the magazine's staff had used. When they asked for it, the staff refused to provide it.

The *US News* staff made a concession to the disgruntled university administrators. They would reveal some of the reasons for a particular university's rank and give advice on how to raise it. However, they required the administrators to pay for this information.

The university administrators still wanted the formula. They eventually were able to figure it out on their own. They realized that it relied heavily on LSAT scores.

The disgruntled administrators detected a major fault with the LSAT. They noted that talented African American and Hispanic students had been earning unusually low scores on it.

Some of these administrators served at universities that had highly competitive and highly ranked law schools. They wished to show their displeasure with the LSAT. They announced that they would cease making it a condition for student admission.

The disgruntled administrators braced for a storm of resistance. They knew that some of this resistance would come from their accrediting association, the American Bar Association (ABA). They were aware that the ABA required law schools to collect and compile applicants' LSAT scores. They had to convince the ABA's members that this requirement was inappropriate.

The disgruntled administrators knew the LSAT annually generated more than 30 million dollars. They anticipated that the publisher would push back against efforts to make it nonmandatory. They were sure that the many LSAT-preparation businesses would join the publisher.

Enthusiasts

Some university administrators had decided to eliminate the LSAT and avoid the annual *US News* rankings. They were eager to see how students would respond to their decisions. They waited to see if they would lose interest in their law schools.

Students recognized that highly regarded law schools had walked away from *US News* and abandoned the LSAT. They still had confidence in those schools. They were as eager as ever to attend them. Those students with low LSAT scores now hoped they would have better chances of admission.

The university administrators kept an eye on student applicants. They also kept one on their academic accrediting association—the ABA. They watched to see if this association was softening its position on mandatory LSAT scores. They were sure that it eventually would because some ABA leaders came from non-LSAT schools.

The university administrators had prodded the ABA to make changes to its law school accreditation requirements. Although they were confident that it eventually would make those changes, they were disappointed at the slow speed. They wondered how journalists were responding to the ABA's reluctance. They focused on journalists because of the influence they had on student admissions.

Journalists had called attention to the allegations about racial biases in the LSAT. They quoted remarks from law school faculty and students who shared that view. Many of them praised the schools that dropped their LSAT requirements. They predicted that this change in the admission procedures would increase the number of African American and Hispanic students at high-profile law schools.

The university administrators were interested in the reactions of parents to their decisions to drop the LSAT and walk away from the rankings to which it was linked. They anticipated that many of them, including African American and Hispanic parents, would support them. They were correct.

Skeptics

The university administrators who eliminated the LSAT were pleased that some groups supported their decision. However, they soon discovered that other groups were unhappy. They listened carefully to the unhappy groups.

Some law school students were unhappy. They explained that they had done well on the LSAT, received admission to top schools, and earned scholarships. They valued the rigorous competition to enter highly regarded law schools. They wanted to preserve the procedures that had benefited them.

Some of the unhappy students represented minority groups. Those who were Asian American and Indian American had been doing extremely well on the LSAT. They were being admitted to the best law schools at disproportionately high rates. They worried that the elimination of the LSAT would reverse this trend. Some speculated that the elimination had been designed for this purpose.

The unhappy students expressed their concerns to the university administrators. They pleaded with them to reverse their decision to eliminate the LSAT. They were disappointed when they refused.

The unhappy students then went to journalists. They were excited when some listened attentively to their arguments, agreed with them, and repeated their arguments to a broad audience of readers and viewers.

TESTING PUBLIC SCHOOL STUDENTS

School boards wished to gauge how students were progressing. They wanted to know whether they were struggling to reach standards, meeting them, or exceeding them. They directed their educational administrators to assess students and report back with the results.

The educational administrators realized that they were responsible for student assessment. Nonetheless, they expected their teachers to take the lead. They noted that the teachers were already assessing students' responses to teacher-made tests, classroom questions, and homework assignments.

Although educational administrators had relied historically on teachers to assess students, they eventually began to rely more on commercial companies. They hired them to develop standardized tests and calculate students' scores.

President George W. Bush was an ardent advocate for standardized testing. He believed that all students should be assessed through a nationally orchestrated program.

Bush and Congress enacted the 2002 No Child Left Behind Act (NCLB). They directed state officials to develop standardized achievement tests for science, math, English, and reading. They also specified the grades in which they were to administer them.

The US Office of Education monitored NCLB's provisions. It ensured that tests were administered and that the scores publicized. It then identified the school districts with exemplary test scores and gave them monetary rewards.

Some educational administrators were enthusiastic about NCLB. They believed the process was educationally sound and able to be implemented without major problems. However, they had colleagues who disagreed.

Some educational administrators were not at all enthusiastic about NCLB. They were critical of the tests that it employed. They doubted that they were valid. They predicted they would demoralize teachers, confuse parents, and harm students.

The critical administrators had additional reasons to be wary of NCLB's testing provisions. They did not want to use federal funds to create a massive assessment bureaucracy. They preferred to hire teachers, expand educational technology, and improve textbooks.

Congressional leaders dismissed this criticism. They repeatedly expressed their commitment to large-scale standardized testing during George W. Bush's administration. However, they were nervous when Barrack Obama was elected.

President Barrack Obama tried to calm the congressional leaders. He hoped that his *Race to the Top Act* (RttT) of 2012 would assure them that he was as committed to large-scale testing as his predecessor.

Within RttT, the president and Congress set aside money for schools that tested students and published their scores. They added a caveat. They insisted that schools should link teachers' performance evaluations to students' scores. They contended that meritorious evaluations should be reserved for teachers who raised scores.

Some educational administrators were impressed by RttT and its testing regimen. They liked the notion of channeling federal funds to schools with high test scores rather than those with low test scores.

Not all educational administrators were impressed by RttT's testing regimen and reward structure. Some were disgruntled.

The disgruntled educational administrators worried that RttT would have negative consequences. For example, they worried that it would demoralize teachers who were working with inner-city students and who would not have the same chances to raise test scores as their colleagues in wealthy suburbs. However, they detected an even more serious problem.

The disgruntled educational administrators noted that African American and Hispanic students historically had struggled on standardized tests. They were able to document that they had had special difficulties with English-language arts tests and mathematics tests. They wished to prevent biased tests from harming these students.

The disgruntled administrators wished to reduce the impact of biased tests. They had practical suggestions. For example, some wished to change the minimum scores that students needed to pass the tests. Others wished to reduce the lengths of the tests.

The disgruntled educational administrators presented their recommendations to state boards of education. They had difficulty getting their interest during the Obama administration. However, they later believed that they would have had greater success.

The educational administrators had closed their schools during the COVID-19 pandemic. They then kept them shuttered for varying durations. Many had initiated the lockdowns during the 2019 school year and then continued them into the 2020 school year.

The educational administrators had substituted online instruction for face-to-face instruction during the lockdowns. They also had substituted teacher-directed testing for large-scale standardized testing. They waited until their students were back in school before they resumed standardized testing.

The educational administrators were eager to see the new standardized test scores. After all, they wondered how much their students had learned from their online courses. They wished to compare their scores with those from earlier tests.

The educational administrators were surprised when they saw the scores. They noted that they were much lower than they had been earlier. They publicly reported them.

Parents read the reports about declining test scores. They were upset. They went to their principals and superintendents. They wanted an explanation.

The educational administrators contemplated how they should respond. Some had been critical of standardized tests before the post-pandemic decline in scores. They still were critical.

The critical educational administrators had contended that standardized tests were biased against African American and Hispanic students. They believed the public commotion over declining test scores could be an ideal pretext for restating that contention.

The critical educational administrators stated that the declining test scores might be partially due to school lockdowns. However, they insisted that they were primarily due to flaws in the tests.

Enthusiasts

The educational administrators who were critical of standardized tests kept an eye on their state boards of education. They wished to see if they were shifting their attitudes in response to the post-pandemic declining scores. They beamed after California's board shortened the lengths of some tests. They continued to beam after New York's board lowered passing scores for some tests.

Not all educational administrators were interested in modifying tests. Some believed that the tests were too flawed to be salvaged. They urged elected officials to completely retire standardized testing programs. They beamed when Florida's governor, legislators, and State Board of Education retired their statewide testing program.

Educational administrators had alerted state boards of education to testing problems. Although they were pleased with the way that some had responded, they wondered how journalists were reacting to their allegations. They focused on journalists because of the influence they had on parents.

Journalists had been struck by the allegations of racially biased standardized tests. They restated these allegations. They also restated the calls for testing changes. In fact, they called for even more dramatic changes. They were able to influence many parents.

Educators were another group that reacted positively to the allegations about racially biased standardized tests. Many of them had disapproved of large-scale standardized tests from the start. They especially had disapproved of the attempts to link the scores from those tests to their professional evaluations.

The educators who opposed standardized assessment were under pressure to identify an alternative. They suggested standards-based assessment (SBA). They explained that teachers who used SBA did not assign numerical scores or letter-based scores to students. They instead assigned a numeral from 1 to 4.

SBA educators might assign the numeral 1 to students who exhibited little mastery of a learning standard, the numeral 2 to those who had partially mastered it, the numeral 3 to those who had mastered it, and the numeral 4 to those who had mastered it with advanced degrees of understanding.

The educators characterized SBA as a type of assessment quite different from standardized testing. They explained that SBA practitioners could be sensitive to the unique situations of students and adjust their grading accordingly.

The educators who championed SBA were sure that they could assess and grade minority students fairly. They insisted that they could replace "biased grading" with "equitable grading." In fact, many of them referred to SBA as "equitable grading."

The educational administrators were interested in reactions of parents to SBA. They anticipated that many of them, including African American and Hispanic parents, would support it. They were correct.

Skeptics

The educational administrators had listened carefully to the parents who supported SBA. However, they soon were confronted by parents who were skeptical of it. They listened attentively to their concerns as well.

The non-SBA parents did not want to reduce the rigor of standardized tests. They explained that many students had done well on these tests. They identified students who had earned high scores and received scholarships or admissions to elite colleges. They wanted to preserve these opportunities.

Some of the non-SBA parents represented minority groups. Those who were Asian American and Indian American noted that their children had done extremely well on standardized tests. They questioned whether SBA was a veiled attempt to reverse this trend.

The non-SBA parents expressed their concerns to the educational administrators. Some of them were disappointed after they had limited success with this group. They therefore went to journalists. They asked them to present their arguments to readers and viewers. They were excited after many did.

QUESTIONS ABOUT ACADEMIC TESTING

This section focuses on the preceding two cases. The first case involved university administrators.

University administrators tried to lure students to their law schools. They were certain they would be attracted if their schools had sterling academic reputations.

The administrators knew that the reputations of law schools could be linked to numerous factors. Nonetheless, they believed their annual rankings by *US News & World Report* were important. They resolved to secure the highest possible rankings.

The *US News* staff had begun to rank undergraduate colleges in the early 1980s. They quickly developed a large audience. They later decided to expand their rankings to include law schools.

The *US News* staff ranked the law schools by a process like that which they had used to rank undergraduate colleges. They began by asking university administrators to supply details about their students, faculty, and resources. They also asked them to evaluate the schools with which they competed for students.

The university administrators carefully considered the requests from *US News*. They realized they could benefit if they participated and earned a rank that would impress applicants. Although they also realized they could be damaged if they earned a low rank, they still agreed to cooperate. They submitted the requested data.

The university administrators waited anxiously for the results. After they had received them, some were pleased. They smiled with satisfaction when their law schools were highly ranked. They took steps to retain and possibly raise their future rankings.

Not all university administrators were pleased with the rankings. Those at low-ranked schools were disgruntled. They questioned the accuracy of the magazine's assessment.

The disgruntled administrators were ready to challenge *US News*. However, they realized their challenge would not be credible unless they could convince colleagues at highly ranked schools to join them. They were excited after they persuaded them.

The disgruntled administrators challenged the validity of the information on which the rankings depended. For example, they challenged the self-reported data about class sizes. They believed that they had been deliberately misrepresented by individuals with conflicts of interest. They also challenged the evaluations of peer institutions. They believed that they also were misrepresented because of conflicts of interest.

The disgruntled administrators detected numerous faults with the *US News* rankings. However, they found one to be particularly disturbing. They noted that the rankings relied heavily on scores from the LSAT. They were convinced that this test was biased against some ethnic and racial groups. They believed that it was particularly unfair to African Americans and Hispanics.

The disgruntled administrators believed that some law schools had rejected African American and Hispanic applicants with low LSAT scores. They assumed that they had rejected these students not because they were academically unfit but because they would damage their institutions' rankings by *US News*.

Some disgruntled administrators announced that they would withdraw from the rankings. They anticipated that the magazine's publishers would put pressure on them to change their minds. However, they were ready to resist that pressure.

The disgruntled administrators made another controversial announcement. They stated that they no longer would require applicants to take the LSAT. They realized that the ABA had mandated the use of this test as a condition for professional accreditation. They anticipated that the ABA staff would be extremely upset.

The disgruntled administrators were eager to see how *US News* and the ABA would respond to their announcements. However, they were interested in the responses from other groups as well.

The disgruntled administrators kept a focus on minority applicants. They expected those who had struggled with the LSAT to applaud their announcements. They had African American and Hispanic students in mind. However, they were not sure how minority applicants who had excelled at the LSAT would respond. They were aware that Asian Americans and Indian Americans had scored extremely high.

While the first case in this chapter concerned university administrators, the next case focused on K–12 educational administrators. These administrators had to assess the academic progress of their students. They relied on informal measures such as classroom quizzes, recitations, and homework assignments. They also relied on standardized tests.

Members of the public had little trouble finding students' scores on standardized tests. They noted that many scores were summarized, shared with the media, and then discussed in public forums. They also read reports about high-scoring students who had received awards, qualified for scholarships, or earned admissions to elite colleges.

Federal elected officials specified the standardized tests that all students had to take in 2002. Within the NCLB, they directed them to take tests for reading, mathematics, and science. They then required schools to publish the scores.

Some educational administrators were disgruntled by NCLB's testing provisions. Those at low-score schools worried that parents might react by withdrawing their children. They worried that legislators might react by reducing their funding.

The educational administrators from low-score schools were nervous. However, they were not alone. Even their colleagues at high-score schools were nervous. Both groups were unsure that the tests were valid.

The disgruntled educational administrators contacted federal elected officials. They challenged the standardized tests that they had mandated.

The disgruntled educational administrators had little luck changing the minds of federal elected officials during the administration of George W. Bush. However, they hoped that they would have greater success after Barack Obama followed Bush.

The disgruntled educational administrators urged President Barack Obama to abandon the tests-centered provisions of NCLB. They were disheartened when he ignored their advice and backed another test-centered piece of legislation, the RttT of 2012.

The disgruntled educational administrators resisted Obama's testing initiative for the same reasons that they had resisted those of Bush. They detected fundamental problems with the tests themselves. They questioned whether they truly measured the skills that they purported to measure. They concluded that the tests could not differentiate effective schools and teachers from ineffective ones.

The disgruntled educational administrators detected numerous faults with the standardized tests. However, they found one fault to be particularly disturbing. They were convinced these tests were biased against some ethnic and racial groups. They believed they were particularly damaging to African American and Hispanic students.

The disgruntled educational administrators had tried to convince federal officials to abandon national standardized testing programs. When they did not have success, they tried to convince state boards of education to make changes to regional testing programs. They again made little progress.

The educational administrators who were upset with standardized tests had failed to limit them. Nonetheless, they later were ready to try again. They waited until the pandemic-related school lockdowns had ended.

The disgruntled administrators noted that the 2022 testing results had declined. They noted that they had declined sharply among some minority groups. They kept an eye on the political, social, and journalistic commotion accompanying this decline. They saw a chance to use the commotion to restate their concerns about standardized tests.

The disgruntled administrators were not willing to attribute declining test scores to the lockdowns. They stood by their pre-pandemic convictions. They insisted they were the result of racially biased standardized tests.

The disgruntled administrators at low-scoring schools made suggestions for reducing the biases in standardized tests. They were joined by the administrators at high-scoring schools. They urged their state boards of education to modify standardized tests. Some went further and urged them to replace standardized tests with informal teacher-centered assessments.

The disgruntled administrators waited to see how groups would respond to the changes for which they were lobbying. They focused on minority groups. They expected the minority groups that had struggled with standardized tests, such as African American and Hispanic students, to applaud the changes. They were not sure how minority groups that had excelled at standardized tests, such as Asian Americans and Indian Americans, would respond.

The following questions will assist you if you are going through this book alone. They provide opportunities like those you would have in a college classroom where the professor is using the case method. They also will help you if you are in an actual college classroom with a professor using this approach.

Question 1: Why Did University Administrators Embrace the LSAT?

University administrators had to demonstrate that law schools and the students in them were meeting standards. They relied on the LSAT. They admitted students with high scores on this test to their programs. They also participated in the LSAT-dependent program rankings of *US News*.

How did different groups respond to the university administrators? Focus on two groups: journalists and law school applicants.

Did the journalists have low confidence, moderate confidence, or high confidence in the way that the university administrators were behaving? How did the law school applicants feel? Explain the basis for your answers.

When answering these questions, and those that follow, you can rely on the information in this chapter. You also might rely on some of the sources identified in the references at the rear of the book. If you are reading this chapter with colleagues, you are encouraged to converse with them about the best way to answer the questions.

Question 2: Why Did University Administrators Later Abandon the LSAT?

University administrators became convinced the LSAT discriminated against minority applicants. They stopped using it for admissions. They also stopped participating in the *US News* program rankings.

How did different groups respond to the university administrators? Focus on two groups: journalists and law school applicants.

Did the journalists have low confidence, moderate confidence, or high confidence in the way that the university administrators were behaving? How did the law school applicants feel? Explain the basis for your answers.

Question 3: Why Did Educational Administrators Embrace Standardized Tests?

Educational administrators had to demonstrate that their students, teachers, and schools were meeting standards. They relied on standardized tests. They directed teachers to prepare students to excel on these tests.

How did different groups respond to the educational administrators? Focus on two groups: journalists and parents.

Did the journalists have low confidence, moderate confidence, or high confidence in the way that the educational administrators were behaving? How did parents feel? Explain the basis for your answers.

Question 4: Why Did Educational Administrators Later Abandon Standardized Tests?

Educational administrators became alarmed when post-pandemic standardized test scores declined. After noting especially sharp declines among some minority groups, they contended that the tests were discriminatory. They pleaded for permission to abandon standardized tests when assessing students, teachers, and schools.

How did different groups respond to the educational administrators? Focus on two groups: journalists and parents.

Did the journalists have low confidence, moderate confidence, or high confidence in the way that the educational administrators were behaving? How did parents feel? Explain the basis for your answers.

SUMMARY

University administrators used LSAT scores to select students for admission. They also used them to rank law schools. However, they worried that the LSAT was biased against some minority students. They therefore designated different approaches for student admissions and law school rankings.

Educational administrators used standardized test scores to assess students, teachers, and schools. They were surprised when post-pandemic scores declined, especially among some minority groups. Worried that the tests were biased, they pleaded for permission to use different assessment techniques.

Chapter 6

The Web Filter Feuds

The Children's Internet Protection Act (CIPA) . . . addresses . . . access to obscene or harmful content over the Internet.
     —Federal Communications Commission, 2023

CIPA requires [that] schools . . . filter Internet access.
     —Federal Communications Commission, 2019

[Schools] must certify compliance with . . . CIPA to be eligible for . . . discounts on . . . internet access.
     —Universal Service Administrative Company, 2023

Inappropriate websites can be blocked [with web filters].
     —CurrentWare *Software Company, 2023*

[Web filtering protects children from] persistent predators, con artists, and fraudsters.
     —Bloski *Software Company, 2023*

Over-filtering . . . creates barriers to learning.
     —American Library Association
     Consultant Kristen Batch, 2014

[Web] filters pose particular problems for LGBT teenagers.
     —National Coalition Against Censorship, 2023

If you [wish to] bypass a school firewall . . . here are several methods.

—Tech Writer Simon Batt, 2022

Schools' efforts to block the Internet are so laughably lame.

—*Science* Journalist Annie Murphy Paul, 2014

> The executives at HBO Max approved *Gone with the Wind* for streaming. Although they realized this film contained racial stereotypes, they believed it still should be available to viewers. They later changed their minds and banned it from their network.
>
> School boards approved open access for school computers. Although they realized it might lead students to inappropriate sites, they believed it still should be available to them. They later changed their minds and installed web filters to block open access.

FILTERING FILMS

Home Box Office (HBO) was a fledgling network in 1972. It had only 365 subscribers. However, it expanded at an impressive rate. Fifty years later, it had over 97 million subscribers.

The executives at HBO eventually changed their company's name to HBO Max. They had a keen sense of the entertainment viewers were craving. They offered them musical performances, comedy routines, specially commissioned programs, and recent films.

The HBO Max executives did not doubt the value of recent and trendy entertainment. However, they also valued the classic films that had fascinated audiences during earlier eras. They knew the Turner Classic Movies (TCM) network maintained a large library of classic films.

The HBO Max executives discovered TCM's managerial staff had been struggling to attract more viewers. They offered to help them in 2021. They would provide a link from HBO Max to TCM.

The HBO Max executives believed a link from their station to TCM would benefit both networks. It would benefit TCM by increasing their viewership, generating income, and enabling them to stay in business. It would benefit HBO Max by letting it showcase the artistic works of earlier eras. They were excited about the partnership.

The HBO Max executives were aware that many of the films on TCM contained racially and culturally biased language, images, and plots. They were sure their viewers would notice the difference between those historical films and the original programs they had been commissioning.

The HBO Max executives allowed their staff to select the classic films featured on their network. They may have been unaware that they selected *Gone with the Wind* to air during the fall of 2020.

Audiences relished *Gone with the Wind* when it was released in 1939. They were drawn to its complex characters, engrossing plot, large-scale reenactments, and tragic ending. Critics also were drawn to the film. They praised the film's acting, directing, cinematography, screenplay, production sets, musical score, film editing, and visual effects.

The voters for the 1939 Hollywood Oscars validated the audiences and the critics. They designated *Gone with the Wind* for eight Academy Awards.

Not all viewers were pleased by *Gone with the Wind*. Some of them did not agree with its depiction of Confederate states. They were especially censorious of how it represented plantation owners and slaves. They noted that the original production staff members had argued about that content.

The critics of *Gone with the Wind* had been upset when the film played in theaters in 1939. They were no less upset when it was scheduled to air on HBO Max in the fall of 2020. John Ridley, a prominent African American director, demanded that the HBO Max executives abandon their hands-off scheduling policy, get involved, and cancel the film.

The HBO Max executives were unprepared for the turmoil that accompanied *Gone with the Wind*. They had commissioned numerous films and series that had highlighted the injustice and damage caused by racial discrimination. They did not want their efforts to be tarnished by a single film.

The HBO Max executives had been urged to take charge of *Gone with the Wind*. They followed this advice. They took charge and canceled the film.

Enthusiasts

The HBO Max executives had made a bold decision when they canceled *Gone with the Wind*. They anticipated they would be supported by the journalists covering the dispute about this film.

The fiercest critics of *Gone with the Wind* did support the executives. They saw no reason to air it on a media platform that had a solid reputation for combating racism and discrimination. They hoped the executives would make comparable decisions about the many other classic films exhibiting racial biases.

The executives were pleased when their critics changed their tone and complimented them. They hoped viewers would compliment them as well.

Some viewers were pleased with the cancellation of this controversial film. Although they had not intended to watch it, they did not want others to watch it. They worried that the film still had the potential to reinforce racism.

Skeptics

Some film VIPs, film critics, and viewers were delighted when the HBO Max executives canceled *Gone with the Wind*. They expressed confidence in them. However, others made it clear that they were skeptical.

The skeptics doubted that the cancellation of this controversial film was intended to change social or racial attitudes. They believed it was another example of the self-censorship that the entertainment industry had exhibited for decades. They contended that these self-censorship decisions had been intended to generate income rather than change attitudes.

The skeptics conceded that the cancellation of *Gone with the Wind* could inconvenience viewers who had intended to watch it on HBO Max. However, they noted that viewers still could view it on a different network or purchase it on DVD.

The skeptics had another objection to the cancellation. They had hoped viewers would watch the film on HBO Max and then make their judgments about it. They believed the cancellation would prevent viewers from forming opinions and benefiting from the process.

Many viewers took the side of the skeptics. They contended that the cancellation amounted to censorship. They compared the cancellation to historical and contemporary attempts to censor films, books, plays, and works of art.

The skeptics did not question that audiences needed to be educated about the racial inaccuracies in classic films. However, they cautioned against indiscriminately censoring those films. They contended that censoring prevented viewers from seeing how early generations had dealt with politically and socially contentious issues.

The skeptics proposed alternative ways of dealing with the inappropriate content in *Gone with the Wind*. They suggested that teachers present this film to students but make sure to precede and follow it with discussions of its strengths and weaknesses.

The skeptics had similar advice for the executives at HBO Max. They urged them to withdraw their directive to cancel *Gone with the Wind*. They suggested that they air the film to general audiences just as they originally had intended. However, they encouraged them to precede the film with a message about its merits, weaknesses, and reasons it deserved to be available to viewers.

FILTERING WEBSITES

School boards wanted to be responsive to parents. They listened attentively when they identified educational priorities. They were not surprised when they identified computer literacy as one of their highest priorities.

The parents had been bombarded with editorialized information about the importance of computer literacy. They were convinced that children who were computer literate could achieve high goals while they were in school and then continue to achieve them after they had moved into the workplace.

Many parents had computers and Internet services in their homes. They made these tools available to their children. However, they still wanted their children to have computers and Internet services at school.

Some parents did not have computers or Internet services at home. They believed their children were at a huge educational advantage compared to their peers from technology-rich homes. They demanded that their children have access to computers and Internet services at school.

The school boards agreed wholeheartedly with the parents. They repeatedly affirmed the importance of computer literacy.

The school boards assured the parents they were ready to promote computer literacy. However, they were shocked by the cost. They had to find the funds for the computers themselves. They also had to find funds for technology-equipped classrooms, ergonomic furniture, technology maintenance, software, on-site technicians, and Internet services.

Many school boards viewed Internet-connected computers as digitized textbooks. They were excited because digitized textbooks, unlike paper ones, provided readers with unlimited information. They therefore reallocated a portion of their printed-textbook budgets to purchase e-textbooks. However, they still had to find the funds for the desktop computers, laptop computers, and tablets on which e-textbooks could be displayed.

The school boards were pleased with the e-textbooks and equipment that they acquired. They were sure the students also were excited.

The school boards assumed that parents shared the excitement about e-textbooks and equipment. They seemed surprised after quite a few parents indicated that they were not pleased. They soon realized that these parents were genuinely distraught.

The distraught parents doubted that their children were being adequately supervised on school computers. They feared their children might be using them to access inappropriate websites. They urged the school boards to limit the Internet sites their children couldvisit.

The distraught parents had another concern about school computers. They had read reports about students who had been distracted by computers during class time. They discovered that these students chatted with friends, made social posts, or played computerized games. They urged the school boards to take steps to prevent these behaviors.

The school boards agreed with the distraught parents. They enacted policies stating that students should use school computers solely for educational reasons. They directed teachers to advise their students of this policy and then follow it.

The teachers did their best to monitor students when they were on school computers. However, they admitted that they could observe them intermittently at best.

The school boards had promised to reduce inappropriate use of classroom computers. They also had promised to prevent students from accessing inappropriate websites. After they had made only limited progress, they turned to business entrepreneurs for help.

The school boards learned that entrepreneurs had devised web filters for the workplace. They discovered that the filters could restrict the sites that employees could access. They asked the entrepreneurs if they could adapt these filters for students on school computers.

The entrepreneurs assured the school boards that they could help. They conceded that their web filters had not been effective in blocking all inappropriate websites. However, they quickly added that they had been remarkably effective in blocking pornographic websites. They contended that they could adapt these filters to block any websites that the school boards identified.

The school boards were intrigued by the web filters. They hoped they would appease distraught parents. They hoped they also would appease irascible federal officials.

Federal elected officials had passed the Children's Internet Protection Act (CIPA) in 2000. They had wished to ensure that students focused exclusively on reputable educational websites. They prodded the schools to install web filters to prevent students from accessing disreputable sites.

The Federal Communications Commission was designated to enforce CIPA compliance. Its staff urged school boards to install web filters. They promised that those who complied would receive a reward. They would give them a discounted rate (E-rate) on Internet services.

The school boards had struggled to create adequate technology budgets. They had difficulty finding the money for computers, tech-savvy teachers, technicians, software, and Internet services. They were sure the bargain-priced E-rate would help them balance their budgets.

The school board purchased the web filters. They then installed them on all student computers. They knew elected officials would be pleased. They anticipated parents also would be pleased. They were eager to observe the parents' reactions.

Enthusiasts

Parents were excited about the web filters. They were impressed that they could block websites with sexually explicit content. However, they wanted them to block additional sites.

Some parents wanted the filters to block students' email accounts, messaging apps, and social media sites. They explained that students seemed obsessed with reading and responding to information on these sites. They suspected they were logging into them when they should have been logging into educational websites.

Some parents worried about websites with graphically depicted violent images. They were concerned that students would access these sites, view the images, and then suffer emotionally. They wanted the schools to block those sites.

Some parents were concerned about political issues. They feared that students would view websites that misrepresented or demeaned progressive values. Others had this apprehension about websites that misrepresented or demeaned conservative values. Although both groups wanted filters, they could not agree about the websites they should block.

Elected state officials paid attention to their constituents. They believed that the constiuents supported laws requiring filters on all school computers. They enacted these laws in more than a dozen states.

Rhode Island's state officials supported the web filter movement. They insisted that all school computers in their state have them. They demanded that these filters block pornographic websites. However, they could not agree on the additional websites they should block. They deferred to the Rhode Island State Department of Education, which required local school boards to specify those sites.

Skeptics

Some parents championed web filters. However, others were skeptical of them.

The filter skeptics doubted that the devices were effective. They conceded that they could block some sites with obscene text and images. However, they doubted that they would block all of them.

The skeptics believed the filters would underperform and allow students to access objectionable websites. However, they added that they would over-filter as well as under-filter. They explained that they would over-filter by blocking students from websites that did not have objectional content and that were appropriate for them.

Many groups took the side of the skeptical parents. These groups included journalists, scholars, educators, political activists, and librarians. They judged that web filtering amounted to Internet censorship. They opposed it for the same reasons that they opposed book censorship.

The skeptics did not question that schools needed to protect children while they were using the Internet. However, they cautioned them to avoid commercial web filters. They gave examples of the harm that these filters had caused when they had prevented students from accessing websites with vital information about safe sex, LGBTQ issues, teenage pregnancy, and venereal disease.

The skeptics found another problem with commercial web filters. They explained that they could easily be circumvented with techniques available to students online.

The skeptics proposed alternative ways that teachers could deal with inappropriate Internet content. They suggested that they keep an eye on students while they were online, identify those visiting inappropriate sites, counsel them, and specify consequences if they continued to visit those sites.

QUESTIONS ABOUT FILTERED INFORMATION

This section focuses on the preceding two cases. The first case involved the executives at HBO Max.

The HBO Max executives streamed a diverse range of entertainment, including films. They were pleased when some of their films turned out to be viewer favorites.

The HBO Max executives primarily streamed contemporary films. Nonetheless, they also streamed some classic films from the 1930s and the 1940s. They streamed these classic films through a link to another network—the TCM network.

The executives realized that Hollywood's VIPs, cinema professionals, and film journalists were committed to preserving and airing classic films. They took pains to satisfy them. They assumed that they were pleased with the classic films that they featured.

The executives did not personally select classic films for streaming. They delegated this task to knowledgeable staff. Since they rarely heard criticism, they believed the staff were making noncontroversial selections.

The executives cared about approval from elite members of the Hollywood community. They also cared about approval from the patrons who subscribed to their network. Although they realized that relatively few patrons watched classic films, they believed that most of them still wanted these films to be available.

The executives knew that classic films could have drawbacks. For example, they were aware that many contained racial stereotypes. They still allowed them to stream. They believed that the benefits of these films outweighed their drawbacks.

The executives did not review all the films their staff selected for streaming. They may not have even been aware when they selected *Gone with the Wind* to stream in 2020.

John Ridley, a prominent African American director, learned of the decision to stream *Gone with the Wind*. He disagreed with that decision. He noted that the film was filled with racial stereotypes. He demanded that the HBO Max executives abandon their hands-off scheduling policy, get involved, and cancel the film.

Ridley attracted the attention of scores of journalists. He must have been pleased by the many who agreed with his recommendations and who placed additional pressure on the HBO Max executives. He had to be just as pleased by the many viewers who agreed with him and who exerted still more pressure.

The executives succumbed to the pressure from critics and viewers. They canceled the film. They assumed that they had suppressed the commotion. However, they soon realized that the commotion was far from over.

While the first case in this chapter concerned HBO Max executives, the next case focused on school boards. The boards were responsible for regulating the Iternet websites students could access on school computers.

The school boards had given their students open access to the Internet. Although they realized that the students might inadvertently view inappropriate websites, they believed they would benefit because they would be developing the skills to recognize inappropriate sites and avoid them.

The school boards were excited about Internet-linked computers. They considered them to be gateways to invaluable information. Nonetheless, they were dismayed by their cost.

The school boards had to come up with funds to purchase computers. They then needed additional funds for printers, software, and Internet access. They needed still more funds to hire specially trained teachers and technicians. They were not sure where to get these funds. They pleaded with federal government officials for financial help.

The government officials were willing to help. They announced that they would provide low-cost Internet service for students. However, they would require that schools follow a code to qualify for this service.

The school boards would be eligible for low-cost Internet service if they followed the code specified within the CIPA. They discovered that this code required them to limit children's access to Internet sites with obscene or harmful information.

The CIPA code was quite specific. It detailed how school boards were to limit children's access to Internet sites. It directed them to install web filters.

The school boards agreed to the web filters. They assumed some students would be frustrated and try to get around them. They were correct.

The school boards anticipated that parents would see the benefits of web filters and then support them. This time they were incorrect. Although some parents did see the benefits, others detected too many drawbacks to support them.

The following questions will assist you if you are going through this book alone. They provide opportunities like those you would have in a college classroom where the professor is using the case method. They also will help you if you are in an actual college classroom with a professor using this approach.

Question 1: Why Did HBO Max Executives Schedule *Gone with the Wind* for Streaming?

HBO Max executives hired expert staff to select classic movies for their network. They initially did not interfere when they selected *Gone with the Wind*. They believed that they had the approval of film critics and viewers.

How did different groups respond to the HBO Max executives? Focus on two groups: film critics and viewers.

Did the film critics have low, moderate, or high confidence in the way that the HBO Max executives were behaving? How did the viewers feel? Explain the basis for your answers.

When answering these questions, as well as those that follow, you can rely on the information in this chapter. You also might rely on some of the sources identified in the references at the rear of the book. If you are reading this chapter with colleagues, you are encouraged to converse with them about the best way to answer the questions.

Question 2: Why Did HBO Max Executives Cancel *Gone with the Wind*?

The HBO Max executives were publicly chastised for scheduling *Gone with the Wind*. They were charged with promoting a film that had glaring racial stereotypes. Fearful of the repercussions from these charges, they changed their minds and canceled the broadcast.

How did different groups respond to the HBO Max executives? Focus on two groups: film critics and viewers.

Did the film critics have low, moderate, or high confidence in the way that the HBO Max executives were behaving? How did the viewers feel? Explain the basis for your answers.

Question 3: Why Did School Boards Provide Open Internet Access to Students?

School boards hired technical staff to manage computers. They did not interfere when they provided students with open access to Internet sites. They believed that they had the approval of elected officials and parents.

How did different groups respond to the school boards? Focus on two groups: elected officials and parents.

Did the elected officials have low, moderate, or high confidence in the way that the school boards were behaving? How did the parents feel? Explain the basis for your answers.

Question 4: Why Did School Boards Cancel Open Access?

School boards were publicly chastised for providing students with open access. They were charged with putting them at risk to view inappropriate, harmful, or obscene websites. Fearful of repercussions from these charges, they changed their minds and installed web filters.

How did different groups respond to the school boards? Focus on two groups: elected officials and parents.

Did the elected officials have low, moderate, or high confidence in the way that the school boards were behaving? How did the parents feel? Explain the basis for your answers.

SUMMARY

HBO Max executives scheduled *Gone with the Wind* to air on their network. However, they were criticized because this film reinforced racial stereotypes. They therefore changed their minds and banned the film. They then waited to see if the criticism subsided.

School boards provided open access to Internet sites on school computers. However, they were criticized because open access allowed students to view inappropriate websites. They therefore changed their minds and installed web filters. They then waited to see if the criticism subsided.

Chapter 7

The School AI Feuds

[Commerical] companies play a crucial role in advancing the use of AI in the classroom.

—*Edutech Global* CTO Olufemi Shonubi, 2023

[People will be] stunned by how [helpful AI is] with reading . . . [and] writing.

—*Microsoft* Founder Bill Gates, 2023

[AI uses] text that simulates human language.

—Journalist Imad Khan, 2023

[The AI in] ELL classrooms . . . [give students] immediate feedback on [their] pronunciation.

—High School Teacher Larry Ferlazzo, 2023

[AI can] find answers to . . . homework questions.

—*Homework Helper* Webpage, *2023*

[AI can develop] social-emotional learning (SEL) competencies.

—*Prodigy* Spokesperson Mandy Froehlich, 2022

[Classroom AI has been] built without any input from teachers.

—*International Society for Technology in Education* CEO Richard Culatta, 2023

> College students used artificial intelligence (AI) to complete their writing assignments. They claimed that it improved their prose and eased their stress. However, they had a hard time convincing skeptical professors.
>
> School boards used AI to instruct students. They claimed that it enhanced face-to-face instruction and eased instructor stress. However, they had a hard time convincing skeptical teachers.

AI IN COLLEGE

College students had been introduced to artificial intelligence (AI) in their classrooms, laboratories, and textbooks. As a result, they knew quite a bit about it.

The students continued to learn about AI outside of college. They engaged Siri, the iPhone's chatbot, to answer questions about restaurants, video games, music, politics, geography, history, and countless other topics. They engaged other AI chatbots while driving cars, banking online, or filing insurance claims.

The students valued the AI chatbots that they had encountered. They were eager to locate still more. They hoped to find some that could help with their college studies.

The students had no trouble locating chatbots for some specific academic applications. For example, they found ones that could construct animations, enhance photos, or assess the authenticity of antiques. However, only a few of them were enrolled in courses to which these skills were relevant.

The students hoped to locate chatbots that could help with a broad range of courses. For example, they looked for ones that would help them write essay-length passages. They were under pressure to make sure their passages had correct spelling, good grammar, accurate research citations, and appropriate formatting. Although they could rely on word processing programs to attend to these features, they had to generate the content on their own.

The students became excited in 2020. They learned that a group of entrepreneurs at the OpenAI firm had developed a chatbot that could write an essay on virtually any topic.

The students downloaded the AI chatbot, which had been named ChatGPT. They were delighted by its cost: it was free. They also were delighted by its ease of use: they simply posed written questions and waited for an essay to appear.

The students were impressed by the quality of the AI-generated essays. Some of them copied the essays, adapted them, and submitted personalized versions to their professors. Others copied the AI-generated essays verbatim, fixed their names to them, and submitted them.

The students were eager to see how their professors would respond to the AI essays. They beamed after they found few errors and assigned high grades.

The students judged that ChatGPT was the program for which they had been searching. They used it to gather content, fashion faultless prose, and procure high grades. As a result, they were feeling less stress.

The professors soon realized that they had been duped. They became agitated. They warned their students to cease using ChatGPT.

The professors announced that they were able to detect AI-generated essays. They intended to treat culprits as plagiarists. They threatened to assign them failing grades, report them for academic misconduct, suspend them, or even expel them.

The students consulted online blogs to learn whether their professors truly could differentiate AI writing from human writing. They concluded that the professors were bluffing. They therefore ignored their threats and continued to give them AI-written passages.

Enthusiasts

Journalists were in the business of creating clear, precise, and persuasive prose. They were exhilarated by the prospect of investigating ChatGPT.

The journalists realized that the college students had a very positive view of ChatGPT. They were not surprised. After all, they had been using somewhat similar writing tools for decades.

The journalist noted that the college students had been relying on word processing programs to check their spelling, word usage, grammar, style, formatting, and citation structure. They viewed ChatGPT as the progeny of those programs.

Many of the journalists took the side of the students. They described how they relied on ChatGPT in their college courses. However, they also provided details about those who had graduated, taken jobs, devised job-related applications for ChatGPT, and earned praise from their employers.

The journalists reported that some tech entrepreneurs treated AI writing as a novel and powerful communication strategy. They described how they had encouraged workers to learn it and even arranged training to facilitate their learning.

The journalists anticipated that the college students and the tech entrepreneurs would be pleased by their enthusiastic reporting. They were correct.

Skeptics

The journalists identified pro-ChatGPT professors and the reasons why they supported AI writing. However, they also described anti-ChatGPT professors and their basis for opposing this program.

The anti-ChatGPT professors claimed that the students who used AI to write were unethical. They claimed they were no different than students who copied prose from their classmates. They intended to treat them as plagiarists.

Some journalists took the side of the anti-ChatGPT professors. They characterized them as bold warriors defending academic integrity, the sanctity of the English language, and truth. They urged them to continue their efforts to ferret out AI-written assignments and punish the students who submitted them.

AI AT SCHOOL

School boards wished to ensure that the students in their districts received high-quality education. They hired top-notch administrators and directed them to focus on quality.

The school boards realized that the administrators needed funds to maintain and improve quality. They apologized that they could provide them with limited funds to hire additional teachers. They still encouraged them to recruit and retain truly talented teachers.

The school boards recognized the difficulty that their administrators faced in hiring and retaining talented teachers. They were frustrated when they reported how top teachers had resigned to work in districts that paid higher salaries.

The school boards tried to find solutions to their problems. They turned to businesspeople for help.

Some of the businesspeople offered online instructor-directed modules. They explained that certified teachers introduced the modules, guided students through them, tested them, graded their tests, counseled them, and answered their questions.

Some businesspeople offered AI-directed instructional modules. They explained that AI chatbots introduced the modules, guided the students through them, graded their responses, and answered their questions.

The school boards were fascinated by the AI-directed instructional modules. They discovered they were expensive because they required special instructional software, hardware, and maintenance staff. However, they could redirect unused teacher salary funds to cover these expenses.

The school boards were excited. They signed the contracts for AI instruction. They were eager to see the reactions of their teachers. They anticipated they would be excited because AI chatbots would relieve them of some burdensome tasks.

Enthusiasts

The teachers who taught English Language Learners (ELL) were enthusiastic about AI instruction. In fact, these teachers were extremely enthusiastic.

The ELL teachers faced a daunting challenge. They had to provide English instruction and academic instruction simultaneously. They were sure that the AI chatbots could help them with English instruction. They programmed them to introduce target words to students, drill them on those words, and continue the drills until the students were pronouncing the words correctly.

The ELL teachers observed the chatbots listening to students and correcting them when they mispronounced words. They were impressed by their ability to simulate caring attitudes toward the students. They also were impressed by their ability to simulate excitement when students responded correctly.

Special education teachers were another group that enthusiastically welcomed AI chatbots into their classrooms. Some programmed them to drill students on academic tasks. Others programmed them to drill students on life skills. They were impressed by the chatbots' patience, persistence, and attention to detail during these drills.

Some teachers taught extremely large numbers of students. They had been unable to give students the attention they needed. They programmed the AI chatbots to instruct students who were sorted by academic abilities. They welcomed these chatbots.

School administrators carefully weighed the expenses of AI chatbots. They conceded that they were expensive. However, they viewed them as virtual teachers. They calculated that they would turn out to be cheaper than actual teachers. They therefore were enthusiastic. They hoped that parents would share their enthusiasm.

Skeptics

Parents had been flooded with news about the rapid spread of AI technology. They wanted the schools to prepare their children to use this technology in their classrooms, in their daily lives, and, eventually, in their workplaces. Many of them were enthusiastic about the AI chatbots that were introduced into their children's classrooms.

The parents observed their children interacting with the chatbots. Many then remained enthusiastic. However, some changed their minds and became skeptical. The skeptics noted that the chatbots were employing instructional strategies that resembled video game strategies. They questioned their value.

Some teachers agreed with the skeptical parents. They saw hardly any resemblance between their instruction and the AI instruction. They were not surprised because the AI instruction had been designed without their input.

The skeptical teachers had another reason for being nervous. They reported that some of their districts had purchased AI software bundled into Google Chromebooks. They complained that the Chromebooks were poorly constructed, easily damaged, and dependent on faulty operational software.

The skeptical teachers worried that technologically sophisticated students would outsmart chatbots. They predicted that they would figure out ways to solve AI problems without doing ancillary learning activities. They noted that some of them already had figured out how to write essays with ChatGPT-generated passages.

The skeptical teachers had still another reason why they were worried about AI technology. They feared school boards would replace human staff with AI technology. They called on their union leaders for protection.

The skeptical teachers hoped journalists would listen to their objections to AI instructional technology, take their side, and broadcast their objections to a wide audience. Although they were pleased when many did take their side, they were disappointed that most of them focused solely on ChatGPT.

The school boards listened to the arguments of those teachers, parents, and journalists urging them to stop AI instruction. However, they ignored them and announced that they would not place limitations on AI instruction. They directed skeptical teachers to suppress their concerns and use AI instruction in their classrooms.

Some school boards wished to avoid offending the AI skeptics or the AI enthusiasts. They announced that they would impose a ban on AI instruction—but only on AI writing instruction. They sanctioned all other AI instructional programs. They hoped that this tempered response would appease both feuding groups.

The school boards had listened to the arguments from AI enthusiasts and the counterarguments from skeptics. The tech entrepreneurs who had developed the AI instruction also listened to them. The entrepreneurs wished to continue selling their products to schools. They did not want to alienate teachers or parents.

The entrepreneurs agreed with the enthusiasts. However, they did not completely dismiss the concerns of the skeptics. They insisted that they had been making changes to address their concerns. They explained that they were collaborating with computer manufacturers to design products that could run on relatively inexpensive but highly reliable devices. They also were collaborating with teachers to make AI products that were more like classroom instruction. Finally, they were taking steps to protect their products from student hackers.

QUESTIONS ABOUT ERGONOMIC TECHNOLOGY

This section focuses on the preceding two cases. The first case involved college students.

College students were required to write essays for their courses. Many of them viewed these assignments as unnecessarily laborious and stressful.

The students were intrigued when a San Franciso firm, OpenAI, released a Generative Pre-trained Transformer (GPT) program. They hoped that the program would solve their writing problems.

The entrepreneurs at OpenAI introduced their GPT program in 2018. They embedded it within an AI chatbot two years later. They gave the chatbot an amorphous name—ChatGPT. They told users they could submit questions to their chatbot and be rewarded with written answers.

The college students were under pressure to write essay-length responses to questions from their professors. They submitted the questions to the AI chatbot. They were delighted by the passages with which it responded.

Some of the students fashioned the AI passages into personalized essays. However, others submitted them verbatim to their professors. Both groups were excited when the professors assigned high grades to their essays.

The professors were pleased by the quality of the written passages students were submitting in their classes. They initially did not realize the role that AI programs had played. After they discovered this role, they became upset.

The upset professors prohibited their students from using AI writing. They told them that they equated it with plagiarism. They threatened to penalize anyone who disregarded their prohibition.

The students were momentarily stunned. However, they questioned whether their professors could differentiate AI writing from human writing. Confident that they could not, they ignored the prohibition. They were relieved after their professors did not decipher the true origin of their essays.

While the first case in this chapter concerned college students, the next case focused on school boards. The school boards were responsible for teachers, instruction, and student learning.

The school boards were always on the lookout for ways to improve the quality of instruction. They realized a sure way would be to pay high salaries to recruit the most talented teachers. However, many did not have the funds these teachers commanded.

The school boards wondered whether technology could help them solve their personnel shortage. They searched for innovative, affordable, and effective instructional technology. They were particularly excited by technology that relied on AI.

The school boards were already quite familiar with AI outside of the schools. They had interacted with it on their phones and in vehicles, homes, and businesses. They began to peruse reports about the positive impact it was having at some schools.

The school boards met with AI sales agents. They then learned about AI software and hardware for schools. They were assured that these products were interesting, affordable, and effective.

The sales agents had AI software for every academic subject. They also had it for every scholastic level from preschool through high school. They assured hesitant school boards that it would increase their teachers' effectiveness while reducing their stress.

The school boards were intrigued. They realized that they would have to budget for the AI instructional software, the hardware on which to run it, and the technical staff to maintain it. They noted that the budget, although substantial, could be much less than the budget to hire additional teachers.

The school boards eventually were ready to implement AI instruction in their schools. They wondered how their teachers would respond. They knew that some of them had been skeptical from the start.

The skeptical teachers explained why they were nervous. They worried that AI chatbots would eventually replace them. They called on their union leaders to block this new technology.

Some of the skeptical teachers were nervous for another reason. They noted that the AI chatbots had been designed by engineers. They characterized them as error-prone during classroom use. They did not wish to introduce them into their classrooms.

The following questions will assist you if you are going through this book alone. They provide opportunities like those you would have in a college classroom where the professor was using the case method. They also will help you if you are in an actual college classroom with a professor who is using this approach.

Question 1: Why Did College Students Embrace AI Writing?

College students used AI writing programs to generate essays for their classes. They claimed that they improved their prose while reducing their stress.

How did different groups respond to the college students? Focus on two groups: journalists and tech entrepreneurs.

Did the journalists have low confidence, moderate confidence, or high confidence in the way that the college students were behaving? How did the tech entrepreneurs feel? Explain the basis for your answers.

When answering these questions, as well as those that follow, you can rely on the information in this chapter. You also might rely on some of the sources identified in the references at the rear of the book. If you are reading this chapter with colleagues, you are encouraged to converse with them about the best way to answer the questions.

Question 2: How Did College Students Deal with Professors Who Objected to AI Writing?

College students submitted AI-written assignments in their classes. When they were confronted by professors who equated AI writing with plagiarism, they ignored them and continued to submit AI-written assignments.

How did different groups respond to the college students? Focus on two groups: journalists and tech entrepreneurs.

Did the journalists have low confidence, moderate confidence, or high confidence in the way that the college students were behaving? How did the tech entrepreneurs feel? Explain the basis for your answers.

Question 3: Why Did School Boards Embrace AI Instruction?

School boards authorized the use of AI instructional programs. They claimed that they improved student learning while reducing teacher stress.

How did different groups respond to the school boards? Focus on two groups: journalists and tech entrepreneurs.

Did the journalists have low confidence, moderate confidence, or high confidence in the way that the school boards were behaving? How did the tech entrepreneurs feel? Explain the basis for your answers.

Question 4: How Did School Boards Deal with Teachers Who Objected to AI Instruction?

School boards introduced AI instruction. When they were confronted by teachers who objected to instruction developed by engineers, some boards ignored them. Others were willing to compromise by banning just AI writing instruction.

How did different groups respond to the school boards? Focus on two groups: journalists and tech entrepreneurs.

Did the journalists have low confidence, moderate confidence, or high confidence in the way that the school boards were behaving? How did the tech entrepreneurs feel? Explain the basis for your answers.

SUMMARY

College students used AI programs to complete writing assignments. They were convinced that they reduced their stress and improved their prose. Many continued to use them even after their professors disagreed.

School boards used AI programs to instruct students. They were convinced that they reduced teachers' stress and improved their instruction. Many continued to use them even after their teachers disagreed.

Chapter 8

The School Bus Feuds

[Diesel school buses are known for their] safety, energy efficiency, reliability, [and] durability.

—Diesel Technology Forum, 2023

[Diesel school buses] are more than 90% cleaner than they were in 2006.

—Thomasbuiltbuses Company, 2023

[Diesel school buses still] produce fumes that are harmful to children.

—Vermont Energy Investment Corporation, 2023

[When my daughter inhaled diesel school bus fumes], she got headaches and sick to her stomach.

—Parent Areli Sanchez, 2024

[Electric school buses] protect our children from harmful [diesel fumes].

—Environmental Law & Policy Center, 2023

[Electric school buses have] a lot of downtime and performance issues.

—Ann Arbor Public Schools Environmental Sustainability Director Emile Lauzzana, 2023

> Auto dealers tried to persuade customers to visit showrooms, view cars, and make purchases. They acquired as many vehicles as they could from manufacturers. They then priced them flexibly. However, they had to change these strategies after the COVID-19 pandemic disrupted their industry.
>
> School boards tried to transport students efficiently. They acquired as many school buses as they could afford. They preferred those buses with reasonably priced diesel engines. However, they had to change these strategies because of government pressure to acquire electric vehicles.

AUTO LOGISTICS

Car dealers were eager to sell new vehicles to customers. However, they first had to attract customers to their showrooms and car lots.

The dealers copied a strategy from department store managers. They noted that these managers had lured customers by expanding their product inventories.

The dealers expanded the number of vehicles at their showrooms and lots. They ensured that their inventories included multiple models in diverse colors with numerous features. They anticipated that this type of inventory would entice customers to view vehicles sit in them, and drive them.

The dealers were happy with this strategy. They concluded that it was attracting customers. However, they still had to persuade the customers to make purchases. They had another strategy in mind.

The dealers realized that many customers were nervous about closing deals because of the high prices of vehicles. They therefore offered discounted prices. They also offered loans with reduced interest rates, extended payback periods, generous trade-in compensations, and free equipment options.

The dealers were pleased with their financial strategies. They judged that they complemented their large-inventory strategy. They made greater and greater profits each year. They assumed that this pattern would continue indefinitely.

The dealers became unnerved in 2020. They realized they had been too optimistic when they were predicting continued profits. They were caught off guard by the massive COVID-19 pandemic. They watched helplessly as it disrupted the international automobile supply line.

The dealers could no longer maintain the large vehicle inventories to which they had become accustomed. Many of them received only a fraction of their previous supply. Some received no new cars whatsoever.

The dealers had to devise new strategies for luring customers. They relied on marketers to create visually enticing photographs of the new vehicles. They hoped that these images would entice customers to visit their car lots. They were pleased when this strategy turned out to be effective.

The dealers typically had only a vehicle or two on their lots and in their showrooms. They told the customers that they could sit in these cars and interact with them. They even told them that they could test-drive them. However, they made it clear that they could not purchase these vehicles.

Customers discovered that the procedures for purchasing new vehicles had changed. They would have to preorder new vehicles. They then would wait until their vehicles were assembled, transported, and delivered. They learned that this waiting period could take several months or even longer.

The dealers had made additional changes to their purchasing procedures. They would no longer be negotiating prices with customers. They would charge them full retail prices for cars. They even might be adding surcharges to the prices for especially hard-to-procure vehicles.

The dealers explained to their customers that pandemic-caused auto disruptions had forced them to change their traditional purchasing procedures. They asked them to be patient and understanding.

Enthusiasts

Car dealers had been alarmed after the pandemic created an industry-wide shortage of vehicles. They quickly changed the way that they conducted business. They then watched to see how customers were reacting.

The customers were nonplussed when they visited car lots and found no new vehicles on them. They met with sales representatives and asked for an explanation.

The sales representatives told the customers that they still could purchase new vehicles. However, they would have to preorder them and wait for them to be manufactured, painted in the colors they wanted, and equipped with designated options.

The sales representatives were pleased when customers indicated that they understood the industry-wide disruptions and still would be interested in purchasing new cars. The sales representatives then moved on to car prices.

The sales representatives made it clear to customers that they could not negotiate new car prices. They would have to charge them the full list prices. They sometimes added special surcharges for extremely scarce vehicles.

Many customers wanted additional information about vehicle shortages and prices. They turned to journalists. They wanted to see how they were covering the new sales practices by the car dealers.

Most journalists sympathized with the dealers. They reported that they were the victims of the unprecedented events that had disrupted their industry. They concluded that neither the auto dealers nor manufacturers should be blamed for the shortages or the soaring prices of new cars.

Skeptics

Many journalists portrayed the auto dealers sympathetically. They assured their readers, listeners, and viewers that the dealers were not using the pandemic as a pretext to make windfall profits.

Not all journalists were sympathetic to the car dealers. Business journalists carefully analyzed the quarterly financial reports from the dealers. They then questioned whether they were facing genuine financial threats.

The dealers certainly had struggled financially during the early months of the pandemic. However, they quickly recovered. They then began making profits comparable to those they had made before the pandemic. They eventually made greater profits.

The skeptical journalists had assumed that car dealers who recovered their business would revert to earlier sales and financial practices. They were struck by their reluctance. They assumed they retained the pandemic-era practices because they were so profitable.

Some customers agreed with the skeptical journalists. They demanded that the dealers expand their inventories and again negotiate prices with customers. They were annoyed when the dealers resisted.

The skeptical customers were frustrated by the car dealers. They looked for an innovative way to purchase new cars. They went to online car dealers.

The skeptical customers appreciated the online car dealers' mammoth car inventories. They also appreciated their refreshingly candid negotiation practices. For example, they liked the way that the online dealers displayed the prices they had paid to acquire cars and the markups they added to them. They realized that the online dealers were selling cars for thousands of dollars less than the dealers with car lots and showrooms.

SCHOOL BUS LOGISTICS

School boards required superintendents to categorize their districts' annual expenditures. They carefully reviewed the amounts that they allocated for each category. As examples, they considered their amounts for administration, teaching, clerical support, building maintenance, grounds maintenance, athletic facility maintenance, instructional equipment, textbooks, and student transportation. They then approved or modified their budgets.

The school boards ensured that administrators did not exceed their spending target for student transportation. However, they also ensured that they did not sacrifice safety or efficiency. They reminded them that parents had assigned high priority to both features.

Parents frequently had been disappointed by the student transportation in their districts. They complained that transportation was unsafe when children had to leave their homes before dawn, walk to distant stops, and then wait in inclement weather to catch their school buses.

Parents complained that student transportation could be inefficient as well as unsafe. They noted that some children had to wait at their bus stops for hours. They added that they then might have to endure hours-long rides to reach school and later return from it.

School board members listened to parents who were distressed about unsafe and inefficient student transportation. They told them that they shared their distress. They then tried to appease them.

The school boards were not always successful in appeasing parents. They realized that many parents were disappointed by changes they initiated. They became even more distressed after these parents went to journalists and asked them to publicize the school boards' inability to make student transportation safe and efficient.

The school boards did not give up. They insisted that they could solve the transportation problems. They told parents and journalists that they had a straightforward solution for these problems. They would purchase more buses and hire more bus drivers.

The school boards believed they could find addtional money to spend on student transportation. However, they were nervous because they were under pressure from powerful groups to spend more on other school needs. They had to consider the pressure exerted by teachers, state legislators, federal educational officials, and law enforcement officers.

Teachers had been pressuring the school boards about their meager salaries. They expected them to find the money needed to boost them.

State legislators had been pressuring the school boards about declining test scores. They expected them to find a way to raise them. They also expected them to replace outdated textbooks.

Federal educational officials had been pressuring the school boards about diversity-equity-inclusion initiatives. They expected them to find a way to expand and enrich them.

Law enforcement officers had been pressuring the school boards about school safety. They expected them to find better ways to protect students, teachers, and staff.

The school boards needed funds to respond to all these groups, including the parents who wanted them to purchase school buses. They immediately realized that they could not spend an excessive amount per bus.

The school boards met with vendors to discuss school buses. They made it clear that the buses had to be reliable and low-priced. Most of them eventually decided to purchase highly reliable but relatively inexpensive diesel school buses. They viewed the purchases as opportunities to expand their fleets while restraining spending.

The school boards cared about parents. They could not stay in office without their confidence. However, they also cared about state and federal legislators. They could not balance their budgets without the funds they supplied.

School boards were nervous when dealing with legislators. They had seen instances in which the legislators had inadvertently interfered with student transportation. For example, Florida legislators believed that the school boards had set starting times that were too early for high schoolers and middle schoolers. They passed a 2023 law requiring them to start school at 8:30 am or later.

The Florida school boards had been using the 8:30 am start time for young students. They did not have enough school buses or drivers to transport the young students and the high schoolers at the same time. They explained that they would need funds to expand their school bus system. They were disappointed when the legislators turned down this request but still insisted that they switch to the earlier start times for all students.

The Florida legislators had directed the school boards to adjust their schedules to accommodate later school starts for middle schools and high schools. They seemed to be unaware that they had made student transportation more expensive. They also seemed to be unaware that federal legislators were demanding additional changes that would make student transportation more expensive.

The federal legislators were pressuring school boards to abandon diesel school buses. They told them that diesel buses produced exhaust fumes that endangered students' health. They wanted to replace the unhealthy diesel buses with cleaner electric school buses (ESBs).

The school boards had been attempting to assemble the largest fleets of school buses they could afford. They had focused on reasonable-priced diesel buses. They could not afford a shift to more expensive ESBs. They asked the federal legislators to supply the funds needed to make this shift.

The federal legislators agreed to provide five billion dollars for ESB grants and subsidies. They indicated that they would be collaborating with state legislators and private companies to provide still more funds. They calculated that the total funding would make the shift to ESBs quite reasonable.

The school boards were impressed. They indicated they would apply for the federal, state, and private grants. They then would start to acquire the ESBs.

Enthusiasts

The school boards were ready to purchase ESBs. Some of them calculated that they could make the purchases without spending any district funds.

The school boards wondered how the public would respond to their ESB plans. They were particularly interested in parents.

Many parents were eager to convert from diesel school buses to ESBs. They had been worried by the government's warnings about the danger of diesel bus fumes. They viewed conversion to ESBs as an effective way to eliminate that danger.

The pro-ESB parents had considered the high cost of ESBs to be a deterrent. They were overjoyed when they learned that the government and private companies would be picking up some, and possibly all, of the costs.

Environmentally minded journalists applauded the federal legislators, state legislators, and businesspeople who were pro-ESB. They had been reporting on the increasing level of pollution in the environment. They viewed the ESB initiatives as a significant way to combat that pollution. They were eager to change the minds of people who disagreed with them.

Skeptics

Many parents supported the shift from diesel buses to ESBs. However, some were skeptical.

The skeptical parents had been complaining about the inefficiency of current student transportation. They had been excited when the school boards had pledged to acquire more school buses and drivers. They had hoped that these acquisitions would lead to short rides with convenient stops.

The skeptical parents supported the school boards' original plan. They urged them to acquire more school buses and drivers. They doubted they could implement this plan if they transitioned to expensive ESBs.

RESPONDING TO QUESTIONS ABOUT LOGISTICS

This section focuses on the preceding two cases. The first case involved auto dealers.

Auto dealers had ways to lure customers to their lots. For example, they kept large inventories of new vehicles on them. They realized the customers wanted opportunities to view multiple vehicles, test-drive them, and determine which models suited them.

The dealers tried to persuade customers to purchase the vehicles they had viewed and driven. They relied on incentives. For example, they reduced vehicle prices, offered loans at special interest rates, waived down payments, and offered no-cost vehicle options.

The dealers had confidence in their sales strategies. They had employed them for decades. They credited them for increasing their profits year after year.

The dealers pleaded with their suppliers to send as many vehicles as they could to their lots. They explained that they had been extremely successful when they had large inventories. They had been pleased by the suppliers' responses.

The dealers assumed that they would continue to receive large shipments of new vehicles. Consequently, they were unprepared for the problem they encountered in 2020. They listened as their suppliers explained that they were unable to get essential vehicle components because of the worldwide COVID-19 pandemic.

When the dealers met with new car customers, they told them they had few cars to display and fewer still for purchase. They explained that they could not obtain vehicles because of the pandemic. However, they assured customers that they still could purchase new vehicles.

The dealers told the customers they would have to follow a novel procedure to purchase new vehicles. They explained that they would have to place their vehicle orders, make down payments, and then wait until their vehicles were assembled, shipped, and delivered. They told them that they should be prepared to wait for months.

The dealers informed the customers that they had made other novel adaptations to the traditional car-buying procedures. They explained that they should not expect price reductions, complimentary options, or financing incentives. On the contrary, they should anticipate that special surcharges would be added to the list prices of vehicles.

The dealers became excited about their plan. They expected to sell fewer cars but make higher profits. They were eager to see how customers would respond.

While the first case in this chapter concerned car dealers, the next case focused on school boards. These boards had multiple responsibilities, including student transportation.

The boards did not doubt the priority that parents assigned to student transportation. They realized that they wanted it to be problem-free. They expected them to complain if it was not.

Many parents complained regularly about school buses. They were upset when the buses picked up children or discharged them at inconvenient locations. They wanted them to use pickup and drop-off locations in the children's neighborhoods.

The parents had additional reasons for filing school bus complaints. They filed them about safety, schedules, bus route lengths, poorly trained drivers, and limited accessibility for students with disabilities.

The school boards were unnerved when parents complained about school buses. However, they were just as unnerved, and sometimes even more, when federal elected officials complained.

The federal officials provided school boards with a portion of the funding they needed to purchase or rent school buses. They then monitored how they spent that funding.

The federal officials had raised questions about the amounts school boards were spending to purchase buses. They noted that some were spending over a hundred thousand dollars for each diesel vehicle. They emphasized that this price was then augmented by spending for routine maintenance, repairs, storage, fuel, and drivers' salaries.

The school boards had braced for challenges from federal educational officials during several presidential administrations. During the administration of President Joe Biden, they anticipated that these officials would continue to monitor their spending on student transportation and then challenge them if it seemed imprudently high. However, they were wrong.

The federal officials changed their focus. They showed greater interest in transportation safety than they did cost. Although they detected many threats to safety, they singled out diesel engine pollution as one of the greatest. They directed the school boards to solve this problem by replacing diesel vehicles with ESBs.

The school boards investigated the prices of ESBs. They were shocked to discover that they were three to four times higher than the prices for diesel school buses. Many concluded that they could not afford the ESBs.

The federal officials were prepared for this objection. They assured the school boards that they would receive subsidies to purchase ESBs. They predicted that the combination of federal, state, and private subsidies would make ESBs affordable and possibly free.

The school boards became excited about ESB subsidies. However, they hoped that parents would share their excitement. They were eager to meet with them.

The following questions will assist you if you are going through this book alone. They provide opportunities like those you would have in a college classroom where the professor is using the case method. They also will help you if you are in an actual college classroom with a professor who is using this approach.

Question 1: Why Did Auto Dealers Procure Large Inventories of New Vehicles?

Auto dealers wished to sell as many new vehicles as they could. They procured large inventories to draw customers. They then employed flexible pricing to close their deals with them.

How did different groups respond to the auto dealers? Focus on two groups: journalists and customers.

Did the journalists have low confidence, moderate confidence, or high confidence in the way that the auto dealers were behaving? How did the customers feel? Explain the basis for your answers.

When answering these questions, as well as those that follow, you can rely on the information in this chapter. You also might rely on some of the sources identified in the references at the rear of the book. If you are reading this chapter with colleagues, you are encouraged to converse with them about the best way to answer the questions.

Question 2: Why Did the Auto Dealers Switch to Smaller Inventories?

Auto dealers had difficulty procuring new vehicles during the COVID-19 pandemic. They had to settle for smaller inventories. They then had to price the vehicles rigidly to cover their costs. They hesitated to relinquish these strategies after they turned out to be remarkably profitable.

How did different groups respond to the auto dealers? Focus on two groups: journalists and customers.

Did the journalists have low confidence, moderate confidence, or high confidence in the way that the auto dealers were behaving? How did the customers feel? Explain the basis for your answers.

Question 3: Why Did School Boards Procure Large Fleets of Diesel School Buses?

School boards wished to transport students efficiently. They acquired as many school buses as they could afford. They increased the number of buses they could afford by focusing on reasonably priced diesel school buses.

How did different groups respond to the school boards? Focus on two groups: journalists and parents.

Did the journalists have low confidence, moderate confidence, or high confidence in the way that the school boards were behaving? How did parents feel? Explain the basis for your answers.

Question 4: Why Did the School Boards Switch to Smaller Fleets of Electric School Buses?

School boards were under government pressure to switch to clean but expensive electric school buses. They were able to make this switch by downsizing their fleets and financing them with federal, state, and private subsidies. They hesitated to relinquish these strategies after they turned out to be remarkably cost-effective for them.

How did different groups respond to the school boards? Focus on two groups: journalists and parents.

Did the journalists have low confidence, moderate confidence, or high confidence in the way that the school boards were behaving? How did parents feel? Explain the basis for your answers.

SUMMARY

Auto dealers had to sell vehicles. They used two strategies. They maintained large inventories to attract customers. They relied on flexible pricing to close deals. However, they had to switch to new strategies after the COVID-19 pandemic disrupted their industry.

School boards had to transport students efficiently. They used two strategies. They acquired as many school buses as they could afford. They focused on buses with reasonably priced diesel engines. However, they had to switch to new strategies because of government pressure to acquire electric school buses.

Chapter 9

The Student Safety Feuds

[Clear backpacks reveal] prohibited or potentially dangerous items.

—Clear Backpacks *Company, 2023*

[The Broward school board's clear backpack policy] . . . also includes [clear] lunch boxes, purses, duffel bags, and fanny packs.

—*Journalist Jacob Geanous, 2023*

Clear backpacks . . . provide [little more than] emotional security blankets.

—*National School Safety and Security Services President Kenneth Trump, 2023*

[Parents complain that] clear backpacks . . . cost more than alternative [backpacks].

—*HeFei Airscape Textile Trading* Company, *2023*

[Clear backpacks] could have the unintended effect of making students feel less safe.

—*High School Student Emmanuel Thomas, 2023*

[Students complain that clear backpacks display] their private belongings—from tampons to medication.

—*Journalist Sarah Holder, 2019*

[My clear backpack was] a waste of time and money.

—Former Student AJ Cardenas, 2023

[Who believes that clear backpacks are] going to fix [this district's student safety] problem?

—*Broward Teachers Union* President Anna Fusco, 2023

Airline managers wished to keep unaccompanied minor passengers safe. They established regulations and procedures for their protection. However, they were accused of establishing only an illusion of protection.

School boards wished to keep students safe. They established clear backpack policies for their protection. However, they were accused of creating only an illusion of protection.

SAFEGUARDING CHILDREN ON PLANES

Airline managers told their flight crews to ensure that planes were on time and passengers were safe. They gave them checklists of important details.

The airline managers instructed the flight crews to take steps so that passengers boarded planes efficiently, found their designated seats, stored their carry-on luggage appropriately, reviewed safety protocols, and fastened their seat belts. They gave them comparable details on which they were to focus during flights, descents, and deplaning.

The managers depended on the US Department of Transportation to specify the safety procedures that their flight crews were to follow. When they did not have procedures from this department, they developed their own.

The managers regularly received questions from their flight crews about how to treat passengers who required special accommodations. For example, they were asked how to handle minors not accompanied by adults. When they contacted the Department of Transportation for its regulation on this matter, they learned that it had none.

The managers realized that supervising unaccompanied minors could be taxing. They told flight crews to be attentive to children's ages, travel times, travel distances, connecting flights, and international stops.

The managers at Allegiant, Breeze, Avelo, and Frontier Airlines had straightforward responses when parents requested that they transport unaccompanied children on flights. They refused.

The managers at some airlines responded differently to the parents. They were willing to transport unaccompanied minors. They stressed to the parents that they would have to follow their policies.

The managers at Alaska Airlines were willing to book unaccompanied minors as young as eight years old. However, they would transport them, as well as nine- and ten-year-olds, only on nonstop itineraries. They would transport children who were eleven or older on multistop itineraries.

The managers had to specify how they would handle unaccompanied minors at Transportation Security Administration screening sites, within airport concourses, at boarding gates, during flights, during deplaning, and after deplaning. They then added unaccompanied minor fees to cover the cost of these services.

The managers could have hired professional escorts to look after unaccompanied minor travelers. However, they realized that this plan would be too expensive. They devised an alternative plan. They directed their current staff not only to continue attending to their primary duties but also to look after unaccompanied minors. They insisted that this plan would be inexpensive but effective.

The managers kept an eye on their airport staff and flight crews to see how they were responding to their new responsibilities. They also kept an eye on parents to see if they were purchasing tickets for unaccompanied minors.

Enthusiasts

Some parents wanted to send their unaccompanied children on flights. They were disappointed with those airlines that refused to provide these opportunities. They were grateful to those that did provide them.

Parents had different reasons for sending children on flights alone. Some had conflicting responsibilities that made it difficult for them to accompany their children on flights. They chose to send their children alone. They were willing to pay surcharges to ensure their children received supervision and care. They supported the unaccompanied minor policies.

Some parents were trying to save money. Although they had to pay a surcharge, they figured they would be paying less for the surcharge than an adult guardian's ticket. They therefore supported the unaccompanied minor policies.

Skeptics

Some parents were excited when they purchased tickets for unaccompanied child flyers. They paid the surcharges with the belief that they were safeguarding their children. However, they became skeptical after they had sent their children alone on flights.

The skeptical parents had been disappointed after their children had flown alone. They reported that they had not received the attention, supervision, and care that they had expected in airports and on planes. They noted that they had felt confused, anxious, and distressed.

Some skeptical parents complained to the airlines. Others posted angry remarks on blogs. Others hired lawyers to sue the airlines for emotional damage totheir children.

The airline managers paid attention to parents complaining about unaccompanied child flyer policies. They were distressed that these parents lost confidence in them. However, they still wanted to hear how their staff were reacting to the policies.

The ground personnel and flight crews told their managers that unaccompanied minors needed extraordinary care. They reported that they were too understaffed to provide this care. They were unhappy with the new policies.

SAFEGUARDING CHILDREN AT SCHOOL

School boards did not doubt that parents cared about their children in public schools. They listened to their advice.

The school boards listened to advice from numerous other groups. They listened to administrators, teachers, and professional staff in their districts. They listened to police officers, health professionals, journalists, elected officials, and state educational officials. They realized that these groups had distinctive views. Nonetheless, they concluded that all of them set student safety as their top priority.

The school boards agreed that student safety should be their top priority. They pledged to review their current safety measures, take steps to enhance them, and add additional safety measures. However, they needed advice from one more group—the sales agents who marketed safety products and services.

The school boards told the sales agents that they wanted to purchase school safety products. They added that they already had a hunch about the types of products that would suit their needs. They were interested in innovative electronic devices.

The sales agents described some of their popular electronic safety devices. For example, they told the school boards to consider X-ray machines. They explained that these machines could rapidly scan backpacks, purses, and lunch boxes for dangerous items such as guns, knives, and ammunition.

The sales agents had no doubt that X-ray machines were highly effective. However, they stressed that they were costly. They told the school boards to recognize their benefits when they considered their costs.

The Chicago School Board members had faced this problem in 2023. They had wished to purchase new X-ray machines for all their elementary schools and high schools. Although they would need 500 machines, they could afford only 70.

The school boards in other districts were in the same situation as the board in Chicago. They judged that X-ray machines would improve student safety. However, they did not have enough money to furnish all their schools with them.

The school board in Broward County Florida felt intense pressure to improve student safety. It may have felt this pressure because of the 2018 assault that had taken place at the Marjory Stoneman Douglas High School.

The Broward County school board wished to take steps to reassure parents about student safety. It already had implemented an expensive safety measure by assigning an armed security officer to every school.

The Broward County school board had implemented another safety measure that was less expensive than armed security guards. It had purchased the license to a safety technology app. The board's members directed teachers, school professionals, administrators, and staff members to download the app to their smartphones. They told them to use this app during an emergency to send out a campuswide alert and to summon the police.

The Broward County school board members wanted to implement still another safety measure. They were interested in one that would be affordable. They contemplated whether they should require students to carry transparent plastic backpacks.

The school board members believed that transparent backpacks would decrease the number of violent student-on-student altercations at school. They explained that transparent backpack inspections for guns, ammunition, and knives would prevent students from using these weapons during altercations.

The school board members decided to implement the new backpack policy. They announced that clear backpacks would be mandatory for the 2023–2024 school year.

Critics immediately pointed to a flaw in the new policy. They noted that transparent backpacks would not be very effective if students continued to carry non-transparent purses, lunchboxes, fanny packs, and gym bags.

The school board members modified their clear backpack policy. They specified that students had to make sure that all the items they brought to school were encased in clear plastic containers.

The school board members expected the entire community to contribute to their new clear backpack policy. They expected parents to purchase clear backpacks. They expected students to carry them. They expected teachers and staff to inspect them. They expected elected officials to applaud them. They were eager to observe the actual reactions from these groups.

Enthusiasts

Some Broward County parents were excited about the clear backpack policy. They hoped that it would complement the safety policies that required the presence of armed guards and the use of the smartphone warning app. They were supportive.

Elected state officials were pleased with the Broward County school board after it decided to use armed officers. They also were pleased when it decided to convert smartphones into panic buttons. They mandated that every Florida school board enact similar measures. However, they had not realized how costly these safety measures would be.

Florida's elected officials had pledged to subsidize the school boards' costs for armed officers and panic buttons. Surprised by the expense, they only subsidized a portion of those costs. They were relieved to discover that clear backpack policies did not require state funding. They were supportive of them.

Skeptics

Some parents were enthusiastic about a local policy requiring clear backpacks in their children's schools. However, many were skeptical.

The skeptical parents had discussed the clear backpack policy with their children. They recounted how their children had become upset when they learned that clear backpacks would display extremely private items. They gave examples of the items their children did not wish to share, such as medications and personal hygiene products. They claimed the mandate to use clear backpacks would violate their children's privacy rights.

The skeptical parents cited reports from school safety experts who had little confidence in clear backpack policies. They encouraged their school boards to read these reports before they implemented these policies.

Many teachers and staff agreed with the skeptical parents that clear backpack policies would not enhance student safety. However, they also had a personal reason for taking this stance. They were too overworked and understaffed to take on the new role as backpack inspectors.

The teachers and staff assumed that clear backpack policies were intended to ease parental anxiety. However, they predicted that they would be poorly implemented and then have the opposite effect.

RESPONDING TO CHILD SAFETY QUESTIONS

This section focuses on the preceding two cases. The first case involved airline managers.

The airline managers were concerned about minor passengers. They realized that they could be especially vulnerable on flights. They strictly enforced the US Department of Transportation's child safety rules. They directed their flight attendants to brief parents and adult guardians about those rules and monitor whether they were complying with them.

The airline managers typically dealt with children who were traveling with their parents. However, they also dealt with some whose parents had requested that they travel without them or any accompanying adult. Some of them categorically denied these requests. However, others were willing to cooperate with the parents. They develop unaccompanied minor policies to guide this type of travel.

The managers made sure that their unaccompanied minor policies set surcharges for tickets. They intended to use this revenue to cover the cost of child-appropriate snacks, handpicked seats, special attention, and escorts to connecting flights.

The managers made sure that their unaccompanied minor policies set age limitations for flyers. They set a minimum age for those flyers who had itineraries without connecting flights. They raised that age when the flyers had itineraries with connections.

Some managers had unaccompanied minor policies that required parents to book preteen flyers and teenage flyers as adults. Others gave them the option of booking them as unaccompanied minors and then paying surcharges.

The managers conceded that their unaccompanied minor tickets were expensive. However, they believed they had to be expensive to pay for the extra safety measures they had implemented.

The managers were eager to see what parents thought of the policies. They were pleased when some of them responded positively.

The managers also needed to know what airport staff and flight crews thought of the unaccompanied minor policies. They hoped these overextended professionals could still shoulder additional responsibilities.

While the first case in this chapter concerned airline managers, the next case focused on school boards. The school boards were responsible for educating the students in their districts. They paid special attention to the educational priorities that parents set.

The school boards discovered that parents viewed safety as their top priority. They agreed with the parents. They pledged to keep students safe. However, they needed help.

The school boards asked for help from agents who sold commercial school safety services and products. They learned from them about high-priced safety services such as private security guards and sniffer dogs. They also learned about high-priced safety products such as electronic surveillance technology, weapon-detecting radar, and clear backpacks.

Although the school boards were impressed by high-priced safety products and services, they frequently could not afford them. They therefore considered low-priced safety measures.

The school boards realized that a safety policy that centered on transparent plastic backpacks would be affordable. However, they wondered whether it would be effective. They consulted with school safety experts.

The school safety experts had examined districts where students were using transparent backpacks. They had concluded that these backpacks had not made the students safer. They judged that they had been little more than placebos designed to suppress parental anxiety.

The school boards that had been contemplating clear backpacks had to decide how they would treat the caustic reports from safety experts. Some announced that they still intended to require clear backpacks. Others changed their minds. Still others were undecided.

The undecided school boards conceded that clear backpacks, even though they were problematic, still might keep students safe. They needed to hear whether parents were supportive. They also were eager to hear whether teachers, who already were overextended, would be able to inspect students' backpacks and confiscate dangerous items in them.

The following questions will assist you if you are going through this book alone. They provide opportunities like those you would have in a college classroom where the professor is using the case method. They also will help you if you are in an actual college classroom with a professor who is using this approach.

Question 1: How Did Airline Managers Protect Unaccompanied Minor Passengers?

Airline managers wished to keep unaccompanied minor passengers safe. They established policies that identified the types of flights on which they could fly, the people who would look after them, the services they would receive, and the fees they would incur.

How did different groups respond to the airline managers? Focus on two groups: parents and airline workers.

Did the parents have low confidence, moderate confidence, or high confidence in the way that the airline managers were behaving? How did the airline workers feel? Explain the basis for your answers.

When answering these questions, and those that follow, you can rely on the information in this chapter. You also might rely on some of the sources identified in the references at the rear of the book. If you are reading this chapter with colleagues, you are encouraged to converse with them about the best way to answer the questions.

Question 2: How Did Airline Managers Deal with Challenges to Their Unaccompanied Minor Policies?

Airline managers were challenged about the effectiveness of their unaccompanied minor policies. Although some disagreed with these challengers, others agreed with them and refused to transport unaccompanied minors.

How did different groups respond to the airline managers? Focus on two groups: parents and airline workers.

Did the parents have low confidence, moderate confidence, or high confidence in the way that the airline managers were behaving? How did the airline workers feel? Explain the basis for your answers.

Question 3: How Did School Boards Protect Students?

School boards wished to keep students safe. They established policies requiring them to carry clear backpacks and openly display the items in them.

How did different groups respond to the school boards? Focus on two groups: parents and teachers.

Did the parents have low confidence, moderate confidence, or high confidence in the way that the school boards were behaving? How did the teachers feel? Explain the basis for your answers.

Question 4: How Did School Boards Deal with Challenges to their Clear Backpack Policies?

School boards were challenged about the effectiveness of their clear backpack policies. Although some disagreed with these challengers, others agreed with them and refused to require clear backpacks.

How did different groups respond to the school boards? Focus on two groups: parents and teachers.

Did the parents have low confidence, moderate confidence, or high confidence in the way that the school boards were behaving? How did the teachers feel? Explain the basis for your answers.

SUMMARY

Airline managers were concerned about the safety of unaccompanied minor travelers. They established policies to protect them. However, they were accused of merely creating the illusion of protection.

School boards were concerned about the safety of students. They established clear backpack policies to protect them. However, they were accused of merely creating the illusion of protection.

Chapter 10

The School Funding Feuds

All Florida residents who are eligible to be enrolled in public schools can receive . . . vouchers [to enroll in private schools instead].

—Journalist Victoria De Cardenas, 2023

[Florida's voucher program] means that every school has a chance to compete for students.

—Florida Senate President Kathleen Passidomo, 2023

[Florida's voucher program will] cost the state about $4 billion dollars in the initial year.

—*Education Law Center* Researcher Mary McKillip, 2023

[Florida's voucher program diverts] public money to unaccountable, corporate-run private schools.

—*Florida Education Association* President Andrew Spar, 2023

[Florida's voucher program] is a glaring example of lawmakers giving yet another benefit to those who don't need it.

—Letter-to-the-Editor Writer Dan Dundon, 2023

[Florida's voucher program is the] Wild West of taxpayer-funded education.

—Journalist Scott Maxwell, 2023

Airline executives traditionally set prices for flights and then kept them stable. However, they later began to increase prices as tickets became scarce. They paid attention to how key groups reacted to their new ticketing strategy. They paid special attention to passengers.

Elected officials in Florida traditionally offered school vouchers to students who met specific criteria. However, they later began to offer them to everyone. They paid attention to howkey groups reacted to their new voucher strategy. They paid special attention to parents.

MANAGING YIELDS AT AIRLINES

Airline executives had complex responsibilities. They had to ensure that their airlines had optimal routes, equipment, and staff. However, they had one overarching responsibility: they had to ensure that they were profitable.

The executives had enormous operational expenses. After they had paid for those expenses, they might have meager profits. They noted that their profit margin was smaller than the margin in other major industries.

The airline executives continually carped about the difficulty of generating profits. Nonetheless, they had done remarkably well. Except for a temporary downturn during the COVID-19 pandemic, they had made enormous amounts of money for their investors.

The executives realized they could generate profits by cutting back on operational expenses or by bringing in a greater amount of income. They therefore had to be extremely diligent when they did their budgetary planning.

The executives were intent on expanding their profit margin. Because they detected few opportunities to cut back on operational expenses, they had to increase their income. They searched for opportunities.

During the 1980s, airline executives became intrigued by strategies to improve profit yields. They noted that these strategies were ideal for businesses that did not have the resources to expand their companies. In their case, they generated most of their income from passenger fares. However, they did not have the resources to serve more passengers. They wondered whether they could use profit yield strategies to extract more money from current passengers.

The airline executives had been setting their ticket prices when flights were scheduled. They then left the prices stationary until the flights departed. They were ready to extract a greater profit yield: they would switch to dynamic pricing.

The executives directed their staff to monitor the number of people who purchased flight tickets. They explained that they should increase the prices as tickets became scarce. They encouraged them to increase the prices several times during a single day. They told them that they might begin selling tickets for 100 dollars but then dynamically increase the prices until the last few tickets sold for twice that amount.

The executives had enormous success with dynamic pricing. They asked their technology staff if they could make the process run even more efficiently. They were excited when they responded with remarkable computerized software.

Enthusiasts

The executives kept an eye on their customers. They had used dynamic pricing to collect more money from them. However, they did not want to alienate them.

The customers soon noticed that they were paying higher ticket prices. Those who had been flying the same routes regularly were paying significantly more when they delayed their ticket purchases.

Some of the customers figured out how to game the new pricing system. They read online blogs in which tech enthusiasts identified the optimal number of weeks before flights to purchase tickets. They even learned the days of the week and the times of the day at which to get bargains. They were gratified when they then secured tickets at lower prices.

Airline stockholders were informed that the airlines had implemented dynamic pricing. They had been assured that it would increase corporate profits and stock values. They were pleased when these predictions turned out to be correct. They encouraged the airline executives to expand their new pricing strategy.

Skeptics

Customers were aware that the airlines were extracting more money from them. They had listened to their executives explain that they were doing this to avoid catastrophic financial problems. However, they noted that the airlines were enormously profitable.

The skeptical passengers were not convinced by the airlines' rationale for raising ticket prices. They believed airline executives were using this strategy to increase their profit yield. They pleaded with other customers to band with them and confront the executives.

The skeptical passengers tried to get the attention of the airline executives. They created blogs to challenge them. However, they did not make an impression on the executives.

The skeptical passengers were ready to turn to another group as allies. They pleaded with journalists to sound an alarm about the airlines' indefensible pricing practices.

Many journalists agreed with the skeptical passengers. They reported the enormous amount of money the airlines were earning through dynamic pricing. They also reported that they were inspiring the tourism industry and recreation industry to adopt dynamic pricing.

MANAGING YIELDS AT SCHOOLS

Florida's school boards reviewed the budgets for the districts they governed. They made sure that they contained enough money to meet their annual goals for hiring, equipment purchases, and school operations.

The school board realized that the budgets relied on some locally raised funds. However, they noted that they relied primarily on state-allocated funds.

Florida's school boards were accustomed to the *formula* with which their state dispensed funds. They expected that formula to provide them with about 10,000 dollars annually for every student served. They expected a bit more when students needed special attention because of disabilities.

The school boards were accountable to the parents who enrolled children in public schools. They made it clear to them that they needed to secure the state funds to educate their children.

The school boards were not accountable to those parents who enrolled their children in private schools. They expected most of these parents to use their personal funds to cover the cost of private school tuition. They assumed that some of these parents had qualified for state-awarded educational vouchers.

Florida's voucher program had emerged in the late 1990s. It provided parents with several thousand dollars per child to help pay for annual private school tuition. It stipulated that the recipients had to have children who were enrolled in failing public schools.

Florida's legislators later modified the 1990s vouchers. However, they continued to stipulate conditions that voucher recipients had to meet.

Parents who had not qualified for vouchers were disgruntled. Many of them were struggling to pay private school tuition. Some had to disenroll their children from private schools and send them to public schools.

The disgruntled parents contacted their state legislators. They urged them to make private school vouchers available to everyone with school-age children.

The legislators sympathized with the disgruntled parents. They pledged to take their advice, craft a universal voucher program, and forward it to the governor.

The Florida State Senate's president, Kathleen Passidomo, shepherded the universal voucher program through the legislature. She stated that it would take money that would have funded children in the public schools and divert it to "education savings accounts." She told parents that they could then draw money from these accounts to "customize their children's education."

Passidomo indicated that the amount in a voucher account would be over 8,000 dollars. She acknowledged that this would be several thousand dollars less than the per-pupil amount that would have been allocated by the state's funding formula. Nonetheless, she hoped that it still would please parents.

Enthusiasts

Some parents had been sending their children to private schools and struggling to pay the tuition. They were extremely pleased with the new vouchers.

Other parents had been unable to send their children to private schools that they could not afford. They had not qualified for the original vouchers. When they realized that they now would qualify, they were very pleased.

The directors at for-profit private schools were excited about the new voucher program. They anticipated that they would see an influx of new students. Those who were charging modest tuition raised their rates to match the amounts in the new voucher accounts. They hoped that they then would be able to pay higher salaries to their staff, purchase current textbooks, and acquire modern equipment.

The directors at nonprofit private schools were as excited as their colleagues at for-profit schools. Like them, they were likely to draw many more students. They increased their tuition rates to match the amounts in the new voucher accounts. They then intended to improve salaries, purchase learning materials, and increase their operating budgets.

Skeptics

Some parents were skeptical of Florida's universal voucher program. They explained that they had been sending their children to public schools and were pleased with them. They worried how the new vouchers would affect their children's schools.

The skeptical parents directed their questions to the state officials who had championed universal vouchers. They feared a budgetary shortfall if large numbers of students left public schools to attend private schools instead. They asked if the officials would adjust the state's funding formula to compensate for the shortfall.

The officials told the parents that they had considered the impact of the new voucher program on public school budgets. They assured them that the statewide shortfall would be less than a million dollars.

The skeptical parents were not as calm as their state officials. They noted that fiscal analysts at the *Education Law Center* had calculated a statewide shortfall of billions of dollars.

The skeptical parents felt that the state elected officials had ignored them. They realized that they needed broader support to get their attention. They asked public school teachers for their support.

The public school teachers were highly skeptical of the new vouchers. They were sure that they would cause damage to their students. They eagerly joined the skeptical parents. They added that the leaders of their union, the Florida Education Association (FEA), would also join them.

The FEA leaders characterized the new vouchers as poorly disguised efforts to increase the profit yields at private schools. They enlisted sympathetic journalists to help them raise a ruckus over them.

RESPONDING TO QUESTIONS ABOUT FINANCIAL STRATEGIES

This section focuses on the preceding two cases. The first case involved airline executives.

Airline executives expected their staff to create schedules with the times, dates, destinations, and prices for flights. They directed them to then sell the tickets.

The executives realized that customers had considered times of departures, dates of departures, and destinations before they purchased tickets. However, they wondered if they considered any other factors. They hired marketers to investigate.

The marketers investigated the reasons that customers chose one carrier over another. They discovered that all customers preferred carriers with reputations for safety. However, they discovered several other traits, including affordability, convenience, efficiency, and staff courtesy.

The executives were impressed by the marketers' research. They resolved to set high standards in the areas that mattered to customers. They directed the marketing firms to develop advertising campaigns to highlight their success in those areas.

The executives knew that they had to please customers to stay in business. However, they also had to please corporate investors. They hoped that investors would retain their corporate shares and purchase additional shares.

The executives knew that investors were interested in profitable airlines. They resolved to demonstrate that their airlines were highly profitable. They therefore highlighted their *profit yields.*

The executives expressed profit yields as summative figures. They compared their current profit yields with those from previous periods. They emphasized the growth over time. They also compared their profit yields to those of less successful rivals. They emphasized the differentials between them.

The executives wished to retain high-profit yields and possibly increase them. They asked experts in business analytics to identify the strategies that would help them achieve these goals.

The analytics experts were able to isolate the factors influencing airline profit yields. They noted that these included the amounts spent on personnel, crafts, fuel, maintenance, and airport access. They warned the executives that tampering with any of these factors could trigger sharp passenger losses.

The experts highlighted an additional factor that influenced product yields. They believed that this factor, the price of tickets, could be manipulated safely.

The executives decided to take the analytics experts' advice. They directed their sales agents to set the prices for flights at the times at which those flights were scheduled. They told them to retain those prices when seats were plentiful but raise them as they became scarce.

The executives then kept an eye on their profit yields. They noted with pleasure that they were growing. However, they also kept an eye on their passengers. They wondered how they were reacting to the higher ticket prices.

While the first case in this chapter concerned airline executives, the next case focused on Florida's elected officials. These officials allocated the funds on which their state's public schools depended for personnel, equipment, and facilities.

The officials annually determined the funding that they would provide to school districts. They geared the amount to the number of students that individual districts were serving.

The officials were accountable to voters for budgetary actions. They genuinely cared how they would react to their actions. Nonetheless, they were especially concerned about parents. They did not underestimate the influence that they wielded during elections. They were on the lookout for ways to improve their standing with them.

Some parents were extremely pleased with Florida's public schools. They applauded their legislators when they provided them with funding for teachers, equipment, and textbooks.

Not all parents were pleased with the public schools. Some were discontented. Some of them were so discontented that they would have preferred to send children to private schools instead. However, they had to calculate whether they could afford to pay private school tuition.

The discontented parents came up with a plan to make private schools more affordable. They wanted the state's per-pupil school funding to be available to them in parent-accessible "vouchers." They contended that the vouchers would enable them to reclaim some of the state dollars that would have been targeted for their children were they in the public schools.

The Florida officials were not surprised by this plan. They already had enacted a voucher plan of their own. However, they had limited their vouchers to certain students, such as those enrolled in "failing" schools. They noted that the new plan would make vouchers available to all students.

Florida officials endorsed the parents' plan. They incorporated it into a 2023 piece of legislation, passed it, and sent it to their governor. They beamed when he signed it.

The legislators were elated by their success in enacting universal vouchers. Nonetheless, they were nervous about their total annual cost. They realized that they could reduce the state's public school budget by millions, and possibly billions, of dollars.

The legislators were eager to see how their constituents were reacting to the new vouchers. Of course, they wanted to know how teachers felt. However, they especially wanted to know how parents felt.

The following questions will assist you if you are going through this book on your own. They provide opportunities like those you would have in a college classroom where the professor is using the case method. They also will help you if you are in an actual college classroom with a professor using this approach.

Question 1: Why Did Airline Executives Use Fixed Ticket Pricing?

Airline executives set the prices for tickets when they scheduled flights. They then kept the prices fixed until the flights departed. They explained that fixed pricing generated enough revenue for them to not only cover their expenses but also make significant profits.

How did different groups respond to the airline executives? Focus on two groups: journalists and passengers.

Did the journalists have low confidence, moderate confidence, or high confidence in the way that the airline executives were behaving? How did the passengers feel? Explain the basis for your answers.

When answering these questions, as well as those that follow, you can rely on the information in this chapter. You also might rely on some of the sources identified in the references at the rear of the book. If you are reading this chapter with colleagues, you are encouraged to converse with them about the best way to answer the questions.

Question 2: Why Did Airline Executives Switch to Dynamic Ticket Pricing?

Airline executives switched to dynamic ticket pricing. They kept prices stable when plane seats were unfilled but raised them as they filled. They explained that dynamic pricing generated more revenue than fixed pricing.

How did different groups respond to the airline executives? Focus on two groups: journalists and passengers.

Did the journalists have low confidence, moderate confidence, or high confidence in the way that the airline executives were behaving? How did the passengers feel? Explain the basis for your answers.

Question 3: Why Did Florida's Officials Offer Private School Vouchers to Select Families?

Florida's officials originally offered private school vouchers to select families. For example, they offered them to those with children at failing public schools. They explained that this strategy benefited families and was cost-effective.

How did different groups respond to the state officials? Focus on two groups: journalists and parents.

Did the journalists have low confidence, moderate confidence, or high confidence in the way that the state officials were behaving? How did parents feel? Explain the basis for your answers.

Question 4: Why Did Florida's Officials Switch to Private School Vouchers for All Families?

Florida's officials switched to private school vouchers for all families. They explained that the new strategy promoted parental choice more effectively than the previous one.

How did different groups respond to the state officials? Focus on two groups: journalists and parents.

Did the journalists have low confidence, moderate confidence, or high confidence in the way that the state officials were behaving? How did parents feel? Explain the basis for your answers.

SUMMARY

Airline executives adopted a new ticketing strategy: they adjusted prices as the seats on flights became scarce. They then kept an eye on how key groups were reacting.

Florida's elected officials adopted a new school voucher system: they offered private school vouchers to all students. They then kept an eye on how key groups were reacting.

Chapter 11

The School Athletics Feuds

The Connecticut Interscholastic Athletic Conference has allowed males who identify as girls to compete in high school women's sports.

—*Alliance Defending Freedom* Web Editor Maureen Collins, 2023

[Connecticut's high school] girls lose nothing from the participation of transgender girls [in women's sports].

—*ACLU* Attorney Joshua Block, 2023

I am a girl and I love to run [with other girls.]

—Transgender Connecticut High School Student Andraya Yearwood, 2019

[Connecticut's cisgender girls] deserve . . . an equal opportunity to excel and win in [high school] athletics.

—*Alliance Defending Freedom* Attorney Christiana Kiefer, 2023

The "fastest girl in Connecticut" . . . [is suing] after losing to trans athletes.

—Journalist Rikki Schlott, 2023

When a transgender female athlete wins a girls [sic] sporting event, some . . . raise questions about the fairness and integrity of the event . . . [while others raise them about that athlete's] social and emotional well-being.

—*National Federation of State High School Associations* Communications Coordinator Luke Modrovsky, 2022

The United States Rowing Association (USRowing) determined who could participate in women's races. It allowed transgender females to race as individuals. It also allowed them to race on all-women crews. However, it did not allow them to fill the women's slots on mixed-gender crews. It insisted that these decisions were in everyone's best interests.

The Connecticut Interscholastic Athletic Conference (CIAC) determined who could participate in women's high school track and field events. It allowed transgender females to compete in all events. It insisted this decision was in everyone's best interests.

ADULT ROWING

USRowing is an enormously influential organization. It prepares athletes for World Cups, World Championships, the Olympics, and other elite rowing contests.

The leaders at USRowing had to ensure that rowing competitions were fair, safe, and inclusive. Although they established the rules and regulations to achieve these goals, they conferred with their members about them.

The USRowing leaders conferred with members about the minimum age for participants at major events. In this case, they decided that they would not set age restrictions. They assumed that restrictions were unnecessary because younger racers would not be able to qualify for those events.

The USRowing leaders wished to nurture younger races. They therefore arranged special competitions for them. They assumed that these competitions would prepare them to qualify for major competitions someday.

The USRowing leaders conferred with their members about another important matter: the genders of participants at major competitions. They decided to offer some races exclusively for men, others exclusively for women, and others for mixed-gender crews.

The USRowing leaders kept their members informed about changes to regulations, policies, rules, and procedures. They highlighted them in publications such as *Rules of Rowing, Referee Procedures Manual*, and *Local Organizational Committee [LOC] Guidance Manual*.

The USRowing leaders tried to anticipate the questions that members could pose. They then could try to find a resolution before those questions became controversial. Nonetheless, they were caught off guard when some members asked them to clarify the organization's policy on gender-restricted events.

The members explained that they had read the official regulations for gender-restricted events. However, they were unsure about events in which transgender females could compete. They explained that transgender female athletes had petitioned to compete in the women's races and to fill the women's slots on mixed-gender crews.

The USRowing leaders deliberated carefully before responding. They realized that some sports leagues had allowed transgender females to compete in women's divisions. They were impressed with the athleticism that the transgender females had then displayed.

The USRowing leaders were sensitive to the discrimination that transgender females historically had sustained. They wanted to take a stand that would advance their interests. They therefore announced that they would permit transgender females to compete in women's rowing races. They also would permit them to fill the female slots on mixed-gender rowing crews.

The USRowing leaders anticipated some resistance to their announcement. They were not disappointed.

Many oarswomen protested. They pointed out that the transgender females had changed their gender but not their sex. They worried that they would have an unfair advantage because they still had the bodies of males.

The USRowing leaders were prepared for resistance from oarswomen. However, they were not sure how oarsmen would respond. They hoped that they would not object to the new policy.

The oarsmen did object to the new policy. They explained that they would have had no objections to transgender males competing against them in the men's division races. They noted that transgender males would not have a biological advantage in stamina or strength.

The oarsmen felt differently about transgender females filling the women's slots on mixed-gender crews. They explained that mixed-gender crews with four males and four transgender females could be unbeatable. They threatened to boycott mixed-gender races if they had to compete against crews of this type.

The USRowing leaders were in a bind. They were unsure that the disgruntled male oarsmen would follow through on their threat to boycott mixed-gender racing. Nonetheless, they did not want to test them.

The USRowing leaders capitulated to the disgruntled oarsmen. They announced that mixed-gender racing would keep its traditional rule and limit the female crew slots to cisgender women.

The USRowing leaders still had to deal with the disgruntled oarswomen. They told them they had not changed their minds about transgender females competing in their division. They explained that they did not want to miss this chance to advance transgender rights.

Enthusiasts

The USRowing leaders were in an uncomfortable position. They were sure that many disgruntled oarswomen would continue to protest their decisions.

They hoped they would keep their protest within the organization and not make it public. They were wrong.

The disgruntled oarswomen wanted to inform the public about the unfair way that they had been treated. They asked sports reporters to highlight their treatment. They posted their own remarks on sports websites.

The USRowing leaders decided that they needed to defend themselves. They used the same strategy as the disgruntled oarswomen. They identified journalists who had advocated for greater participation of transgender female athletes in women's sports. They noted that they had been particularly eloquent advocates for transgender female swimmers on college teams. They pleaded with them to advocate for USRowing's new policy.

Some journalists advocated for USRowing's new policy. However, they learned that their audiences had little interest in competitive rowing. They realized that they had a much greater interest in competitive swimming. Consequently, they gave limited coverage to the rowing dispute and emphasized the swimming dispute.

The USRowing leaders were disappointed that the journalists did not generate more public support for them. They hoped that elected officials would be of greater help.

The USRowing leaders identified elected officials who had fervently supported female transgender swimmers. They expected them to show the same degree of fervor for transgender oarswomen. However, they were disappointed when these officials did not switch their focus from the hyperpublicized cases of swimmers to the less-publicized cases of rowing crews.

Skeptics

The USRowing leaders had been proud of their new policy. They had been confident that it had pleased transgender females and their advocates. However, they had acknowledged that it was controversial.

The USRowing leaders had not been surprised when the oarswomen in their organization opposed the new policy. However, they had been genuinely surprised when the oarsmen opposed it as well. In fact, they had noted that the oarsmen were so upset that they threatened to withdraw from all mixed-gender rowing competitions.

The USRowing leaders had suppressed the oarsmen rebellion by making a concession. They had exempted mixed-gender rowing events from the new policy. They were not willing to make this exemption for either women's individual rowing events or women's team rowing events.

The disgruntled oarswomen wrote blistering letters to the organization's leaders. They scolded them for showing a concern about fairness only when males were affected.

The disgruntled oarswomen had one more argument. They hoped that it would change the minds of their organization's leaders. They told them that they would be placing US transgender female rowers in a bind when they tried to compete in the qualifying regattas for the Olympics. They pointed out that these regattas had transgender rules that were incompatible with those of USRowing.

HIGH SCHOOL TRACK

School boards recognized the importance of team sports. They believed they were essential components of high school education. They gladly acknowledged their responsibility for them.

Although the school boards were responsible for team sports, they relied heavily on their state athletic associations to help them. For example, they expected these associations to specify the rules and regulations for high school team sports.

The state athletic associations were ready to establish rules and regulations for high school sports. They had several goals to guide them. They wanted these sports to be personally rewarding to the student participants. They also wanted them to provide the participants with chance to compete in public events. Finally, they hoped to allow some participants to get ready and qualify for college sports.

The state athletic associations belonged to a larger organization—the National Federation of State High School Associations (NFHS). They collaborated with this organization to update the rules for sports, including those in track and field.

The national federation released its annual track and field rule book at the beginning of each school year. It made sure that coaches and students had plenty of time to find out about new rules it may have introduced.

The national federation had enjoyed a harmonious and stress-free relationship with its state associations. It had for decades collaborated with them on the rules they featured in their *Track & Field Rules Book*.

The national federation's staff eventually had to deal with a controversial and potentially divisive question. They had been asked to respond to a situation involving transgender high school athletes in Connecticut. They had to clarify how to deal with transgender high school girls who wished to compete in women's track and field events.

The national federation's staff realized that Connecticut had a law protecting transgender individuals from discrimination. They also realized that its state athletic association, the Connecticut Interscholastic Athletic Conference (CIAC), had authorized transgender high school girls to compete in women's track and field events.

The national federation's staff had to articulate their organization's policy on transgender female athletes competing in the women's division track and field events. They could have duplicated the policy of CIAC. However, they had to be careful because they would be setting a precedent that would affect states other than Connecticut. For example, they had to consider how their policy would affect Iowa.

The Iowa High School Athletic Association had taken the same stance on transgender female athletes as CIAC. However, it was in a different situation. It did not have a state law affirming transgender high school girls' right to compete in women's track and field events. It instead had an incongruous state law—one that banned transgender high school girls from these events.

Iowa was not the only state with a law that kept transgender high school girls out of women's athletic events. Twenty-three states had similar laws. More states were contemplating laws of this sort.

The national federation's staff deliberated carefully before announcing its policy on transgender female athletes. It did not want to create tension with its state associations. It also did not wish to create tension with its parent organization—World Athletics (WA).

WA is the organization that establishes the regulations for international track and field events. It recognizes that the world's elite track and field athletes attend those events and abide by its regulations.

The WA leaders were distressed by the bickering among member nations about cisgender and transgender female athletes. They realized that they had to take a side on this issue.

The WA leaders announced that they would ban transgender females from competing in the women's events that it arranged. They made it clear to members that they took no joy in making this decision. They explained that they made it because they detected an "overarching need" to protect sports competition among females.

The national federation's leaders were struck by WA's stand on transgender females. They realized that the WA had no choice but to make a decisive statement on this controversial issue. They resolved that they also had to take a stand on that issue. They knew their colleagues at CIAC were waiting for them to announce their position.

The national federation's leaders noted that some of their members, who were concerned about fairness, adamantly opposed the participation of transgender girls in women's high school track events. They contrasted these members with those in Connecticut, who were concerned about the social inclusion of a marginalized group and who supported full participation.

The NFHS leaders announced that they took the side of CIAC. They urged members to affirm that transgender girls had the right to participate in all women's high school sports. However, they did not provide any practical advice about how they should implement this policy in states that had banned the participation of transgender girls.

Enthusiasts

The CIAC leaders had authorized the full participation of transgender female athletes in women's track and field events. They anticipated that the state officials would applaud them. After all, they had been pressured by them to enact this policy.

The CIAC leaders were gratified when the elected officials responded with supportive statements. However, they were just as concerned about the public. They had learned from polls that the public's attitudes toward this issue were complex and volatile.

The CIAC leaders knew that the public was heavily influenced by journalists. They asked them to articulate the rationale for the full inclusion of transgender female athletes in women's track and field sports.

Many journalists were eager to assist the CIAC leaders. They reported that the full inclusion of transgender female athletes in women's sports would improve the mental health of transgender girls. They added that it would benefit everyone else who then could observe the athletic efforts and achievements of these girls.

Skeptics

Not all members of the public supported Connecticut's policy for transgender female high school students. Polls showed significant opposition.

The CIAC leaders recognized that their new policy was controversial. They were not surprised when it was opposed by some members of the public. They also were not surprised when it was opposed by talented female athletes who had lost competitions to transgender female athletes.

The CIAC leaders refused to back away from their new policy. They reaffirmed their commitment to it. They hoped that they eventually could change the minds of skeptics.

QUESTIONS ABOUT ATHLETIC REGULATIONS

This section focuses on the preceding two cases. The first case involved adult rowing competitions in the United States.

USRowing decided who could participate in rowing competitions. They traditionally had allowed only cisgender females to participate in the women's division at these competitions. However, they had not specifically addressed whether transgender females could participate. They came under increasing pressure to answer this question.

Transgender female athletes needed to know whether they were eligible for women's rowing events. The non-transgender female athletes against whom they would be competing also needed to know. The rowing coaches who trained the athletes needed this information. The university sports administrators who organized rowing teams on their campuses needed it.

The USRowing leaders had to answer whether transgender females could participate as individual racers in the women's division rowing events. They also had to answer whether they could be members of all-female crews in this division. Finally, they had to decide whether they could fill the slots designated for females on mixed-gender crews.

The USRowing leaders were familiar with the transgender females who had competed in the women's division at high school athletic competitions. They realized that they had been extraordinarily competitive in track and field events. They predicted that transgender female rowers would be equally competitive in women's rowing events.

Advocates for transgender females wanted the USRowing leaders to confirm that transgender females had the right to compete against other females. They were joined by federal and state officials, who demanded that the USRowing leaders treat transgender females no differently than they treated other females.

The advocates highlighted the social and emotional challenges that transgender women had faced when they were in high school. They believed participation in female rowing had helped them deal with those challenges. They believed they should continue to have these opportunities.

The USRowing leaders were under pressure from the advocates for transgender females. However, they also were under a different type of pressure from advocates for non-transgender females.

The advocates for non-transgender females wanted only cisgender females to compete in women's rowing. They explained that cisgender females were at a disadvantage when they were racing against females with the strength and stamina of men.

The advocates for cisgender females wanted to keep women's rowing the way that it traditionally had been. They stated that they wished to ensure that cisgender females were treated fairly.

The USRowing leaders listened respectfully to this debate. However, they sided with the advocates for transgender women. They were moved by their argument that everyone needed to help transgender women deal with their serious emotional and social challenges. They also were moved by an antidiscrimination directive from the US president's office.

The USRowing leaders announced that they were opening women's competition to transgender females. They were sure that many citizens would be enthusiastic. They looked forward to their reactions.

The USRowing leaders knew that some people would be disappointed with their decision. They braced for their reactions.

The USRowing leaders had anticipated negative criticism. However, they were shocked by the amount of it. They attempted to counter it by publicizing the basis for their stance.

The USRowing leaders located journalists and elected officials who were eager to speak in their defense. They were pleased by the impact that they had.

The USRowing leaders had to deal with the cisgender women who were affected by their decision to allow transgender women to participate in women's events. They realized that these women were extremely upset. Although they did not appease them, they refused to budge from their decision.

The USRowing leaders also had to deal with the males who disagreed with their decision to change the composition of crews for mixed-gender racing. They were disappointed when these males said they would not accept their decision. They were even more disappointed when they threatened to boycott mixed-gender rowing.

The USRowing leaders relented. They walked back their decision about the women's slots on mixed-gender racing teams. They announced that only cisgender women could fill them.

The USRowing leaders knew many people would be disappointed with them after they gave in to the male rowers. They braced for their reactions.

While the first case in this chapter concerned rowing, the next case focused on high school track and field events. CIAC determined which students in Connecticut were eligible for these events.

The CIAC leaders traditionally had restricted women's track and field to cisgender females. However, they had not specifically addressed whether transgender students could participate. They came under increasing pressure to answer this question.

Transgender high school girls needed the answer. The non-transgender girls against whom they competed needed the answer. So did parents, teachers, coaches, school administrators, journalists, and elected officials.

The CIAC leaders had received inquiries about whether they would allow transgender girls to play on the women's teams. They were not surprised by the frequency of these inquiries or the urgent tone in which they were expressed.

The CIAC leaders were aware that transgender girls had been competing in women's track and field events at some schools. They noted that they had been extremely competitive and even dominated these events.

Advocates for transgender girls wanted the CIAC leaders to confirm that the transgender girls had the right to race in women's events throughout the state. They were joined by like-minded state and federal officials.

The advocates for transgender girls highlighted the social and emotional challenges that these girls faced in high school. They believed participation in women's track and field would help them deal with those challenges.

The CIAC leaders were under pressure from the advocates for transgender girls. However, they also were under pressure from advocates for cisgender girls.

The advocates for cisgender girls wanted only these girls to compete in women's track and field. They explained that the cisgender girls were unable to compete fairly against opponents who had the strength and stamina of boys.

The advocates for cisgender girls wanted to keep women's high school sports the way that they had been for decades. They argued that cisgender girls needed to be treated with fairness.

The CIAC leaders listened respectfully to both groups. However, they sided with the advocates for transgender girls. They were moved by the argument to help these girls adapt emotionally and socially. They also were moved by their state's antidiscrimination law and a complementary US Department of Education directive.

The CIAC leaders announced that they were opening women's high school track to transgender girls. They were sure many constituents would be enthusiastic. They looked forward to their responses. However, they also braced for the reactions from disappointed constituents.

The CIAC leaders were ready for negative publicity. However, they were shocked by its volume. They decided to counter with their own publicity campaign. They reached out to elected officials and journalists to come to their defense.

The following questions will assist you if you are going through this book alone. They provide opportunities like those you would have in a college classroom where the professor is using the case method. They also will help you if you are in an actual college classroom with a professor who is using this approach.

Question 1: Why Did USRowing Restrict Women's Races to Cisgender Females?

USRowing regulated women's rowing races. It allowed only cisgender females to participate in women's individual races, in women's team races, and in the women's slots during races with mixed-gender crews. It explained that this regulation ensured competitive fairness for females.

How did different groups respond to USRowing? Focus on two groups: crews and elected officials.

Did the crews have low confidence, moderate confidence, or high confidence in the way that USRowing was behaving? How did elected officials feel? Explain the basis for your answers.

When answering these questions, as well as those that follow, you can rely on the information in this chapter. You also might rely on some of the sources in the references at the rear of the book. If you are reading this chapter with colleagues, you are encouraged to converse with them about the best way to answer the questions.

Question 2: Why Did USRowing Open Women's Races to Transgender Females?

USRowing changed its regulation on women's races. It allowed transgender females to participate in the single races and team races. However, it would not allow them to fill the women's slots during mixed-gender races. It contended that the new regulation promoted social acceptance without undermining competitive fairness.

How did different groups respond to USRowing? Focus on two groups: crews and elected officials.

Did the crews have low confidence, moderate confidence, or high confidence in the way that USRowing was behaving? How did elected officials feel? Explain the basis for your answers.

Question 3: Why Did CIAC Restrict Women's High School Track to Cisgender Females?

CIAC regulated high school track and field events in Connecticut. It allowed only cisgender females to participate in women's events. It explained that this regulation ensured competitive fairness for females.

How did different groups respond to CIAC? Focus on two groups: high school female athletes and elected officials.

Did the high school female athletes have low confidence, moderate confidence, or high confidence in the way that CIAC was behaving? How did elected officials feel? Explain the basis for your answers.

Question 4: Why Did CIAC Open Women's High School Track to Transgender Females?

CIAC changed its regulation for women's high school track and field. It allowed transgender females to participate in all of the women's events. It contended that the new regulation promoted social acceptance without undermining competitive fairness for females.

How did different groups respond to CIAC? Focus on two groups: high school female athletes and elected officials.

Did the high school female athletes have low confidence, moderate confidence, or high confidence in the way that CIAC was behaving? How did elected officials feel? Explain the basis for your answers.

SUMMARY

USRowing regulated women's rowing races. It allowed transgender females to compete as individuals or as members of all-women crews. However, it forbade them from filling the female slots on mixed-gender crews. It contended that these regulations were in the best interests of the sport and the participants.

CIAC regulated high school track and field events in Connecticut. It allowed transgender females to compete in all the women's events. It contended that this regulation was in the best interest of the sports and the participants.

Chapter 12

The Social-Emotional Learning Feuds

The vast majority of K-12 school districts have invested in SEL [Social Emotional Learning].

—*Education Week*'s Research Center
Director Holly Yettick, 2018

How do you understand your feelings? [SEL question in a fifth-grade math textbook].

—*quoted by* Dana Goldstein & Stephanie Saul, 2022

[Schools need to help students] develop healthy identities . . . show empathy . . . maintain supportive relationships, and make . . . caring decisions.

—Collaborative for Academic, Social, and Emotional Learning, 2023

[SEL requires teachers] to serve as psychologists, which they are not equipped to do.

— *Manhattan Institute for Policy Research*
Fellow Christopher Rufo, 2022

Math is about getting the right answer, not about feelings.

—Florida Governor Ron DeSantis, 2022

Business executives commissioned ads with overweight models. They believed these ads helped their businesses by boosting customer approval ratings and product sales. They contended that they also helped overweight customers by reducing their fat insecurity, anxiety, and shame.

School boards purchased math textbooks with an SEL (Social Emotional Learning) emphasis. They believed these books helped their districts by boosting parent approval ratings and student test scores. They contended that they also helped struggling students by reducing their math insecurity, anxiety, and shame.

NEUTRALIZING FAT SHAME

Business executives were always on the lookout for new products to manufacture, distribute, and sell. When they found them, they were eager to request the financing needed to move ahead with their projects. However, they had to take several steps before they could make this request.

The executives had to document robust consumer demand for their new products. They then had to explain how they would control costs for those products without sacrificing quality. Only then could they request the financing they needed.

The executives eventually manufactured their products and were ready to sell them. However, they needed assistance. They turned to marketers to create ads that would motivate customers to purchase their products.

The marketers had formulas for developing ads. They relied heavily on models. They noted that the models had to be appealing. They reasoned that unappealing models would not be able to engage consumers as effectively as appealing ones.

The marketers still had to devise the optimal situations in which to place their models. Aware that each product had distinctive constraints, they might place their models in restaurants when promoting food items, gas stations when promoting automotive products, or hospitals when promoting medicine.

The marketers adapted advertising situations to fit the products they were promoting. They also adapted the models themselves. They discovered that models with the ideal gender, age, or ethnicity could be invaluable for stimulating sales of their sponsors' products. However, they invariably relied on models with standard body weights—the weights suited to their frames and heights.

The marketers were open to making additional adaptations to their advertising formulas. They were on alert for emerging social trends. They then deliberated carefully about whether to incorporate those trends into their ads.

The marketers eventually began to reconsider the standard bodyweight models on whom they had been relying in ads. They judged that these models were not having the impact they once had. They wished to replace them with models who were fresh and stimulating.

The marketers proposed to use heavy, overweight, and even obese models. They predicted that these models would make a firm impression on viewers. They assured the sponsors that this impression, which would be linked to their products, would stimulate purchases.

The marketers explained why it was the right moment to hire heavier models. They noted that medical doctors, pharmaceutical researchers, and mental health specialists had been characterizing obesity as the result of physical ailments rather than behavioral habits. As a result, they believed that obesity no longer had the negative associations it once had.

The marketers added that politicians had attracted media attention by characterizing obesity in a different fashion. They gave the example of New York City's mayor who had promoted a weight-discrimination ordinance. They singled out politicians in Illinois, Michigan, New York, Wisconsin, and California who had backed similar initiatives.

The marketers created sample ads featuring overweight models. They predicted that consumers would link these ads to a critically important national trend. They were sure they would applaud the companies that used those ads.

The marketers identified overweight consumers as one of the groups that would respond positively to the new ads. They believed they would change the way they viewed themselves and be less likely to feel insecure, anxious, or ashamed. They believed that they then might feel more inclined to exercise and less inclined to overeat.

The marketers predicted that normal-weight consumers also would respond positively to the new ads. They explained that they would respect the businesses that had sponsored them. They anticipated they would purchase products made by those businesses and featured in the ads.

Enthusiasts

Medical professionals met with patients who were obese. They felt prepared to help them lose weight. However, they were less sure about how to handle patients with obesophobia—an extreme degree of bodyweight insecurity, anxiety, or shame. They noted that obesophobic patients were less likely to follow advice about weight reduction. They typically had to refer them to mental health professionals for help.

The mental health professionals met with, examined, and diagnosed patients with obesophobia. They concluded that some of them had developed this disorder because they could not reconcile their views of their bodies with the body images in ads. They commended the marketers who were introducing overweight models in their ads.

The marketers who were using overweight models were pleased by the responses from medical and mental health professionals. However, they judged that these specialists had relatively few opportunities to influence the general public. They therefore went to journalists and asked them to broadcast the conclusions of the medical professionals and mental health professionals.

The marketers were excited when many journalists highlighted the new advertising campaigns and the groups that supported them. They realized that these journalists would increase the impact of those campaigns. They returned to their clients and assured them that they would see significant boosts in their consumer product ratings and sales.

Skeptics

Business executives were intrigued by ads with overweight models. Many were ready to commission them. However, they waited to see how journalists were reacting to the new ads.

Although many journalists supported ads with overweight models, some were critical. The critics contended that the ads could cause obese people to reassess their weight and view it as medically and socially acceptable. They worried that they then would lose any motivation to shed that weight or even control it.

The critical journalist belittled the new ads. They conceded that they might improve the social acceptance of obese individuals. However, they predicted that they inadvertently would increase their number.

NEUTRALIZING MATH SHAME

Parents paid attention to their children's scores on mathematics tests. They worried when their scores dipped.

The parents had good reasons to worry about math test scores. They had seen them influence the high school courses in which students enrolled, the college academic majors that they chose, and even the careers that they eventually pursued. They expressed their concerns at school board meetings.

The school boards tried to appease the worried parents. They told them that they were taking steps to raise their children's math test scores. For example, they were selecting first-rate math textbooks for them.

The school boards relied on local committees to help them select math textbooks. Many of them made sure that these committees comprised parents as well as educators. They advised them to examine the math materials on their states' lists of approved textbooks.

The school boards had collaborated with textbook committees for decades. They had seen committee members bicker when reviewing social studies textbooks. However, they believed they had been extremely cooperative when reviewing math textbooks.

The school boards had an explanation about why social studies textbooks led to committee disputes. They noted that their authors employed narrative organizations that made it easy for them to insert their values and opinions.

The school boards contrasted the social studies textbooks with those for algebra, geometry, and calculus. They noted that their authors employed skills-driven organizations that provided few opportunities for them to interject their values and opinions.

The school boards were generally pleased with the textbook committees. However, they relied on one more group: textbook sales agents.

The sales agents were proud of their mathematics textbooks. They identified books that had been popular for many editions. They noted that these books had been praised by school administrators, math teachers, and parents for boosting students' test scores.

The sales agents claimed that their bestselling mathematics textbooks were already highly effective. Nonetheless, they believed they had become even more effective. They explained that their authors had rewritten them with a greater emphasis on Social and Emotional Learning (SEL). They noted that they were trying to help teachers nurture positive self-concept, empathy, respect, and collaboration. They stated that they had designed their new books to reduce and possibly eliminate math insecurity, anxiety, and shame among students.

The school boards were intrigued by the new math textbooks. They met with their superintendents, who assured them that many of their principals and math teachers were aware of SEL textbooks and supported them.

The school boards had heard enough. They authorized purchases of the SEL textbooks. They then waited to observe the reactions to them. They were especially interested in the reactions of the teachers who would be using those textbooks to enhance their instruction.

Enthusiasts

Many teachers had expressed concern about math anxiety. They believed that it was dampening their students' motivation to learn. They were excited about textbooks that would address this problem.

The teachers dealt with mild cases of math insecurity, anxiety, and shame. However, they were not prepared to handle severe cases. They referred these to mental health professionals.

The mental health professionals met with the emotionally troubled students. They noted that some were troubled because they had failed screening tests and been blocked from advanced classes. They noted that others were troubled after they had been admitted to advanced math classes but then struggled in them. They concluded that both groups were generalizing their negative feelings toward math to other academic subjects and to school in general.

The mental health professionals were confident that SEL textbooks would help teachers identify students with math insecurity, anxiety, or shame. They believed that they could even help them identify students who were psychologically aberrant and potentially dangerous.

Many educators in California were excited about the SEL textbooks. They were even more excited after their state board of education approved them. They hoped that their local school boards would purchase and distribute them.

California educators employed curricular plans to guide their math instruction. They depended on their textbooks to provide these. However, they also depended on their state's curricular plan—the *California Math Framework*.

The educators detected a problem. They noted that the new math textbooks embodied SEL competencies while the *California Math Framework* embodied skills-based competencies.

The educators knew they were accountable for teaching the skills-based competencies in the *California Math Framework*. They wondered how they were to reconcile these competencies with those in the SEL textbooks. They asked the California Board of Education for clarification.

The state board members were stumped when teachers pointed to the discrepancy between the SEL textbooks and the *California Math Framework*. However, they quickly recovered their poise.

The state board members explained that they would develop another math framework. They promised that this new framework would still show a commitment to "mathematical excellence." However, they promised that it also would show a commitment to "mathematical equity."

Skeptics

School boards around the nation were impressed when California embraced SEL math textbooks. They included several school boards in Florida.

The Florida boards were eager to purchase SEL math textbooks. They hoped that their local textbook committees would recommend them. They directed them to search for them on their state's list of approved textbooks.

The members of the Florida State Board of Education kept a list of approved textbooks. They had relied on the *Florida B.E.S.T. Standards in Mathematics* (Benchmarks for Excellent Student Thinking) when compiling that list.

The local textbook committees searched for SEL math textbooks on the state list. They found no SEL math textbooks on it. They reported back to their school boards.

The school boards were not surprised. They were aware that Florida's governor, legislators, and State Board of Education had repeatedly expressed no confidence in SEL math textbooks. Although they were willing to challenge them, they needed the support of teachers and parents in their districts.

The pro-SEL school boards asked their local math teachers if they would support these textbooks. They quickly surmised that the teachers were not unified. Although they found some who were supportive, they detected many who were skeptical.

The skeptical Florida teachers explained why they had reservations about SEL textbooks. They contended that the materials were less challenging than the skills-based textbooks. They predicted that talented students who used them would struggle when taking standardized math tests or advanced math courses. They believed those struggles might disqualify them for scholarships or admission to prestigious colleges.

The pro-SEL school boards listened to the skeptical teachers. They realized they would need their support to move forward on SEL textbooks. They realized they also needed parental support. They were surprised when some parents expressed skepticism.

Many parents of math-anxious students had been hopeful about SEL textbooks. However, some of them changed their minds. These parents conceded that their children might feel less emotional stress with SEL textbooks. However, they suspected they would begin to view low math achievement as normal. They worried about the damage from this view.

The parents of high-achieving students were another Florida group skeptical of SEL textbooks. They were skeptical for a different reason than the parents of low-achieving students.

The parents of high-achieving students contended that the SEL math textbooks were less challenging. They worried that they would limit their children's progress. They concluded that these textbooks, even if they benefited low-achieving students, required too many sacrifices from high-achieving students.

The parents of high-achieving students had another objection to the SEL math textbooks. They insisted that they set unreasonable expectations for teachers. They doubted teachers had the training to identify math insecurity, anxiety, or shame. They predicted that those who assumed this responsibility would do more harm than good.

RESPONDING TO QUESTIONS ABOUT SOCIAL AND EMOTIONAL GOALS

This section focuses on the preceding two cases. The first case involved business executives.

Business executives were eager to manufacture, distribute, and sell new products. However, they first had to assess if those products would be in demand by consumers. They hired marketers to make the assessment.

The marketers assured the executives that they could skillfully assess the current demand for their products. However, they told them that they also could increase that demand. They would rely on expertly tailored ads. They were pleased when the executives hired them for both tasks.

The marketers described the ads that they had in mind. They recommended ads that featured physically fit models. They explained that these ads would appeal to consumers and motivate them to purchase the featured products.

The marketers later changed their advice to the executives. They still believed that ads with fit models were effective. However, they believed that a different type of ad could be even more effective.

The marketers urged the executives to switch to ads with overweight models. They were certain that these ads would appeal to overweight individuals. However, they predicted that they also would appeal to the many people who were not themselves overweight but who were concerned about the marginalization of overweight individuals in our society.

The marketers predicted that the new ads would not only generate business but also provide help to overweight individuals. They explained that they would persuade them to feel less guilt over their body sizes. They added that they also would motivate them to increase their social activity and raise their career aspirations.

The executives were intrigued by ads with heavy models. They directed the marketers to shift to them. They then waited to see how people responded to them.

The executives had been assured that many individuals would applaud the new ads. They were not disappointed. They noted that journalists, medical professionals, mental health specialists, and obese consumers praised the ads.

The executives were encouraged by the many people who were pleased with their new ads. However, they had been warned that some individuals might be skeptical of them. They were surprised by the number of skeptics.

The skeptics chided the executives for the changes to their ads. They assumed that they had made the changes to improve profits. However, they questioned whether they had the expertise to assess the complex psychological consequences of those changes.

The skeptics worried that the new ads had convinced obese consumers that excessive weight was normal and acceptable. They suspected they might have inadvertently encouraged them to sustain unhealthy weights and eating habits.

While the first case in this chapter concerned business executives, the next case focused on school boards. These boards were responsible for designating math textbooks for the students in their districts.

The school boards paid special attention to the connection between math textbooks and scores on standardized math tests. They had seen textbooks given the credit after scores increased. They also had seen them blamed after scores decreased.

The school boards wanted their students to develop the skills they needed to progress in mathematics and earn high test scores. They recognized that the students needed suitable textbooks.

The school boards noted that the publishers traditionally had supplied books that emphasized mathematical skills. They judged that these books appealed to parents, teachers, and school administrators. Furthermore, they seemed to boost the academic performance of mathematically talented students. They concluded that they were effective.

The publishers assessed their textbooks from a different perspective. They did not doubt that their books were effective. However, they believed that they could be replaced by ones that were even more effective.

The publishers urged the school boards to switch to textbooks that fostered SEL. They assured them that these textbooks would help students who felt marginalized in their math classes.

The publishers explained that the SEL textbooks benefited students who had become emotionally insecure, anxious, or ashamed about their mathematics ability. They contended that they would motivate these students, expand their math proficiency, increase their test scores, and raise their academic aspirations.

The school boards consulted with their principals and their staff about the SEL math textbooks. After confirming that they were in favor of them, they advised them to prepare for textbook changes.

The school boards were eager to see how community members responded to the SEL textbooks. They were gratified when many of them praised the books.

The school boards were pleased that many people supported the new textbooks. However, they still were cautious. They were especially cautious about how parents were reacting.

Some of the parents were critical. They did not doubt that students who used SEL textbooks learned how to handle their emotional problems. However, they contended that they replaced those problems with a different problem. They believed that the students had begun to view low mathematics achievement as nothing to fret about.

The critical parents believed that teachers were in a difficult situation. They realized that teachers had to assess whether SEL textbooks were helping students deal with their math insecurity, anxiety, and shame. However, they did not think teachers had the psychological training to make these assessments.

The following questions will assist you if you are going through this book alone. They provide opportunities like those you would have in a college classroom where the professor is using the case method. They also will help you if you are in an actual college classroom with a professor who is using this approach.

Question 1: Why Did Executives Commission Ads with Fit and Trim Models?

Business executives commissioned ads with fit and trim models. They believed the ads benefitted their businesses by boosting customer approval ratings and product sales.

How did different groups respond to the business executives? Focus on two groups: journalists and consumers.

Did the journalists have low confidence, moderate confidence, or high confidence in the way that the executives were behaving? How did consumers feel? Explain the basis for your answers.

When answering these questions, as well as those that follow, you can rely on the information in this chapter. You also might rely on some of the sources identified in the references at the rear of the book. If you are reading this chapter with colleagues, you are encouraged to converse with them about the best way to answer the questions.

Question 2: Why Did Executives Switch to Ads with Overweight Models?

Business executives switched to ads with overweight models. They believed these ads would benefit their business by boosting customer approval ratings and product sales. However, they believed they also would benefit overweight customers by reducing fat insecurity, anxiety, and shame.

How did different groups respond to the business executives? Focus on two groups: journalists and consumers.

Did the journalists have low confidence, moderate confidence, or high confidence in the way that the executives were behaving? How did consumers feel? Explain the basis for your answers.

Question 3: Why Did School Boards Purchase Math Textbooks Emphasizing Academic Skills?

School boards purchased math textbooks that emphasized academic skills. They believed these books helped their districts by boosting parent approval ratings and student test scores.

How did different groups respond to the school board members? Focus on two groups: journalists and parents.

Did the journalists have low confidence, moderate confidence, or high confidence in the way that the school boards were behaving? How did parents feel? Explain the basis for your answers.

Question 4: Why Did School Boards Switch to Math Textbooks Emphasizing SEL?

School boards switched to mathematics textbooks emphasizing SEL. They believed these books would benefit their districts by boosting parent approval ratings and student test scores. However, they believed that they also would benefit struggling students by reducing math insecurity, anxiety, and shame.

How did different groups respond to the school boards? Focus on two groups: journalists and parents.

Did the journalists have low confidence, moderate confidence, or high confidence in the way that the school boards were behaving? How did parents feel? Explain the basis for your answers.

SUMMARY

Business executives commissioned ads with fit and trim models. However, they later switched to ads with overweight models. They believed this switch helped their businesses by boosting customer approval ratings and product sales. They believed it also helped overweight customers by reducing fat insecurity, anxiety, and shame.

School boards purchased mathematics textbooks that emphasized academic skills. However, they later switched to textbooks with an SEL emphasis. They believed this switch benefited their districts by boosting parent approval ratings and student test scores. They believed it also benefited struggling students by reducing math insecurity, anxiety, and shame.

References

REFERENCES FOR *PREFACE EPIGRAPHS*

Hardaker, T.—*quoted by* Patterson, S. (2022, August 6). Duval County School Board, District 6. *Florida Times Union*. Retrieved from: https://jacksonville-fl-app.news-memory.com/?publink=1cb31635e_13485aa.

Prior, I.—*quoted by* Minock, N. (2022, December 21). Outraged Loudoun County parents prepare to oust school board in 2023. Wjla.com. Retrieved from: https://wjla.com/news/crisis-in-the-classrooms/sexual-assaults-loudoun-county-public-schools-outraged-loudoun-county-parents-oust-school-board-2023-grand-jury-report-scott-ziegler-wayde-bayard-abbie-platt-ian-prior-fight-for-schools-nick-gothard-loudoun-4-all.

Tigge, J.—*quoted by* Minock, N. (2023, January 5). Loudoun County man found not guilty for trespassing at heated 2021 school board meeting. Wjla.com. Retrieved from: https://wjla.com/news/local/loudoun-county-jon-tigges-found-not-guilty-trespassing-heated-loudoun-county-school-board-meeting-2021-scott-ziegler.

Wall Street Journal Editorial Board. (2022, May 8). A parental victory on free speech. *Wall Street Journal*. Retrieved from: https://www.wsj.com/articles/a-parental-victory-free-speech-ryder-ohio-big-walnut-school-district-board-crowl-parents-rights-education-11652034063.

REFERENCES FOR CHAPTER 1

References for *Chapter 1 Epigraphs*

Brengle, G.—*quoted in* Banned books. (2023, May 7). *Florida Times-Union*. Retrieved from: https://jacksonville-fl.newsmemory.com/?publink=0abcdb52c_134ab8f.

Caldwell-Stone, D.—*quoted by* Italie, H. (2023, March 23). Banned book attempts hit record high in 2022. *USA TODAY*. Retrieved from: https://www.usatoday.com/story/entertainment/books/2023/03/23/banned-books-banning-attempts-hit-record-high-2022/11531816002.

Nossel, S.—*quoted by* Luhnow, D., & Colchester. M. (2023, February 20). Roald Dahl's children's books changed to make them more inclusive. *Wall Street Journal*. Retrieved from: https://www.wsj.com/articles/roald-dahls-childrens-books-changed-to-make-them-more-inclusive-d6ccc6c4?mod=hp_listb_pos4.

Shah, N. (2023, March 17). Shelves have been left barren: Florida teachers sue DeSantis' government over school library regulations. *USA TODAY*. Retrieved from: https://www.usatoday.com/story/news/education/2023/03/17/florida-school-library-controversy-teachers-sue-desantis-government/11491268002/.

References for *Aerial Surveillance—Introduction*

Abbany, Z. (2020, August 25). Modern spy satellites in an age of space wars. Dw.com. Retrieved from: https://www.dw.com/en/modern-spy-satellites-in-an-age-of-space-wars/a-54691887.

Cast, N. (2023). Military drones: A simple and detailed guide 2023. Remoteflyer.com. Retrieved from: https://www.remoteflyer.com/military-drones-a-simple-and-detailed-guide-2023.

Dienesch, R. M. (2016). *Eyeing the red storm: Eisenhower and the first attempt to build a spy satellite*. Lincoln: University of Nebraska Press.

Drones and aerial surveillance. (2023). Epic.org. Retrieved from: https://epic.org/issues/surveillance-oversight/aerial-surveillance.

Military drone—Surveillance. (2023). Elistair.com. Retrieved from: https://elistair.com/applications/defense-surveillance-drone.

National Museum of the United States Air Force. (2023). *Cold war in space: Top secret reconnaissance satellites revealed*. Author. Retrieved from: https://www.nationalmuseum.af.mil/Visit/Museum-Exhibits/Fact-Sheets/Display/Article/195923/cold-war-in-space-top-secret-reconnaissance-satellites-revealed/.

Stanley, J., & Crump, C. (2011, December). Protecting privacy from aerial surveillance: Recommendations for government use of drone aircraft. American Civil Liberties Union. Retrieved from: https://www.aclu.org/report/protecting-privacy-aerial-surveillance-recommendations-government-use-drone-aircraft.

References for *Aerial Surveillance—Enthusiasts*

Reed, B. (2023, May 11). US and China hold "constructive" talks in effort to move beyond spy balloon incident. *Guardian*. Retrieved from: https://www.theguardian.com/us-news/2023/may/12/us-and-china-hold-constructive-talks-in-effort-to-move-beyond-spy-balloon-incident.

Smith, P. (2023, July 20). Chinese spy balloon exposed gaps in U.S. ability to detect threats, NORAD commander says. *Wall Street Journal.* Retrieved from: https://www.nbcnews.com/news/us-news/chinese-spy-surveillance-balloon-flaws-threat-detection-norad-defense-rcna95094.

US to China: Let's "move beyond" balloon. (2023, May 13). *Florida Times-Union.* Retrieved from: https://jacksonville-fl.newsmemory.com/?publink=00e1ae732_134ab95.

Vincent, B. (2023, March 17). Post-balloon saga, US defense leaders "know a lot more" about China's alleged global surveillance operations. Defensescoop.com. Retrieved from: https://defensescoop.com/2023/03/17/post-balloon-saga-us-defense-leaders-know-a-lot-more-about-chinas-alleged-global-surveillance-operations.

References for *Aerial Surveillance—Skeptics*

Copp, T., Tucker, E., & Long, C. (2023, February 15). Latest downed objects could well be "benign," US says Balloon was believed to be headed for Guam. *Florida Times-Union.* Retrieved from: https://jacksonville-fl.newsmemory.com/?publink=2b11ff99e_134aa6b.

Wall Street Journal Editorial Board. (2023a, February 5). Biden and the Chinese spy balloon— Why did he wait so long to order the airspace intruder shot down? *Wall Street Journal.* Retrieved from: https://www.wsj.com/articles/biden-and-the-chinese-spy-balloon-f22-shooting-airspace-montana-military-pentagon-debris-defense-beijing-trespasser-espionage-intelligence-11675626225.

Wall Street Journal Editorial Board. (2023b, February 6). Seen any other spy balloons lately? *Wall Street Journal.* Retrieved from: https://www.wsj.com/articles/chinese-spy-balloon-biden-administration-trump-administration-pentagon-glen-vanherck-11675724569.

Wall Street Journal Editorial Board. (2023c, February 8). Exposing the Chinese spy balloon fleet. *Wall Street Journal.* Retrieved from: https://www.wsj.com/articles/chinese-spy-balloon-biden-cuban-missile-crisis-beijing-11675898313.

Wall Street Journal Editorial Board. (2023d, February 10). Mystery invasion object of the week. *Wall Street Journal.* Retrieved from: https://www.wsj.com/articles/flying-object-alaska-shot-down-biden-administration-chinese-spy-balloon-1199de88.

References for *Scholastic Surveillance—Introduction*

Florida State Board of Education. (2023, January 13). Rule 6A-7.0715: Certifications and plans for instructional materials and library media. Author. Retrieved from: https://www.fldoe.org/academics/standards/subject-areas/library-media-services-instructional-t/.

Grenn, S. (2023, March 11). Who decides what books to keep. *Florida Times-Union.* Retrieved from: https://jacksonville-fl.newsmemory.com/?publink=275d73ffb_134aacb.

Italie, H. (2023, March 23). Banned book attempts hit record high in 2022. *USA TODAY*. Retrieved from: https://www.usatoday.com/story/entertainment/books/2023/03/23/banned-books-banning-attempts-hit-record-high-2022/11531816002.

Lieberman, M. (2023, February 27). How school libraries buy books, struggle for funds, and confront book bans. *Education Week*. Retrieved from: https://www.edweek.org/teaching-learning/how-school-libraries-buy-books-struggle-for-funds-and-confront-book-bans-an-explainer/2023/02.

McLean, J. (2023, March 7). St. Johns County removes 23 books from library shelves after review. News4jax.com. Retrieved from: https://www.news4jax.com/news/local/2023/02/07/st-johns-county-removes-23-books-from-library-shelves-after-review.

O'Connor, J. (2023, April 10). Ill. seeks pledge against book bans. *Florida Times-Union*. Retrieved from: https://jacksonville-fl.newsmemory.com/?publink=0b2907ca7_134ab2e.

PEN America. (2023, March 10). Florida book bans are no hoax. Pen.org. Retrieved from: https://pen.org/florida-book-bans-not-a-hoax/.

Pendharkar, E. (2023, February 21). Over 300 picture books were banned last school year. *Education Week*. Retrieved from: https://www.edweek.org/teaching-learning/over-300-picture-books-were-banned-last-school-year/2023/02.

Ross, N. (2022, September 26). PEN America: Here are the 411 books banned in Florida school libraries and classrooms. *Fort Myers News-Press*. Retrieved from: https://www.news-press.com/story/news/education/2022/09/26/book-bans-here-411-books-banned-florida-schools-pen-america-districts-banned/10434253002.

Rummler, O. (2023, February 23). Book bans internalize "shame" for young LGBTQ+ people, advocates say. Retrieved from: 19thnews.org. https://19thnews.org/2023/02/book-bans-lgbtq-reading.

Shah, N. (2023, March 17). Shelves have been left barren: Florida teachers sue DeSantis' government over school library regulations. *USA TODAY*. Retrieved from: https://www.usatoday.com/story/news/education/2023/03/17/florida-school-library-controversy-teachers-sue-desantis-government/11491268002/.

Turco, R. (2023, January 18). State education officials pass rule on schools' library book choices. Mynews13.com. Retrieved from: https://www.mynews13.com/fl/orlando/news/2023/01/18/state-education-officials-pass-rule-on-library-book-choice.

USA TODAY Editorial Staff. (2023, March 19). Don't proclaim liberty while banning books. *Florida Times-Union*. Retrieved from: https://jacksonville-fl.newsmemory.com/?publink=2e09dd96c_134aac5.

References for *Scholastic Surveillance—Enthusiasts*

Alter, A., & Harris, E. A. (2021, October 20). Dr. Seuss books are pulled, and a "cancel culture" controversy erupts. *New York Times*. Retrieved from: https://www.nytimes.com/2021/03/04/books/dr-seuss-books.html.

Anderson, Z., & Brugal, S. (2021, December 14). Moms for Liberty. *Florida Times-Union*. Retrieved from: https://jacksonville-fl-app.newsmemory.com/?publink=2e37437bb_1346032.

Banned Books Week: Roald Dahl. (2018, September 27). Aapld.org. Retrieved from: https://ys.aapld.org/archives/4845-banned-books-week-roald-dahl/.

Elassar, A., Romine, T., & Rose, A. (2023, April 1). Judge orders books removed from Texas public libraries due to LGBTQ and racial content must be returned within 24 hours. Cnn.com. Retrieved from: https://www.cnn.com/2023/04/01/us/texas-book-ban-removed-library-replaced-judge/index.html.

Goulis, L. (2021, March 1). Dr. Seuss books banned at school over claims the classic stories are racist. Kidspot.com. Retrieved from: https://www.kidspot.com.au/lifestyle/entertainment/books-tv-and-movies/dr-seuss-books-banned-at-school-over-claims-the-classic-stories-are-racist/news-story/a0e62806a5869bada9a0301de0b00568.

Local libraries begin removal of controversial Dr. Seuss books. (2021, March 2). Wavy.com. Retrieved from: https://www.wavy.com/news/local-news/local-libraries-begin-removal-of-controversial-dr-seuss-books.

Mutchler, K. (2023, April 3). Westport parent wants Staples library books removed, altered. Ctinsider.com. Retrieved from: https://www.ctinsider.com/westport/article/westport-banned-books-removal-17871323.php.

Paradkar, S. (2023 February 23). Equating the Roald Dahl edits to book banning is living in a Willy Wonka fantasy world. *Toronto Star*. Retrieved from: tps://www.thestar.com/opinion/star-columnists/2023/02/23/equating-the-roald-dahl-edits-to-book-banning-is-living-in-a-willy-wonka-fantasy-world.html.

Parents seek to ban Roald Dahl book, "The Witches". (1989 October 19). Apnews.com. Retrieved from: https://apnews.com/article/9d0328715491b36e39ccdf53d6da6a04.

Price, C. (2021, April 23). Library, schools consider whether to keep Dr. Seuss books on shelves. Oxfordobserver.org. Retrieved from: https://oxfordobserver.org/5172/community/dr-seuss-enterprises-pulls-six-books-for-harmful-images.

References for *Scholastic Surveillance—Skeptics*

Amy, J. (2023, May 22). Georgia school's book bans may break civil rights law, federal officials warn. Apnews.com. Retrieved from: https://apnews.com/article/schools-education-book-bans-libraries-civil-rights-bf3494e25528cb2403eaca43c813f684.

Beaumont, H. (2023, April 7). How teachers and librarians are subverting book bans in the US. Aljazeera.com. Retrieved from: https://www.aljazeera.com/amp/news/2023/4/7/how-teachers-and-librarians-are-subverting-book-bans-in-the-us.

Brown, D. J. (2022, February 19). Amid fear and censorship, Florida school districts are pulling books off shelves in public schools. https://www.the74million.org/article/amid-fear-and-censorship-florida-school-districts-are-pulling-books-off-shelves-in-public-schools/.

DeSantis, R. (2023, March 8). Governor Ron DeSantis debunks book ban hoax. Flgov.com. Retrieved from: https://www.flgov.com/2023/03/08/governor-ron-desantis-debunks-book-ban-hoax.

Rozier, A. (2023, March 10). "Hoax": Gov. Ron DeSantis defends book ban. Wpbf.com. Retrieved from: https://www.wpbf.com/article/gov-ron-desantis-debunks-book-ban-hoax-florida/43252164#.

REFERENCES FOR CHAPTER 2

References for *Chapter 2 Epigraphs*

Carvalho, A.—*quoted by* Yilek, C. (2021, August 12). Florida school board to require face masks despite ban. Cbsnews.com. Retrieved from: https://www.cbsnews.com/news/florida-broward-county-schools-face-mask-requirement-desantis-ban-covid-19.

Centers for Disease Control and Prevention.—*quoted by* Smelkinson, M., Bienen, L., & Noble, J. (2022, January 26). The case against masks at school. *Atlantic*. Retrieved from: https://www.theatlantic.com/ideas/archive/2022/01/kids-masks-schools-weak-science/621133.

Corcoran, R.—*quoted by* Mervosh, S., (2021, September 10). Florida withholds money from school districts over mask mandates. *New York Times*. Retrieved from: https://www.nytimes.com/2021/08/30/us/florida-schools-mask-mandates.html.

Mervosh, S. (2021, September 10). Florida withholds money from school districts over mask mandates. *New York Times*. Retrieved from: https://www.nytimes.com/2021/08/30/us/florida-schools-mask-mandates.html.

Parental Lawsuit—*quoted in* Clay County woman takes on national role. (2023, May 8). *Florida Times-Union*. Retrieved from: https://jacksonville-fl.newsmemory.com/?publink=09a8ede72_134ab90.

Smelkinson, M., Bienen, L., & Noble, J. (2022, January 26). The case against masks at school. *Atlantic*. Retrieved from: https://www.theatlantic.com/ideas/archive/2022/01/kids-masks-schools-weak-science/621133.

References for *Hearing Aids—Introduction*

Fla., feds at odds over importing of drugs. (2023, April 25). *Florida Times-Union*. Retrieved from: https://jacksonville-fl.newsmemory.com/?publink=08c7cc66b_134ab3d.

OTC: Debate in Europe on the situation in the US. (2017, July 11). Audiology-worldnews.com. Retrieved from: https://www.audiology-worldnews.com/market2/2348-otc-debate-in-europe-on-the-situation-in-the-us.

Sieber, T. (2023, March 7). How do hearing aids work? Soundguys.com. Retrieved from: https://www.soundguys.com/how-do-hearing-aids-work-57482/.

Treisman, R. (2022, August 16). Millions of Americans will soon be able to buy hearing aids without a prescription. Npr.org. Retrieved from: https://www.npr.org/2022/08/16/1117741695/over-the-counter-hearing-aids.

U.S. Food & Drug Administration. (2022, August 16). FDA finalizes historic rule enabling access to over-the-counter hearing aids for millions of Americans. Author. Retrieved from: https://www.fda.gov/news-events/press-announcements/fda-finalizes-historic-rule-enabling-access-over-counter-hearing-aids-millions-americans.

U.S. National Institute of Health. (2022, August 16). Over-the-counter hearing aids. Author. Retrieved from: https://www.nidcd.nih.gov/health/over-counter-hearing-aids.

References for *Hearing Aids—Enthusiasts*

Musto, J. (2022, November 16). Apple AirPods the cheaper alternative to hearing aids? *Fox News*. Retrieved from: https://www.foxnews.com/tech/apple-airpods-cheaper-alternative-hearing-aids.

Purdy, K. (2022, November 17). Study: AirPods Pro are this close to being full-fledged hearing aids. Arstechnica.com. Retrieved from: https://arstechnica.com/science/2022/11/study-airpods-pro-are-this-close-to-being-full-fledged-hearing-aids.

Scott, D. (2023, April 27). How Ron DeSantis transformed into an anti-public health crusader. Vox.com. Retrieved from: https://www.vox.com/policy/23682263/ron-desantis-covid-19-vaccines-joseph-ladapo.

Thompson, G. (2017, June 20). A worldwide perspective: Evidence for OTC disruption (or lack thereof), Part 4. Hearinghealthmatters.org. Retrieved from: https://hearinghealthmatters.org/hearing-technologies/2017/worldwide-perspective-evidence-otc-disruption-lack-thereof-part-4.

References for *Hearing Aids—Skeptics*

Baird, S. (2023, July13). Wait, are hearing aids cool now? Ask millennials. *Wall Street Journal*. Retrieved from: https://www.wsj.com/articles/wait-are-hearing-aids-cool-now-ask-millennials-629e7e55.

Chappell, B. (2022, August 18). Over-the-counter hearing aids will bring relief, but with some confusion. Npr.org. Retrieved from: https://www.npr.org/2022/08/17/1117934920/hearing-aids-over-the-counter-paying.

Erich Spahr, pivot of Bernafon since 1984, waves goodbye to a "people business". (2021, October 20). Audiology-worldnews.com. Retrieved from: https://www.audiology-worldnews.com/market2/4250-erich-spahr-pivot-of-bernafon-since-1984-waves-goodbye-to-a-people-business.

Solan, M. (2022, November 16). Should you get an over-the-counter hearing aid? Health.harvard.edu. Retrieved from: https://www.health.harvard.edu/blog/should-you-get-an-over-the-counter-hearing-aid-202211162852.

Starkey to launch an OTC hearing aid...reluctantly, and without conviction. (2022, October 11). Audiology-worldnews.com. Retrieved from: https://www.audiology

-worldnews.com/market2/4590-starkey-to-launch-an-otc-hearing-aid-reluctantly-and-without-conviction.

Weiss, C. (2023, February 9). Mayo Clinic Q and A: Are over-the-counter hearing devices a fit for you? Mayoclinic.org. Retrieved from: https://newsnetwork.mayoclinic.org/discussion/mayo-clinic-q-and-a-are-over-the-counter-hearing-devices-a-fit-for-you.

References for *School Facemasks—Introduction*

Freeman, J. (2023, April 26). Fauci and the *New York Times*. *Wall Street Journal*. Retrieved from: https://www.wsj.com/articles/fauci-and-the-new-york-times-6fcecc37?mod=hp_opin_pos_3#cxrecs_s.

Lee, D. (2023, March 10). Covid worsened America rage virus, for which there's no vaccine. *Wall Street Journal*. Retrieved from: https://www.wsj.com/articles/covid-worsened-america-rage-virus-for-which-theres-no-vaccine-lockdown-vaccine-mandates-ron-desantis-stanford-masking-2670cd39?mod=hp_opin_pos_4#cxrecs_s

Lonas, L. (2023, April 4). Teachers union blasts GOP's "misleading claims" ahead of Weingarten's House hearing. *The Hill*. Retrieved from: https://thehill.com/homenews/house/3959421-teachers-union-blasts-gops-misleading-claims-ahead-of-weingarten-house-hearing.

Map: Coronavirus and school closures in 2019-2020 (2021, October 13). *Education Week*. Retrieved from: https://www.edweek.org/leadership/map-coronavirus-and-school-closures-in-2019-2020/2020/03.

Nazaryan, A. (2022, January 5). "We want schools to be open," White House says as Chicago cancels classes. News.yahoo.com. Retrieved from: https://news.yahoo.com/we-want-schools-to-be-open-white-house-says-as-chicago-cancels-classes-201418110.html.

San Francisco Unified School District. (2023). Notice of COVID-19 school closure dates (SY 2020-2021). Author. Retrieved from: https://www.sfusd.edu/covid-19-response-updates-and-resources/preparing-fall-2021/notice-covid-19-school-closure-dates-sy-2020-2021#:~:text=Due%20to%20the%20COVID%2D19,was%20provided%20through%20remote%20learning.

References for *School Facemasks—Enthusiasts*

Durkee, A. (2021, August 25). 10 Florida school districts now defying DeSantis' mask mandate ban. Forbes.com. Retrieved from: https://www.forbes.com/sites/alisondurkee/2021/08/25/10-florida-school-districts-now-defying-desantis-mask-mandate-ban/?sh=3208b42f28fe.

Miller, Z. (2023, May 2). Most federal vaccine mandates to end: Emergency declaration will be lifted next week. *Florida Times-Union*. Retrieved from: https://jacksonville-fl.newsmemory.com/?publink=200b6d145_134ab8a.

School District of Manatee, Florida. (2020, August 14). Operating protocols for policy 8450. Fldoe.org. Retrieved from: https://www.fldoe.org/core/fileparse.php/19861/urlt/0824BestPracticesSlide5-2.pdf.

Wein, H. (2022, March 22). Mandatory masking in schools reduced COVID-19 cases. *NIH Research Matters.* Retrieved from: https://www.nih.gov/news-events/nih-research-matters/mandatory-masking-schools-reduced-covid-19-cases.

References for *School Facemasks—Skeptics*

Anderson, Z., & Brugal, S. (2021, December 14). Moms for Liberty. *Florida Times-Union.* Retrieved from: https://jacksonville-fl-app.newsmemory.com/?publink=2e37437bb_1346032.

Lee, D. (2023, March 10). Covid worsened America rage virus, for which there's no vaccine. *Wall Street Journal.* Retrieved from: https://www.wsj.com/articles/covid-worsened-america-rage-virus-for-which-theres-no-vaccine-lockdown-vaccine-mandates-ron-desantis-stanford-masking-2670cd39?mod=hp_opin_pos_4#cxrecs_s

Lonas, L. (2023, April 4). Teachers union blasts GOP's "misleading claims" ahead of Weingarten's House hearing. *The Hill.* Retrieved from: https://thehill.com/homenews/house/3959421-teachers-union-blasts-gops-misleading-claims-ahead-of-weingarten-house-hearing.

Roche, D. (2021, December 17). CDC's school mask guidelines fuel a culture war that Europe, WHO avoided. *Newsweek.* Retrieved from: https://www.newsweek.com/cdc-school-mask-guidelines-fuel-culture-war-europe-who-avoided-coronavirus-1660469.

REFERENCES FOR CHAPTER 3

References for *Chapter 3 Epigraphs*

Claybrook, R.—*quoted by* Sawchuk, S. (2022, April 28). Are teachers obliged to tell parents their child might be trans? Courts may soon decide. *Education Week.* Retrieved from: https://www.edweek.org/policy-politics/are-teachers-obliged-to-tell-parents-their-child-might-be-trans-courts-may-soon-decide/2022/04.

Deardorff, A.—*quoted by* Rizzo, E. (2023, February 14). "These are human rights issues": Pa. school board directors condemn Central Bucks for apparent anti-LGBTQ actions. Whyy.org. Retrieved from: https://whyy.org/articles/pa-school-board-directors-condemn-central-bucks-anti-lgbt.

Mastroianni, M.—*quoted by* Brown, J. (2022, December 27). Judge dismisses MA parents' lawsuit over school gender policy, scolds district: "Disconcerting". Foxnews.com. Retrieved from: https://www.foxnews.com/us/judge-dismisses-ma-parents-lawsuit-school-gender-policy-scolds-district-disconcerting.

Nelson, A. (2023, February 10). Mom sues after discovering school district identified daughter as male, counseled her on breast binding. Foxnews.com. Retrieved from: https://www.foxnews.com/media/mom-sues-after-discovering-school-district-identified-daughter-male-counseled-breast-binding.

Patrick, W.—*quoted by* Lanum, N. (2023, January 25). Attorneys sound off on teachers transitioning kids without parental consent: "Playground, not pronouns". Foxnews.com. Retrieved from: https://www.foxnews.com/media/attorneys-teachers-transitioning-kids-without-parental-consent-playground-pronouns.

References for *Airline Boarding—Introduction*

Explorer-C. (2020, October 12). Military boarding policy. Southwest.com. Retrieved from: https://community.southwest.com/t5/Travel-Policies/Military-Boarding-Policy/td-p/112385.

Explorer-C. (2022, August 30). Retired veterans. Southwest.com. Retrieved from: https://community.southwest.com/t5/Check-In-Boarding/Retired-Veterans/td-p/148048.

Leff, G. (2023, May 8) The game theory of choosing seats on southwest airlines. Viewfromthewing.com. Retrieved from: https://viewfromthewing.com/the-game-theory-of-choosing-seats-on-southwest-airlines.

Passy, J. (2023, May 21). Want a printed airline boarding pass—Be ready to shell out $25. *Wall Street Journal*. Retrieved from: https://www.wsj.com/articles/airline-fees-paper-boarding-pass-spirit-4d23b6d1?mod=hp_featst_pos5.

References for *Airline Boarding—Enthusiasts*

Dukovski, K. (2021, January 11). How to get priority boarding with American Airlines. Finder.com. Retrieved from: https://www.finder.com/american-airlines-priority-boarding.

Measom, C. (2021). 6 airline fees that are worth paying. Gobankingrates.com. Retrieved from: https://www.gobankingrates.com/saving-money/airlines/airline-fees-that-are-worth-paying.

Rawson, C., & Hostetler, J. (2023, May 8). The best credit cards with priority boarding of 2023. Businessinsider.com. Retrieved from: https://www.businessinsider.com/personal-finance/credit-cards-priority-boarding-airline-flight.

References for *Airline Boarding—Skeptics*

Kline, D. (2023a, May 13). Delta follows American, JetBlue Airlines in making unpopular move. Thestreet.com. Retrieved from: https://www.thestreet.com/travel/delta-follows-american-jetblue-airlines-in-cutting-flights.

Kline, D. (2023b, June 29). Southwest Airlines passengers angry over key boarding policy. Thestreet.com. Retrieved from: https://www.thestreet.com/travel/southwest-airlines-passengers-angry-over-key-boarding-policy.

Passy, J. (2023a, January 15). Travelers with food allergies fight for early boarding. *Wall Street Journal.* Retrieved from: https://www.wsj.com/articles/allergies-travel-early-boarding-peanuts-tree-nuts-11673627555.

Passy, J. (2023b, June 8). Frequent fliers wonder: Is elite status worth it anymore? *Wall Street Journal.* Retrieved from: https://www.wsj.com/articles/frequent-flier-loyalty-programs-free-flights-upgrades-7c94c48d.

References for *Parenting—Introduction*

Abrams P. (2009). *Cross purposes: Pierce v. Society of Sisters and the struggle over compulsory public education.* Ann Arbor, MI: University of Michigan Press.

American School Counselor Association. (2022). *Ethical standards for school counselors.* Alexandria, VA: Author.

Giordano, G. (2003). *Twentieth-century textbook wars: A history of advocacy and opposition.* New York: P. Lang.

Giordano, G. (2005). *How testing came to dominate American schools: The history of educational assessment.* New York: Peter Lang.

Giordano, G. (2009). *Solving education's problems effectively: A guide to using the case method.* Lanham, MD: Rowman & Littlefield Education.

Giordano, G. (2010). *Lopsided schools: Case method briefings.* Lanham, MD: Rowman & Littlefield Education.

Giordano, G. (2011). *Capping cost: Putting a price tag on school reform.* Lanham, MD: Roman & Littlefield Education.

Giordano, G. (2016). *Common sense questions about tests: The answers can reveal essential steps for improvement.* Lanham, MD: Rowman & Littlefield Education.

Giordano, G. (2019). *Parents and textbooks: Answers that reveal essential steps for improvement.* Lanham, MD: Rowman & Littlefield Education.

Giordano, G. (2022). *Parents and school violence: Essential steps to improve schools.* Lanham, MD. Roman & Littlefield Education.

Longnecker, E. (2023, May 9). Brownsburg school board votes to fire employees accused of mistreating a student with special needs. Wthr.com. Retrieved from: https://www.wthr.com/article/news/local/brownsburg-school-board-votes-to-fire-employees-accused-of-mistreating-a-student-with-special-needs-brown-elementary-staff/531-b4a1e190-c849-48fa-869e-323bc192a4e1.

Mahoney, D. (1984), Justifying school searches—The problems with the doctrine of "in loco parentis." *Journal of Juvenile Law,* 8(1), 140–148. Retrieved from: https://www.ojp.gov/ncjrs/virtual-library/abstracts/justifying-school-searches-problems-doctrine-loco-parentis.

Russo C. J., & Osborne A. G. (2012). *School law.* Thousand Oaks, CA: SAGE.

Russo C. J., Osborne A. G., Massucci J. D., & Cattaro G. M. (2009). *The law of special education and non-public schools: Major challenges in meeting the needs of youth with disabilities.* Lanham, MD: Rowman & Littlefield Education.

References for *Parenting—Enthusiasts*

Baker, K. J. (2023, January 22). When students change gender identity, and parents don't know. *New York Times.* Retrieved from: https://www.nytimes.com/2023/01/22/us/gender-identity-students-parents.html.

Berman S. B. (2022). *LGBTQ history in high school classes in the United States since 1990.* London: Bloomsbury Academic.

Brangham, W., & Hastings, D. (2022, September 20). Critics say new school policies in Florida ostracize LGBTQ students. Pbs.org. Retrieved from: https://www.pbs.org/newshour/show/critics-say-new-school-policies-in-florida-ostracize-lgbtq-students.

Lavietes, M. (2022, June 30). As Florida's "Don't Say Gay" law takes effect, schools roll out LGBTQ restrictions. Nbcnews.com. Retrieved from: https://www.nbcnews.com/nbc-out/out-news/floridas-dont-say-gay-law-takes-effect-schools-roll-lgbtq-restrictions-rcna36143.

Roth J. C., & Erbacher T. A. (2022). *Developing comprehensive school safety and mental health programs: An integrated approach.* New York. Routledge.

References for *Parenting—Skeptics*

Bloch, E. (2022, May 4). Duval School Board tables Joyce's Parental Rights resolution after hundreds show up at meeting. *Florida Times-Union.* Retrieved from: https://www.nbcnews.com/nbc-out/out-news/floridas-dont-say-gay-law-takes-effect-schools-roll-lgbtq-restrictions-rcna36143.

Carabina R. V. (2023). *The hijacking of American education: How cancel culture and critical race theory destroyed our educational system.* Pennsauken Township, NJ: BookBaby.

REFERENCES FOR CHAPTER 4

References for *Chapter 4 Epigraphs*

Green, J. (2023, March 19). Notable & quotable: Chicago's mayoral race. *Wall Street Journal.* Retrieved from: https://www.wsj.com/articles/notable-quotable-chicagos-mayoral-race-brandon-johnson-green-vallas-teachers-unions-710492a4?mod=hp_opin_pos_4#cxrecs_s.

Wall Street Journal Editorial Board. (2022a, October 4). Illinois's shocking report card. *Wall Street Journal* Retrieved from: https://www.wsj.com/articles/illinois-shocking-report-card-reading-math-grade-level-decatur-teachers-school-board-11664722519?mod=trending_now_opn_1.

Wall Street Journal Editorial Board. (2023a, January 13). Chicago's newest union workers. *Wall Street Journal* Retrieved from: https://www.wsj.com/articles/chicagos-newest-union-workers-principals-illinois-amendment-1-j-b-pritzker-schools-education-11673534256?mod=hp_opin_pos_4#cxrecs_s

Wall Street Journal Editorial Board. (2023b, March 1). Who will save Chicago? *Wall Street Journal.* Retrieved from: https://www.wsj.com/articles/chicago

-mayor-election-lori-lightfoot-paul-vallas-brandon-johnson-crime-teachers-unions-schools-6956202c?mod=hp_opin_pos_1.

Wall Street Journal Editorial Board. (2023c, March 19). The Chicago Teachers Union power play. *Wall Street Journal*. Retrieved from: https://www.wsj.com/articles/the-chicago-teachers-union-power-play-brandon-johnson-dues-money-election-campaign-ctu-chicago-donor-52a37d2b?mod=hp_opin_pos_5#cxrecs_s.

Wall Street Journal Editorial Board. (2023d, April 2). Chicago teachers fight a union political ploy. *Wall Street Journal*. Retrieved from: https://www.wsj.com/articles/chicago-teachers-fight-a-union-ripoff-candidate-race-brandon-johnson-political-fund-dues-ctu-mayoral-election-7201a542?mod=hp_opin_pos_2#cxrecs_s.

References for *DC's Commuters—Introduction*

Llorico, A., & Goncalves, D. (2022, December 6). DC approves making buses free, but what happens next? Wusa9.com. Retrieved from: https://www.wusa9.com/article/traffic/mission-metro/what-does-metro-for-dc-amendment-act-of-2022-do-free-buses-dc-fact-check-2022/65-3b6ed5d7-2faf-4a9c-9df2-63986e2938d6

Metro installs new gates to crack down on fare evasion, starting with Fort Totten station. [Video]. (2023, July 25). Nbcwashington.com. Retrieved from: https://www.nbcwashington.com/news/local/metro-installs-new-gates-to-crack-down-on-fare-evasion-starting-with-fort-totten-station/3390746/.

Wall Street Journal Editorial Board. (2022b, October 9). In D.C., the bus fare is merely a polite suggestion. *Wall Street Journal*. Retrieved from: https://www.wsj.com/articles/the-d-c-bus-fare-is-a-polite-suggestion-evasion-budget-shortfall-enforcement-action-virginia-maryland-11665341012.

Washington Metropolitan Area Transit Authority. (2022, December 7). Metro improves service on popular routes in DC, effective Sunday, Dec. 11. Wmata.com. Retrieved from: https://www.wmata.com/about/news/Metrobus-service-changes-Dec-11-2022.cfm.

Washington Metropolitan Area Transit Authority. (2022). Remember to pay your fare before riding—If you don't pay your fare, Metro Transit Police could fine you. Author. Retrieved from: https://www.wmata.com/fares/paythefare.cfm.

Wells, C. (2023, July 25). Metro rolls out new, higher fare gates in attempt to curb gate jumpers. Onedrive.live.com. Retrieved from: https://onedrive.live.com/edit.aspx?resid=FEAD42B7A85048FC!2349&ithint=file%2cdocx&ct=1690302094817&wdOrigin=OFFICECOM-WEB.MAIN.EDGEWORTH&wdPreviousSessionSrc=HarmonyWeb&wdPreviousSession=e2110f04-138d-435d-9603-706aee363a54&wdo=2.

References for *DC's Commuters—Enthusiasts*

Andrews, H. (2023, February 8). Fare evasion is still bad. Theamericanconservative.com. Retrieved from: https://www.theamericanconservative.com/fare-evasion-is-still-bad/.

Brune, M. (2023, May 24). Breakfast links: WMATA holding in-person feedback sessions on 8000-series trains. Ggwash.org. https://ggwash.org/view/89732/breakfast-links-wmata-holding-in-person-feedback-sessions-on-8000-series-trains.

Schulz, D. M. (2022, May 3). The gentrification of fare evasion. *City Journal.* Retrieved from: https://www.city-journal.org/article/the-gentrification-of-fare-evasion.

References for *DC's Commuters—Skeptics*

Alpert, D. (2020, February 24). WMATA can't measure fare evasion, but still says it's a big problem. Retrieved from: https://ggwash.org/view/76263/wmata-metro-fare-evasion-measurement-rail-bus-kids-ride-free.

Demsas, J. (2022, December 9). Buses shouldn't be free. *Atlantic.* Retrieved from: https://www.theatlantic.com/ideas/archive/2022/12/washington-dc-free-bus-transit/672407.

Goncalves, D. (2022, October 5). Legal, civil rights advocates keeping a close eye on how Metro's fare evasion campaign is enforced. Wusa9.com. Retrieved from: https://www.wusa9.com/article/traffic/mission-metro/metro-to-issue-fines-fare-evasion/65-07f0a0ae-7f5b-40ae-9077-ccb97bc9d0b1.

Hamburg, D. (2023, June 29). Police use pepper spray on fare evaders. Dcnewsnow.com. Retrieved from: https://www.dcnewsnow.com/news/local-news/virginia/arlington-county/police-use-pepper-spray-on-fare-evaders-4-arrested-at-pentagon-city-metro-station.

Oberg, T., Leslie, K., Olazagasti, C., & Piper, J. (2023, January 3). Two tickets in DC—Metro says "pleasant surprise" as fare evasion crackdown starts slow. Nbcwashington.com. Retrieved from: https://www.nbcwashington.com/investigations/two-tickets-in-dc-metro-says-pleasant-surprise-as-fare-evasion-crackdown-starts-slow/3245942.

Smith, J. (2023, April 19). Fare evasion crackdowns make for a stressful commute for some Howard students. Truthbetold.news. Retrieved from: https://truthbetold.news/2023/04/fare-evasion-crackdowns-make-for-a-stressful-commute-for-some-howard-students.

Surico, J., & Byington, L. (2023, April 19). The real costs of curbing fare evasion. Bloomberg.com. Retrieved from: https://www.bloomberg.com/news/features/2023-04-19/budget-strapped-subways-get-tougher-on-turnstile-jumpers.

Wall Street Journal Editorial Board. (2023e, May 21). Escape from New York, Etc. *Wall Street Journal.* Retrieved from: https://www.wsj.com/articles/progressive-cities-population-decline-census-bureau-chicago-new-york-san-francisco-e803562c?mod=hp_opin_pos_6#cxrecs_s.

Wilcox, C. (2018). *Onward Christian soldiers: The religious right in American politics.* Philadelphia: Routledge.

Zilckuhr, K. (2020, February 20). What is the impact of fare evasion in D.C.? Dcpolicycenter.org. Retrieved from: https://www.dcpolicycenter.org/publications/fare-evasion-data.

References for *Chicago's Unionized Teachers—Introduction*

Andriesen, P. (2022, January 14). Chicago teachers unions illegal strike is over but parents sue to stop next one. Illinoispolicy.org. Retrieved from: https://www.illinoispolicy.org/chicago-teachers-unions-illegal-strike-is-over-but-parents-sue-to-stop-next-one.

Chapoulie, J. M., Kornblum W., & Wazer, C. (2020). *Chicago sociology.* New York: Columbia University Press.

Charters for Change. (2023). Elevate Chicago's schools: Enrollment facts. Author. Retrieved from: https://chartersforchange.org/enrollment-facts.

Chen, G. (2023, February 14). Chicago schools: What happens after the teachers strike? Publicschoolreview.com. Retrieved from: https://www.publicschoolreview.com/blog/chicago-schools-what-happens-after-the-teachers-strike.

Kehrer, D. (2022, May 10). A quick guide to owned, earned and paid media. Score.org. Retrieved from: https://www.score.org/resource/article/a-quick-guide-owned-earned-and-paid-media?gclid=CjwKCAjw9pGjBhB-EiwAa5jl3CtsinFwFJ7O0PDk9s5-SRd6JgusdMS4MEIgwlVgXYeTx08pdgZouRoCe_UQAvD_BwE.

Levy, C. (2023, February 10). Is it too late to save Chicago from progressive misrule? *Wall Street Journal.* Retrieved from: https://www.wsj.com/articles/is-it-too-late-to-save-chicago-from-progressive-misrule-crime-police-mayoral-race-bussiness-flight-candidates-lori-lightfoot-d0defb65.

Public officials vow to make improvements at CPS a decade after mass school closures. (2023, May 27). Abc7chicago.co. Retrieved from: https://abc7chicago.com/chicago-public-schools-cps-school-closures-rahm-emanuel-better-government-association/13303704.

Smith, M., & Davey, M. (2019, October 31). Chicago teachers' strike, longest in decades, ends. *New York Times.* Retrieved from: https://www.nytimes.com/2019/10/31/us/chicago-cps-teachers-strike.html.

Stefanski, R. (2021, July 21). 9 Examples of earned media. Burrelles.com. Retrieved from: https://burrelles.com/9-examples-of-earned-media.

Todd-Breland, E. (2018). *A political education: Black politics and education reform in Chicago since the 1960s.* Chapel Hill, NC: University of North Carolina Press.

References for *Chicago's Unionized Teachers—Enthusiasts*

Kapos, S., & Olander, O. (2023, May 5). Pogressive Brandon Johnson wins Chicago mayor's race. *Politico.* Retrieved from: https://www.politico.com/news/2023/04/04/chicago-mayors-race-results-00090504.

Masterson, M. (2023, May 24). CTU leader touts "historic reset" labor relations between union and chicago public schools. Wttw.com. Retrieved from: https://news.wttw.com/2023/05/24/ctu-leader-touts-historic-reset-labor-relations-between-union-and-chicago-public-schools.

Teachers union-backed candidate Brandon Johnson was elected mayor of Chicago. (2023, May 16). *Politico.* Retrieved from: https://www.politico.com/2023-election/results/chicago-mayor.

References for *Chicago's Unionized Teachers—Skeptics*

Cardona-Maguigad, A. (2020, March 6). One year after a wave of Chicago charter strikes, schools are forced to cut back. Npr.org. Retrieved from: https://www.npr.org/local/309/2020/03/06/812836710/one-year-after-a-wave-of-chicago-charter-strikes-schools-are-forced-to-cut-back#:~:text=New%20charter%20contract%20costs,126%20charter%20schools%20in%20Chicago.

Freeman, J. (2023, May 17). Worst job description in Chicago. *Wall Street Journal.* Retrieved from: https://www.wsj.com/articles/worst-job-description-in-chicago-f3cc1221?mod=hp_opin_pos_2#cxrecs_s.

Wall Street Journal Editorial Board. (2023f, May 23). Will Illinois still "invest in kids"? *Wall Street Journal.* Retrieved from: https://www.wsj.com/articles/illinois-invest-in-kids-scholarship-progam-general-assembly-school-choice-teachers-union-1659dc2?mod=hp_opin_pos_5#cxrecs_s.

Wall Street Journal Editorial Board. (2023g, May 24). A Chicago self-destruction plan. *Wall Street Journal.* Retrieved from: https://www.wsj.com/articles/chicago-budget-plan-brandon-johnson-saqib-bhatti-acre-peoples-unity-platform-95c775c7?mod=hp_opin_pos_6#cxrecs_s.

REFERENCES FOR CHAPTER 5

References for *Chapter 5 Epigraphs*

Associated Press. (2022, October 24). Test scores dropped to lowest levels in decades during pandemic, according to nationwide exam. Nbcnews.com. Retrieved from: https://www.nbcnews.com/news/us-news/test-scores-dropped-lowest-levels-decades-pandemic-according-nationwid-rcna53659.

Braga, D., & Parker, K. (2022, October 26). Most K-12 parents say first year of pandemic had a negative effect on their children's education. Pewresearch.org. Retrieved from: https://www.pewresearch.org/short-reads/2022/10/26/most-k-12-parents-say-first-year-of-pandemic-had-a-negative-effect-on-their-childrens-education.

Carr, P.—*quoted by Wall Street Journal* Editorial Board. (2022a, September 1). Randi Weingarten flunks the Pandemic. *Wall Street Journal.* Retrieved from: https://www.wsj.com/articles/randi-weingarten-flunks-the-pandemic-naep-test-scores-decline-schools-covid-american-federation-of-teachers-11662069418.

Carvalho, A.—*quoted in* Test scores dropped to lowest levels in decades during pandemic, according to nationwide exam. (2022, October 24). Nbcnews.com. Retrieved from: https://www.nbcnews.com/news/us-news/test-scores-dropped-lowest-levels-decades-pandemic-according-nationwid-rcna53659.

New York Post Editorial Board. (2023, June 21). Latest grim NAEP news should raise red flags. *New York Post.* Retrieved from: https://nypost.com/2023/06/21/latest-grim-naep-news-should-raise-red-flags.

Wall Street Journal Editorial Board. (2022a, September 1). Randi Weingarten flunks the Pandemic. *Wall Street Journal.* Retrieved from: https://www.wsj.com/articles/randi-weingarten-flunks-the-pandemic-naep-test-scores-decline-schools-covid-american-federation-of-teachers-11662069418.

References for *Testing College Students—Introduction*

Boyington, A. (2023, March 31). How to prepare for the LSAT: Resources and common questions. Forbes.com. Retrieved from: https://www.forbes.com/advisor/education/how-to-prepare-for-the-lsat.

Campbell, C. M. (2023, March 30). Should you use college rankings to pick a good school—Here's a critical factor they miss. *USA Today*. Retrieved from: https://www.usatoday.com/story/opinion/2023/03/30/what-college-rankings-get-wrong-universities/11550436002.

College rankings rebellion. (2023, May 14). Theweek.com. Retrieved from: https://theweek.com/education/1023446/the-college-rankings-rebellion.

Create your U.S. News account. (2023). Usnews.com. Retrieved from: https://secure.usnews.com/commerce/checkout/college-compass-with-digital?int=compass-signup-button.

Gertler, E. J. (2023, February 28). Why elite law and medical schools can't stand *U.S. News*. *Wall Street Journal*. Retrieved from: https://www.wsj.com/articles/why-elite-schools-cant-stand-us-news-law-medical-affirmative-action-ranking-diversity-transparency-supreme-court-29170776.

Hiebert, P. (2016, April). *Consumer Reports* in the age of the amazon review. *Atlantic*. Retrieved from: https://www.theatlantic.com/business/archive/2016/04/consumer-reports-in-the-age-of-the-amazon-review/477108.

Hufford, A. (2022, November 26). Employers rethink need for college degrees in tight labor market. *Wall Street Journal*. Retrieved from: https://www.wsj.com/articles/employers-rethink-need-for-college-degrees-in-tight-labor-market-11669432133.

Korn, M. (2022a, November 16). Yale and Harvard law schools abandon *U.S. News* rankings. *Wall Street Journal*. Retrieved from: https://www.wsj.com/articles/yale-law-school-abandons-u-s-news-rankings-citing-flawed-methodology-11668607649.

Korn, M. (2022b, December 20). University of Southern California sued over education-school rankings claims. *Wall Street Journal*. Retrieved from: https://www.wsj.com/articles/university-of-southern-california-sued-over-education-school-rankings-claims-11671561070?mod=hp_listb_pos5.

Korn, M. (2023a, March 21). The unraveling of the *U.S. News* college rankings. *Wall Street Journal*. Retrieved from: https://www.wsj.com/articles/u-s-news-college-rankings-yale-law-fe24f0b2.

LSAT test: Online prep & review. (2023). Study.com. Retrieved from: https://study.com/academy/course/lsat-test.html.

Morse, R., & Brooks, E. (2022, September 11). How U.S. News calculated the 2022–2023 best colleges rankings. Usnews.com. Retrieved from: https://www.usnews.com/education/best-colleges/articles/how-us-news-calculated-the-rankings.

Mueller, J. (2023, June 7). Columbia University no longer submitting data to *US News* college ranking. Thehill.com. Retrieved from: https://thehill.com/homenews/education/4038410-columbia-university-no-longer-submitting-data-to-us-news-ranking.

Sage, A. (2023). What are college rankings: An expert's guide. Collegeadvisor.com. Retrieved from: https://www.collegeadvisor.com/resources/college-rankings-experts-guide.

Stoll, I. (2023, January 29). Medical schools bail on academic merit and intellectual rigor. *Wall Street Journal.* Retrieved from: https://www.wsj.com/articles/medical-schools-bail-on-academic-merit-and-intellectual-rigor-us-news-rankings-diversity-equity-inclusion-race-students-11675005330.

References for *Testing College Students—Enthusiasts*

Ebadolahi, M. (2023). Law schools that don't require the LSAT. Testmaxprep.com. Retrieved from: https://testmaxprep.com/blog/lsat/law-schools-that-dont-require-lsat?v=3#/.

Fortin, J. (2023, February 17). Do law schools need the LSAT—Here's how to understand the debate. *New York Times.* Retrieved from: https://www.nytimes.com/2023/02/17/us/law-schools-lsat-requirement.html.

Mulvaney, E. (2022, November 18). Law school accrediting panel votes to make LSAT optional. *Wall Street Journal.* Retrieved from: https://www.wsj.com/articles/law-school-accrediting-panel-to-consider-making-lsat-optional-11668778730.

Sloan, K. (2022, November 18). ABA votes to end law schools' LSAT requirement, but not until 2025. Reuters.com. Retrieved from: https://www.reuters.com/legal/legalindustry/aba-votes-end-law-schools-lsat-requirement-not-until-2025-2022-11-18/.

References for *Testing College Students—Skeptics*

Bauer-Wolf, J. (2022, August 26). Mixed reactions as ABA considers tossing LSAT mandate. Highereddive.com. Retrieved from: https://www.highereddive.com/news/mixed-reactions-as-aba-considers-tossing-lsat-mandate/630460.

Korn, M. (2023b, April 11). Yale law still no. 1 on *U.S. News & World Report*'s rankings despite leading revolt. *Wall Street Journal.* Retrieved from: https://www.wsj.com/articles/yale-law-still-no-1-on-u-s-news-world-reports-rankings-despite-leading-revolt-426f2194.

Patrice, J. (2022, August 12). Company profiting off LSAT deeply concerned about prospect of not forcing everyone to take the LSAT. Abovethelaw.com. Retrieved from: https://abovethelaw.com/2022/08/company-profiting-off-lsat-deeply-concerned-about-prospect-of-not-forcing-everyone-to-take-the-lsat.

Ruiz, N. G., Tian, Z., & Krogstad, J. M. (2023, June 8). Asian Americans hold mixed views around affirmative action. Pewresearch.org. Retrieved from: https://www.pewresearch.org/race-ethnicity/2023/06/08/asian-americans-hold-mixed-views-around-affirmative-action.

Wall Street Journal Editorial Board. (2022b, November 24). Law schools without LSATs. *Wall Street Journal.* Retrieved from: https://www.wsj.com/articles/lawyers-without-lsats-american-bar-association-11669157733.

Wall Street Journal Editorial Board. (2023, June 9). The deception of "affirmative action". *Wall Street Journal.* Retrieved from: https://www.wsj.com/

articles/affirmative-action-pew-research-survey-asian-americans-supreme-court-5a202926.

Zumbrun, J. (2023, January 27). Rebellion over college rankings seems likely to fail. *Wall Street Journal*. Retrieved from: https://www.wsj.com/articles/rebellion-over-college-rankings-seems-likely-to-fail-11674794247.

References for *Testing Public School Students—Introduction*

Camera, L. (2022, October 24). Pandemic prompts historic decline in student achievement on nations report card. Usnews.com. Retrieved from: https://www.usnews.com/news/education-news/articles/2022-10-24/pandemic-prompts-historic-decline-in-student-achievement-on-nations-report-card.

Giordano, G. (2005). *How testing came to dominate American schools: The history of educational assessment*. New York: P. Lang.

Giordano, G. (2010). *Cockeyed education: A case method primer*. Lanham, MD: Rowman & Littlefield Education.

Giordano, G. (2016). *Common sense questions about tests: The answers can reveal essential steps for improvement*. Lanham, MD: Rowman & Littlefield Education.

Karp, S., Issa, N., & Spielman, F. (2023, July 5). Mayor Brandon Johnson replaces most of Chicago Board of Education. *Chicago Sun Times*. Retrieved from: https://chicago.suntimes.com/education/2023/7/5/23784856/chicago-school-board-replaced-brandon-johnson.

Philadelphia Inquirer Editorial Board. (2023, July 4). Reversing pandemic-related learning loss must be a top priority. *Philadelphia Inquirer*. Retrieved from: https://www.inquirer.com/opinion/editorials/low-test-scores-report-card-education-crisis-pandemic-math-reading-20230704.html?outputType=amp.

Randazzo, S. (2023a, February 17). To increase equity, school districts eliminate honors classes. *Wall Street Journal*. Retrieved from: https://www.wsj.com/articles/to-increase-equity-school-districts-eliminate-honors-classes-d5985dee.

Randazzo, S. (2023b, March 11). Parents challenge lottery systems used to diversify elite high schools. *Wall Street Journal*. Retrieved from: https://www.wsj.com/articles/parents-challenge-lottery-systems-used-to-diversify-elite-high-schools-f46824c7?mod=hp_listb_pos3.

Randazzo, S. (2023c, April 26). Schools are ditching homework, deadlines in favor of "equitable grading". *Wall Street Journal*. Retrieved from: https://www.wsj.com/articles/schools-are-ditching-homework-deadlines-in-favor-of-equitable-grading-dcef7c3e.

School responses in Florida to the coronavirus (COVID-19) pandemic. (2023). Ballotpedia.org. Retrieved from: https://ballotpedia.org/School_responses_in_Florida_to_the_coronavirus_(COVID-19)_pandemic.

Sgueglia, K., & Dolan, L. (2023, June 21). Test scores for 13-year-olds drop several points since the start of pandemic, building on decade-long decline, report says. Cnn.com. Retrieved from: https://www.cnn.com/2023/06/21/us/test-scores-decline-nations-report-card/index.html.

St. George, D. (2023, June 21). National test scores plunge with no signs of pandemic recovery. *Washington Post*. Retrieved from: naephttps://www.washingtonpost.com/education/2023/06/21/national-student-test-scores-drop-naep.

References for *Testing Public School Students—Enthusiasts*

Bouchrika, I. (2023, April 24) Standards-based grading: Definition, benefits & comparison with traditional grading. Research.com. Retrieved from: https://research.com/education/standards-based-grading.

California Department of Education. (2020, November 6). State Board of Education approves shorter standardized tests to give schools flexibility amidst COVID-19 uncertainties. Author. Retrieved from: https://www.cde.ca.gov/nr/ne/yr20/yr20rel90.asp.

Delandro, T. (2023, April 27). Equitable grading: What is it and how is it helping students. Newsnationnow.com. Retrieved from: https://www.newsnationnow.com/us-news/education/equitable-grading-what-is-it-and-how-is-it-helping-students.

DeSantis signs overhaul of student testing. (2022, March 15). Winknews.com. Retrieved from: https://winknews.com/2022/03/15/gov-ron-desantis-will-hold-a-news-conference-in-st-petersburg.

Person, Y. (2023, March 17). NYSED, Board of Regents examining potential changes in Regents Exams. Wkbw.com. Retrieved from: https://www.wkbw.com/news/local-news/nysed-board-of-regents-examining-potential-changes-in-regents-exams.

References for *Testing Public School Students—Skeptics*

Barakat, M. (2023, January 5). Virginia attorney general investigating elite school. *Florida Times-Union*. Retrieved from: https://jacksonville-fl-app.newsmemory.com/?publink=1d9fb7ae3_134a9fd.

Barnum, M. (2019, October 28). No thanks, Obama: 9 states no longer require test scores be used to judge teachers. Chalkbeat.org. Retrieved from: https://www.chalkbeat.org/2019/10/8/21108964/no-thanks-obama-9-states-no-longer-require-test-scores-be-used-to-judge-teachers.

Dailey. R. (2022, March 17). DeSantis signs testing overhaul. *Florida Times-Union*. Retrieved from: https://jacksonville-fl-app.newsmemory.com/?publink=38e1ef388_13483c1.

Greene, P. (2021, November 30). This decade-long experiment in teacher evaluation is a failure. Forbes.com. Retrieved from: https://www.forbes.com/sites/petergreene/2021/11/30/this-decade-long-experiment-in-teacher-evaluation-is-a-failure/?sh=4063f3951737.

Li, M. (2022, April 4). I wanted to know what my high school peers thought about the SHSAT, so I asked them. Chalkbeat.org. Retrieved from: https://ny.chalkbeat.org/2022/4/4/23003866/shsat-asian-students-specialized-high-school-admissions.

NYC Parent slams "mindful breathing program" amid poor test scores: "Its [sic] hard to take it seriously". Komonews.com. Retrieved from: https://komonews

.com/news/nation-world/nyc-parent-slams-mindful-breathing-program-amid-poor-test-scores-its-hard-to-take-it-seriously-mayor-eric-adams-place-maud-maron-national-assessment-of-educational-progress-math-reading-proficiency.

Riley, J. L. (2022, March 1). Asian-Americans fight back against school discrimination. *Wall Street Journal.* Retrieved from: https://www.wsj.com/articles/asian-american-fight-school-discrimination-affirmative-action-racial-justice-admissions-standards-testing-charter-schools-achievement-gap-harvard-supreme-court-11646172518.

Riley, J. L. (2023, February 7). Black students need better schools, not lower standards. *Street Journal.* Retrieved from: https://www.wsj.com/articles/black-students-need-better-schools-not-lower-standards-college-board-african-american-studies-ap-course-11675807002.

Struggling with schoolwork. (2023, March 20). *Florida Times-Union.* Retrieved from: https://jacksonville-fl.newsmemory.com/?publink=01f3b7883_134aad4.

Wexler, N. (2022, September 9). Covid hasn't disrupted educational progress—Test scores were already falling. *Forbes.* Retrieved from: https://www.forbes.com/sites/nataliewexler/2022/09/05/covid-hasnt-disrupted-educational-progress-test-scores-were-already-falling/?sh=3e4f2cf751e6.

REFERENCES FOR CHAPTER 6

References for *Chapter 6 Epigraphs*

Batch, K. (2023). *Fencing out knowledge.* American Library Association. Retrieved from: https://www.ala.org/aboutala/sites/ala.org.aboutala/files/content/oitp/publications/issuebriefs/cipa_report.pdf.

Batt, S. (2022, December 28). How to bypass a school firewall: Tips and warnings. Makeuseof.com. Retrieved from: https://www.makeuseof.com/tag/how-to-bypass-school-firewall.

Bloski. (2023). Keywords your school's content filter should block and why. Author. Retrieved from: https://www.blocksi.net/blocksi-news/keywords-your-schools-content-filter-should-block-and-why.

CurrentWare. (2023). Computer monitoring and web filtering software for schools. Author. Retrieved from: https://www.currentware.com/industries/web-filtering-in-schools.

Federal Communications Commission. (2019). What CIPA requires. Author. Retrieved from: https://www.fcc.gov/consumers/guides/childrens-internet-protection-act.

Federal Communications Commission. (2023). Children's Internet Protection Act (CIPA). Author. Retrieved from: https://www.fcc.gov/consumers/guides/childrens-internet-protection-act.

National Coalition Against Censorship. (2023). Internet filters. Author. Retrieved from: https://ncac.org/resource/internet-filters-2.

Paul, A. M. (2014, July 2). Why schools' efforts to block the Internet are so laughably lame. *Hechinger Report*. Retrieved from: https://hechingerreport.org/schools-efforts-block-internet-laughably-lame.

Universal Service Administrative Company. (2023). Author. Retrieved from: https://www.usac.org/e-rate/applicant-process/starting-services/cipa.

References for *Filtering Films—Introduction*

Fox, A. (2022, July 3). 15 Best Films of the 1930s. Slashfilm.com. Retrieved from: https://www.slashfilm.com/915730/best-films-of-the-1930s.

Gone with the Wind removed from HBO Max. (2020, June 10). Bbc.com. Retrieved from: https://www.bbc.com/news/entertainment-arts-52990714.

Kubincanek, E. (2023, July 13). A world without Turner Classic Movies. Filmschoolrejects.com. Retrieved from: https://filmschoolrejects.com/turner-classic-movies.

Smith, J. (2023, July 5). Spielberg, Scorsese, and PTA can't save TCM—There's only one way to keep it alive. Slashfilm.com. Retrieved from: https://www.slashfilm.com/1330029/spielberg-scorsese-pta-cant-save-tcm-one-way-keep-it-alive.

References for *Filtering Films—Enthusiasts*

Blanchet, B. (2023, March 2). Original "Gone with the Wind" script reveals behind-the-scenes "war" over depiction of slavery. *People*. Retrieved from: https://people.com/movies/original-gone-with-the-wind-shooting-script-depiction-of-slavery.

Donaldson, K. (2020, June 10). Why *Gone with the Wind* is (& always was) a problematic movie. Screenrant.com. Retrieved from: https://screenrant.com/gone-with-wind-movie-problematic-slavery-racism-reason.

Jolly, J. (2023, October 14). Kids are tuning into the violence of the Israel-Hamas war: What parents should do. *USA TODAY*. Retrieved from: https://www.usatoday.com/story/tech/columnist/2023/10/14/kids-violence-videos-gaza-israel/71146557007.

Masters, K. (2023, June 28). After filmmaker outcry over TCM cuts, Warner Bros. reverses course (sort of). *Hollywood Reporter*. Retrieved from: https://www.hollywoodreporter.com/business/business-news/zaslav-reverses-tcm-changes-1235525256.

Ridley, J. (2020, June 8). Op-Ed: Hey, HBO, "Gone with the Wind" romanticizes the horrors of slavery: Take it off your platform for now. *Los Angeles Times*. Retrieved from: https://www.latimes.com/opinion/story/2020-06-08/hbo-max-racism-gone-with-the-wind-movie.

References for *Filtering Films—Skeptics*

Biesen, S. C. (2018). *Film censorship: Regulating America's screen*. New York: Columbia University Press/Wallflower.

Biltereyst, D., & Vande Winkel, R. (eds.). (2013). *Silencing cinema: Film censorship around the world*. Camden, GB: Palgrave Macmillan.

Fronc J. (2017). *Monitoring the movies: The fight over film censorship in early twentieth-century urban America*. Austin, TX: University of Texas Press.
Sacco, D. (2023). *Film censorship in a cultural context*. Great Britian: Edinburgh University Press.
Spangler, T. (2020, June 10). "Gone With the Wind" hits No. 1 on Amazon bestsellers chart after HBO Max drops movie. *Variety*. Retrieved from: https://variety.com/2020/digital/uncategorized/gone-with-the-wind-amazon-best-seller-hbo-max-1234630577.
Wittern-Keller L. (2008). *Freedom of the screen: Legal challenges to state film censorship 1915—1981*. Lexington, KY: University Press of Kentucky.
Yogerst, C. (2022, September 2). 100 Years ago: How Hollywood's early self-censorship battles shaped the MPA. *Hollywood Reporter*. Retrieved from: https://www.hollywoodreporter.com/business/business-news/100-years-ago-how-hollywoods-early-self-censorship-battles-shaped-the-mpa-1235210771.

References for *Filtering Websites—Introduction*

Federal Communications Commission. (2023). Children's Internet Protection Act (CIPA). Author. Retrieved from: https://www.fcc.gov/consumers/guides/childrens-internet-protection-act.
Federal Communications Commission. (2023). E-Rate (Schools & Libraries). Author. Retrieved from: https://www.fcc.gov/tags/e-rate-schools-libraries.
Gajanan, M. (2020, June 25). *Gone With the Wind* should not be erased, argue film historians: But it should not be watched in a vacuum. *Time*. Retrieved from: https://time.com/5852362/gone-with-the-wind-film-history.
Giordano, G. (2021). *Parents and school technology: Answers that reveal essential steps for improvement*. Lanham, MD: Rowman & Littlefield Education.
Sawchuk, S. (2021, April 2). Teachers are watching students' screens during remote learning. *Education Week*. Retrieved from: https://www.edweek.org/technology/are-remote-classroom-management-tools-that-let-teachers-see-students-computer-screens-intrusive/2021/04.

References for *Filtering Websites—Enthusiasts*

Copperfasten Technologies. (2023). Advanced DNS web security and content filtering software for education. Author. Retrieved from: https://www.titanhq.com/education-master-lp.
Nikson, M. (2023). Deliver safer online experiences. Securly.com. Retrieved from: https://www.securly.com/filter.
Raymond, S. (2023). Web content filtering. Dnsfilter.com. Retrieved from: https://www.dnsfilter.com/features/content-filtering.
Rhode Island Department of Education. (2023). Internet filtering laws and guidance. Author. Retrieved from: https://ride.ri.gov/teachers-administrators/other-tools-information/internet-filtering.

References for *Filtering Websites—Skeptics*

American Library Association. (2023). Guidelines to minimize the negative effects of internet content filters on intellectual freedom. Author. Retrieved from: https://www.ala.org/advocacy/intfreedom/filtering/filtering_guidelines.

Anderson, M. D. (2016, April 26). How Internet filtering hurts kids. *Atlantic*. Retrieved from: https://www.theatlantic.com/education/archive/2016/04/internet-filtering-hurts-kids/479907/.

Fox, S. (2022, March 8). How to unblock Instagram at school: Gramming in 2023. Retrieved from: Cloudwards.net. https://www.cloudwards.net/unblock-instagram-at-school.

Means, S. P. (2018, July 26). Utah law says libraries and schools should have filters against internet porn—A new study says filtering doesn't work. *Salt Lake Tribune*. Retrieved from: https://www.sltrib.com/news/2018/07/26/utah-law-says-libraries.

Prothero, A. (2023, September 20). Monitoring or blocking what students do online poses all kinds of problems. *Education Week*. Retrieved from: https://www.edweek.org/technology/monitoring-or-blocking-what-students-do-online-poses-all-kinds-of-problems/2023/09.

Rees, K. (2023, February 27). How to bypass internet restrictions and blocks and view any website. Makeuseof.com. Retrieved from: https://www.makeuseof.com/tag/how-to-bypass-internet-censorship.

REFERENCES FOR CHAPTER 7

References for *Chapter 7 Epigraphs*

Culatta, R.—*quoted by* Klein, A. (2023, June 22). Schools are "focusing on the wrong things" when it comes to AI, tech leader argues. *Education Week*. Retrieved from: https://www.edweek.org/technology/schools-are-focusing-on-the-wrong-things-when-it-comes-to-ai-tech-leader-argues/2023/06.

Ferlazzo, L. (2023, May 2). How teachers are using artificial intelligence in classes today. *Education Week*. Retrieved from: https://www.edweek.org/technology/opinion-how-teachers-are-using-artificial-intelligence-in-classes-today/2023/05.

Froehlich, M. (2022, April 27). Building social-emotional learning with Prodigy. *Education Week*. Retrieved from: https://www.edweek.org/sponsor/prodigy/building-social-emotional-learning-with-prodigy.

Gates, B., & Huddleston, T. (2023, April 22). Bill Gates says A.I. chatbots will teach kids to read within 18 months: You'll be "stunned by how it helps". Cnbc.com. Retrieved from: https://www.cnbc.com/2023/04/22/bill-gates-ai-chatbots-will-teach-kids-how-to-read-within-18-months.html.

Homework Helper [Webpage]. (2023, May 15). Find answers to homework questions. Homeworkhelper-app.net. Retrieved from: https://www.homeworkhelper-app.net.

Khan, I. (2023, August 28). AI glossary: Basic terms all ChatGPT users should know. Cnet.com. Retrieved from: https://www.cnet.com/tech/computing/ai-glossary-basic-terms-all-chatgpt-users-should-know.

Shonubi, O. (2023, February 21). AI in the classroom: Pros, cons and the role of EdTech Companies. *Forbes*. Retrieved from: https://www.forbes.com/sites/theyec/2023/02/21/ai-in-the-classroom-pros-cons-and-the-role-of-edtech-companies/?sh=22515863feb4.

References for *AI in College—Introduction*

Aten, J. (2023, August 26). With 1 sentence, Google's CEO just explained the biggest downside of A.I., and it's a warning for all of us. Inc.com. Retrieved from: https://www.inc.com/jason-aten/with-1-sentence-googles-ceo-just-explained-biggest-downside-of-ai-its-a-warning-for-all-of-us.html.

Coldewey, D. (2023, August 4). Age of AI: Everything you need to know about artificial intelligence. Techcrunch.com. Retrieved from: https://techcrunch.com/2023/08/04/age-of-ai-everything-you-need-to-know-about-artificial-intelligence.

Crow, K. (2023, February 28). Is this a real Raphael painting—AI says yes—but humans aren't so sure. *Wall Street Journal*. Retrieved from: https://www.wsj.com/story/is-this-a-real-raphael-painting-ai-says-yes-but-humans-arent-so-sure-ede9ed54.

Grad, P. (2023, August 30). Nineteen researchers say AI is not sentient—not yet. Techxplore.com. Retrieved from: https://techxplore.com/news/2023-08-nineteen-ai-sentientnot.html.

Jenkins, H. W. (2023, August 1). AI is Hollywood's fake villain. *Wall Street Journal*. Retrieved from: https://www.wsj.com/articles/ai-is-hollywoods-fake-villain-unions-strike-actors-writers-ai-jobs-studios-9cdb3ab4.

Mims, C. (2022, November 12). Can you tell whether this headline was written by a robot? *Wall Street Journal*. Retrieved from: https://www.wsj.com/articles/can-you-tell-whether-this-headline-was-written-by-a-robot-11668204880.

O'Brien, M. (2022, July 18). As AI language skills grow, so do scientists' concerns. Retrieved from: https://jacksonville-fl-app.newsmemory.com/?publink=2bffe4247_1348552.

Quach, K. (2022, December 27). University students recruit AI to write essays for them. Now what? Theregister.com. Retrieved from: https://www.theregister.com/2022/12/27/university_ai_essays_students.

Reddy, S. (2023, February 28). How doctors use AI to help diagnose patients. *Wall Street Journal*. Retrieved from: https://www.wsj.com/articles/how-doctors-use-ai-to-help-diagnose-patients-ce4ad025.

Roberts, M. (2023, August 7). What does GPT stand for in Chat GPT? Mlyearning.org. Retrieved from: https://www.mlyearning.org/what-does-gpt-stand-for-in-chat-gpt/#:~:text=Share%20this%3A-,What%20Is%20GPT%3F,released%20by%20OpenAI%20in%202018.

Samuel, S. (2023, April 10). What happens when ChatGPT starts to feed on its own writing? Vox.com. Retrieved from: https://www.vox.com/future-perfect/23674696/chatgpt-ai-creativity-originality-homogenization.

Samuel, S. (2023, September 7). Silicon Valley's vision for AI—It's religion, repackaged. Vox.com. Retrieved from: https://www.vox.com/the-highlight/23779413/silicon-valleys-ai-religion-transhumanism-longtermism-ea.

Toonkel, J., & Krouse, S. (2023, April 4). Who owns SpongeBob? AI shakes Hollywood's creative foundation. *Wall Street Journal*. Retrieved from: https://www.wsj.com/articles/ai-chatgpt-hollywood-intellectual-property-spongebob-81fd5d15?mod=hp_lead_pos10&mod=hp_lead_pos10.

Usher, N. (2023, May 4). Professors are grappling with an excruciating assignment. Slate.com. Retrieved from: https://slate.com/technology/2023/05/chatgpt-ai-doom-college-essay.html.

Wong, A. (2023, April 3). Paparazzi photos were the scourge of celebrities—Now, it's AI. *Wall Street Journal*. Retrieved from: https://www.wsj.com/articles/ai-photos-pope-francis-celebrities-dfb61f1d.

References for *AI in College—Enthusiasts*

Balasubramanian, S. (2023, September 4). Bayer is rapidly expanding its footprint with artificial intelligence. *Forbes*. Retrieved from: https://www.forbes.com/sites/saibala/2023/09/04/bayer-is-rapidly-expanding-its-footprint-with-artificial-intelligence/?sh=43eb6dd4df85.

Cook, J. (2023, July 19). 7 ChatGPT prompts for writing better content. *Forbes*. Retrieved from: https://www.forbes.com/sites/jodiecook/2023/07/19/7-chatgpt-prompts-for-writing-better-content/?sh=475c7e302952.

Kelly, R. (2023, April 26). More than half of students will use AI writing tools even if prohibited by their institution. Campustechnology.com. Retrieved from: https://campustechnology.com/articles/2023/04/26/more-than-half-of-students-will-use-ai-writing-tools-even-if-prohibited-by-their-institution.aspx#:~:text=In%20a%20recent%20survey%20by,by%20their%20instructor%20or%20institution.

Meet Ernie, China's answer to ChatGPT. (2023, September 9). Economist.com. Retrieved from:https://www.economist.com/business/2023/09/03/meet-ernie-chinas-answer-to-chatgpt.

Noah, A. (2022, October 25). Best AI writers for students—A comprehensive list. Becominghuman.ai. Retrieved from: https://becominghuman.ai/best-ai-writers-for-students-a-comprehensive-list-8ceefc2695e2.

Robinson, B. (2023, September 2). Workers taking wellness into their own hands using AI-backed mental health. *Forbes*. Retrieved from: https://www.forbes.com/sites/bryanrobinson/2023/09/02/workers-taking-wellness-into-their-own-hands-using-ai-backed-mental-health/?sh=3960e7e25ee4.

Rubio-Licht, N. (2022, December 12). At UCLA, professors see "exciting opportunities" in AI writing tools. Dot.la. Retrieved from: https://dot.la/students-using-ai-write-essays-2658944983.html.

Shen-Berro, J. (2023, January 6). New York City schools blocked ChatGPT—Here's what other large districts are doing. Chalkbeat.org. Retrieved from: https://www.chalkbeat.org/2023/1/6/23543039/chatgpt-school-districts-ban-block-artificial-intelligence-open-ai.

References for *AI in College—Skeptics*

Bowman, E. (2023, January 9). A college student created an app that can tell whether AI wrote an essay. Npr.org. Retrieved from: https://www.npr.org/2023/01/09/1147549845/gptzero-ai-chatgpt-edward-tian-plagiarism.

Reich, R. (2022, November 28). Now AI can write students' essays for them, will everyone become a cheat. *Guardian*. Retrieved from: https://www.theguardian.com/commentisfree/2022/nov/28/ai-students-essays-cheat-teachers-plagiarism-tech.

Turnitin, LLC. (2023). Turnitin's AI writing detection available now. Author. Retrieved from: https://www.turnitin.com/solutions/ai-writing.

References for *AI at School—Introduction*

Cohen, G. (2023, September 11). Doubling up on classrooms, using online teachers and turning to support staff: How schools are dealing with the ongoing teacher shortage. Cnn.com. Retrieved from: https://www.cnn.com/2023/09/11/us/ongoing-teacher-shortage-creative-solutions/index.html.

Coldewey, D. (2023, August 31). OpenAI angles to put ChatGPT in classrooms with special tutor prompts. Techcrunch.com. Retrieved from: https://techcrunch.com/2023/08/31/openai-angles-to-put-chatgpt-in-classrooms-with-special-tutor-prompts.

Donohue, C. (ed.). (2020). *Exploring key issues in early childhood and technology: Evolving perspectives and innovative approaches*. New York City. Routledge.

Kewalramani, S., Palaiologou, I., & Dardanou, M. (2023). *The integration of internet of toys in early childhood education: research from Australia England and Norway*. New York City. Routledge.

Lonas, L. (2023, September 3). Facing mounting challenges, schools embrace the 4-day week. Thehill.com. Retrieved from: https://thehill.com/homenews/education/4179739-facing-mounting-challenges-schools-embrace-the-4-day-week.

References for *AI at School—Enthusiasts*

Herman, D. (2023, August). High-school English needed a makeover before ChatGPT. *Atlantic*. Retrieved from: https://www.theatlantic.com/technology/archive/2023/08/chatgpt-rebirth-high-school-english/675189.

Roose, K. (2023, January 12). Don't ban ChatGPT in schools—Teach with it. *New York Times*. Retrieved from: https://www.nytimes.com/2023/01/12/technology/chatgpt-schools-teachers.html?auth=login-google1tap&login=google1tap.

Rosenblatt, K. (2023, May 18). New York City public schools remove ChatGPT ban. Nbcnews.com. Retrieved from: https://www.nbcnews.com/tech/chatgpt-ban-dropped-new-york-city-public-schools-rcna85089.

Sinha, S. (2023, June 22). New *Google for Education* tools for how you teach, learn and manage. Blog.google. Retrieved from: https://blog.google/outreach-initiatives/education/google-for-education-iste-2023.

References for *AI at School—Skeptics*

Castillo, E. (2023, March 27). Banned Chat GPT and similar AI tools. Bestcolleges.com. Retrieved from: https://www.bestcolleges.com/news/schools-colleges-banned-chat-gpt-similar-ai-tools/#:~:text=The%20most%20notable%20K%2D12,on%20content%20safety%20and%20accuracy.

Jimenez, K. (2023, January 30). "This shouldn't be a surprise"—The education community shares mixed reactions to ChatGPT. *USA TODAY*. Retrieved from: https://www.usatoday.com/story/news/education/2023/01/30/chatgpt-going-banned-teachers-sound-alarm-new-ai-tech/11069593002.

Johnson, A. (2023, January 18). ChatGPT In schools: Here's where it's banned—And how It could potentially help Students. *Forbes*. https://www.forbes.com/sites/ariannajohnson/2023/01/18/chatgpt-in-schools-heres-where-its-banned-and-how-it-could-potentially-help-students/?sh=1046c8746e2c.

Kuhns-Boyle, E. (2023, May). ChatGPT and essay writing. *Education Week*. Retrieved from: https://www.edweek.org/technology/opinion-how-teachers-are-using-artificial-intelligence-in-classes-today/2023/05.

Nguyen, N. (2023, May 7). Forget ChatGPT—These are the best AI-powered apps. *Wall Street Journal*. Retrieved from: https://www.wsj.com/articles/forget-chatgpt-these-are-the-best-ai-powered-apps-d927d0bf.

Nguyen, N. (2023, August 27). Chromebooks were once a good deal for schools—Now they're becoming e-waste. *Wall Street Journal*. Retrieved from: https://www.wsj.com/tech/personal-tech/chromebooks-were-once-a-good-deal-for-schools-now-theyre-becoming-e-waste-dc93833b.

REFERENCES FOR CHAPTER 8

References for *Chapter 8 Epigraphs*

Diesel Technology Forum. (2023). School buses. Author. Retrieved from: https://dieselforum.org/school-buses#:~:text=Diesel%20powers%20over%2091%25%20of,low%20acquisition%20and%20operating%20costs.

Enviornmental Law and Policy Center. (2023). Accelerating rollout of electric school buses. Author. Retrieved from: https://elpc.org/projects/electric-school-buses-safe-ride-for-kids.

Lauzzana, E.—*quoted by* Kokai, M. (2023, May 25). Bad news about electric school buses. Johnlocke.org. Retrieved from: https://www.johnlocke.org/bad-news-about-electric-school-buses.

Sanchez, A.—*quoted by* St. John, A. (2024, February 24). Tired of diesel fumes, these moms are pushing for electric school buses. Retrieved from: Apnews.com. https://apnews.com/article/electric-school-buses-diesel-exhaust-environmental-justice-4263455c7d55e34acd6f35dceb6db7c0.

Thomasbuiltbuses Company. (2023). Correcting diesel myths. Thomasbuiltbuses.com. Retrieved from: https://thomasbuiltbuses.com/school-buses/diesel.

Vermont Energy Investment Corporation. (2023). What if you could reduce costs and increase reliability through electric school buses? Author. Retrieved from: https://www.veic.org/clients-results/case-studies/ma-pilot-program-shows-electric-school-buses-can-cut-ghg-emissions-in-half.

References for *Auto Logistics—Introduction*

Felton, R. (2023a, May 20). Auto dealers finally have cars to sell again. *Wall Street Journal*. Retrieved from: https://www.wsj.com/articles/auto-dealers-finally-have-cars-to-sell-again-6ecff886.

Felton, R. (2023b, July 28). 5 Ways that buying a car has drastically changed. *Wall Street Journal*. Retrieved from: https://www.wsj.com/articles/5-ways-buying-car-changed-pandemic-643cb2c0.

Jenkins, H. W. (2023, June 2). Car shopping ain't broke, so the FTC will fix it. *Wall Street Journal*. Retrieved from: https://www.wsj.com/articles/car-shopping-aint-broke-so-the-ftc-will-fix-it-lina-khan-auto-sales-dealership-consumer-driver-5ee75129.

References for *Auto Logistics—Enthusiasts*

Wilmot, S. (2022, July 29). Car makers are churning out profits—From the passenger seat. *Wall Street Journal*. Retrieved from: https://www.wsj.com/articles/car-makers-are-churning-out-profitsfrom-the-passenger-seat-11659098251.

References for *Auto Logistics—Skeptics*

Eisen, B. (2023, April 23). Car dealer markups helped drive inflation, study finds. *Wall Street Journal*. Retrieved from: https://www.wsj.com/articles/car-dealer-markups-helped-drive-inflation-study-finds-7c1d5a2d.

Naughton, N. (2021, September 11). Everything must go! The American car dealership is for sale. *Wall Street Journal*. Retrieved from: https://www.wsj.com/articles/everything-must-go-the-american-car-dealership-is-for-sale-11631332812.

Welch, D., & Naughton, K. (2023, February 13). New cars are only for the rich now as automakers rake in profits: The shift to EVs will make things worse. Bloomberg.com. Retrieved from: https://www.bloomberg.com/news/features/2023-02-14/new-car-prices-are-so-high-only-rich-americans-can-afford-them.

References for *School Bus Logistics—Introduction*

Bill to make Florida schools start later becomes law. (2023, May 20). *Florida Times-Union*. Retrieved from: https://jacksonville-fl.newsmemory.com/?publink=1b1ea91ca_134ab9c.

Bird Bus Sales Company. (2023). Blue bird school buses. Birdbussales. Retrieved from: https://www.birdbussales.com/blue-bird-school-buses.

Blanco, S. (2023, May 6). You're about to see way more electric school buses—Here's why. Caranddriver.com. Retrieved from: https://www.caranddriver.com/news/a43795823/electric-school-buses-latest-details.

Change in school start times in Florida raises questions. (2023, May 23). *Florida Times-Union*. Retrieved from: https://jacksonville-fl.newsmemory.com/?publink=027fc09c7_134ab9f.

Goñi-Lessan, A. (2023, March 11). Bill would require later school start times for teens. *Florida-Times Union*. Retrieved from: https://jacksonville-fl.newsmemory.com/?publink=19d2be145_134aacb.

Shahan, Z. (2023, July17). Blue Bird electric school bus gets better. Retrieved from: https://cleantechnica.com/2023/07/17/blue-bird-electric-school-bus-gets-better.

Wixon, C. (2023, May 22). New law sets mandated start times for schools, but no changes are coming before 2026. Tcpalm.com. Retrieved from: https://www.tcpalm.com/story/news/education/2023/05/22/new-florida-law-mandates-a-later-start-time-for-middle-high-schools/70213593007.

References for *School Bus Logistics—Enthusiasts*

Clarke, M. (2023, July 16). Federal grants to help city of Alexandria make electric-bus history. Wjla.com. Retrieved from: https://wjla.com/news/local/federal-grants-to-help-city-of-alexandria-make-electric-bus-history-emissions-federal-transit-administration-wmata-metro-randy-clarke-fairfax-alexandria-transit-company.

Environmental Defense Fund. (2021, February). Electric school bus fact sheet. *Blogs.edf.org*. Retrieved from: *Chrome-extension://efaidnbmnnnibpcajpcglclefindmkaj/ https://blogs.edf.org/energyexchange/wp-content/blogs.dir/38/files/2021/02/ElectricSchoolBusFactSheet.pdf.*

Garcia, L. (2023, July 13). EQT bets billions on electric school buses. *Wall Street Journal*. Retrieved from: https://www.wsj.com/articles/eqt-bets-billions-on-electric-school-buses-2ac6e04a.

Muller, J. (2022, December 19). Electric school buses are practically free now. Axios.com. Retrieved from: https://www.axios.com/2022/12/19/electric-school-buses.

Propane Energy and Research Council. (2023). Every child deserves a safe, clean, and healthy ride to school. Author. Retrieved from: https://propane.com/propane-products/buses.

References for *School Bus Logistics—Skeptics*

Athans, E. (2023, July 25). Wake County parents begging for bus routes as district faces "severe" school bus driver shortage. [Video]. Abc11.com. Retrieved from: https://abc11.com/school-bus-driver-shortage-wcpss-wake-county-north-carolina/13546998.

Benish, J. (2022, July 29). Back to school with biodiesel. Retrieved from: https://stnonline.com/blogs/back-to-school-with-biodiesel.

Diesel Technology Forum. (2023). School buses. Retrieved from: https://dieselforum.org/school-buses.

DOJ weighs charging driver in 7th grader's death at school bus stop. [Video]. (2023, July 14). Nbc15.com. Retrieved from: https://www.nbc15.com/video/2023/07/14/doj-weighs-charging-driver-7th-graders-death-school-bus-stop.

Ekbatani, T. (2021, June 15). New data indicates biomass diesel reduces carbon intensity better than electric. Stnonline.com. Retrieved from: https://stnonline.com/news/new-data-indicates-biomass-diesel-reduces-carbon-intensity-better-than-electric.

Heaton, E. (2023, May 19). Gov. DeSantis signs Florida bill that changes school start times. Winknews.com. Retrieved from: https://winknews.com/2023/05/15/desantis-changes-florida-school-start-times.

Henry, M. (2023, January 4). Late buses, students stranded: Columbus school bus route changes lead to parent complaints. *Columbus Dispatch*. Retrieved from: https://www.dispatch.com/story/news/education/2023/01/04/today-is-the-first-day-of-the-new-columbus-city-schools-busing-routes/69775870007.

Rosevear, J. (2022, December 10). Electric school buses are giving kids a cleaner, but costlier, ride to class. Cnbc.com. Retrieved from: https://www.cnbc.com/2022/12/10/electric-school-buses-give-kids-a-cleaner-but-costlier-ride-.html.

REFERENCES FOR CHAPTER 9

References for *Chapter 9 Epigraphs*

Cardenas, A.—*quoted by* Holder, S. (2019, November 6). The empty promise of the clear plastic backpack. Bloomberg.com. Retrieved from: https://www.bloomberg.com/news/articles/2019-11-06/the-empty-promise-of-the-clear-plastic-backpack.

Clear Backpacks. (2023, June 19). Clear backpack policy at school: Addressing parents [sic] concerns. Author. Retrieved from: https://clear-handbags.com/blogs/news/the-clear-backpack-policy-at-school-addressing-parents-concerns.

Fusco, A.—*quoted by* Miller, K. (2023, May 10). These schools are requiring clear backpacks as "security." Yahoo.com. Retrieved from: https://www.yahoo.com/lifestyle/schools-requiring-clear-backpacks-security-155954688.html.

Geanous, J. (2023, May 6). South Florida schools will only allow clear backpacks next year for school safety. *New York Post*. Retrieved from: https://nypost.com/2023/05/06/south-florida-schools-will-only-allow-clear-backpacks-next-year.

HeFei Airscape Textile Trading. (2023). Clear advantages and disadvantages of using a clear backpack. Airscapebag.com. Retrieved from: https://airscapebag.com/advantages-and-disadvantages-of-clear-backpack.

Holder, S. (2019, November 6). The empty promise of the clear plastic backpack. Bloomberg.com. Retrieved from: https://www.bloomberg.com/news/articles/2019-11-06/the-empty-promise-of-the-clear-plastic-backpack.

Thomas, E.—*quoted by* Balingit, M., & Asbury, N. (2023, August 17). Schools afraid of gun violence are requiring clear backpacks. *Washington Post*. Retrieved from: https://www.washingtonpost.com/education/2023/08/17/school-clear-backpacks.

Trump, K. S.—*quoted by* Miller, K. (2023, May 10). These schools are requiring clear backpacks as "security." Yahoo.com. Retrieved from: https://www.yahoo.com/lifestyle/schools-requiring-clear-backpacks-security-155954688.html.

References for *Safeguarding Children on Planes—Introduction*

Gilbertson, D. (2023 February 1). Read the rules before sending your child on a flight alone. *Wall Street Journal*. Retrieved from: https://www.wsj.com/articles/unaccompanied-minor-airlines-flights-age-limit-rules-11675190209.

Harvey, L. (2023, February 17). Flights for unaccompanied minors: Comparing each airline's fees & rules. Tripswithtykes.com. Retrieved from: https://tripswithtykes.com/unaccompanied-minors-your-complete-guide-to-each-airlines-policies-fees-rules.

Hull, S. (2023, July 17). Can kids fly alone? Everything you need to know about unaccompanied minor flights. Thepointsguy.com. Retrieved from: https://thepointsguy.com/guide/unaccompanied-minor-flight-tips.

Hunter, M. (2023, November 19). Airplane etiquette: Dos and don'ts for your next flight. Apple.news. Retrieved from: https://apple.news/APed-I7vKRBuvErerjCmThA.

U.S. Department of Transportation. (2013). *When kids fly alone*. U.S. Department of Transportation Aviation Consumer Protection Division. Retrieved from: https://www.transportation.gov/sites/dot.dev/files/docs/Kids_Fly_Alone.pdf.

References for *Safeguarding Children on Planes—Enthusiasts*

Perkins E. (2022, February 7). Kids on planes: What you should know before booking a flight for unaccompanied minors. *USA TODAY*. Retrieved from: https://www.usatoday.com/story/travel/2022/02/07/unaccompanied-kids-flight/6670011001.

Press-Reynolds, K. (2023, January 23). A mom asked Twitter about the safety of sending her 6-year-old on a plane alone but it sparked a larger conversation about co-parenting. Insider.com. Retrieved from: https://www.insider.com/twitter-divorced-parents-crowdsourcing-child-advice-flying-alone-dangerous-viral-2023-1.

References for *Safeguarding Children on Planes—Skeptics*

Bodell, Y. (2023, July 18). Unaccompanied minor left alone for hours in Baltimore. Simpleflying.com. Retrieved from: https://simpleflying.com/unaccompanied-minor-left-alone-hours-baltimore.

Dean, G. (2022, August 4). A flight attendant says sickness and fatigue levels have gone "through the roof" amid the current travel chaos. Businessinsider.com. Retrieved from: https://www.businessinsider.com/travel-chaos-flight-crew-airlines-workers-sickness-fatigue-wellbeing-work-2022-8.

Koenig, D. (2016, June 23). New incidents raise worry: How to protect kids who fly alone? *Seattle Times*. Retrieved from: https://www.seattletimes.com/life/travel/new-incidents-pose-question-of-how-to-protect-kids-who-fly-alone.

Mann, J. (2022, November 6). Ex-flight attendant: Airlines lose children more than you'd think—But I help families in these dark moments. Businessinsider.com. Retrieved from: https://www.businessinsider.com/this-ex-flight-attendant-is-helping-airlines-stop-losing-children-2022-8.

Muntean, P. (2022, October 4). FAA announces rule allowing more rest for flight attendants. Cnn.com. Retrieved from: https://www.cnn.com/travel/article/faa-new-rule-flight-attendants-more-rest/index.html.

Murphy, B. (2022, August 13). American Airlines flight attendants just made a big complaint, and nobody is very happy. Inc.com. Retrieved from: https://www.inc.com/bill-murphy-jr/american-airlines-flight-attendants-just-made-a-big-complaint-nobody-is-very-happy.html.

Pilots and aviation workers are overworked and understaffed over airline chaos [Video]. (2022). *Wall Street Journal*. Retrieved from: https://youtu.be/p-N5PJx3jY8.

Rychter, T. (2021, August 8). Flight attendants' hellish summer: "I don't even feel like a human". *New York Times*. Retrieved from: https://www.nytimes.com/2021/08/26/travel/flight-attendant-burnout.html.

Steinbuch, Y. (2023, November 7). Florida mom alleges American Airlines "misplaced" kids in jail-like room for night. *New York Post*. Retrieved from: https://nypost.com/2023/11/07/news/florida-mom-alleges-american-airlines-misplaced-kids-in-jail-like-room-for-night.

Wingo, M. (2022, December 28). "A nightmare for the kids": Unaccompanied minors caught in Southwest's cancellation fiasco. Kcra.com. Retrieved from: https://www.kcra.com/article/sacramento-international-airport-minors-southwest-flight-cancellation-dec-28/42358116#.

References for *Safeguarding Children at School—Introduction*

ACLU of Florida. (2023). What does the "Marjory Stoneman Douglas High School Public Safety Act" mean for students? Author. Retrieved from: https://www.aclufl.org/en/what-does-marjory-stoneman-douglas-high-school-public-safety-act-mean-students.

Berlatsky, N. (ed.). (2016). *School safety*. Farmington Hills, MI: Greenhaven.

Broward County Public Schools continues investigation into the Marjory Stoneman Douglas High School tragedy. (2022). Broward County Public Schools. Retrieved from: https://www.browardschools.com/site/default.aspx.

Carter, S. (2023, June 14). Are clear backpacks the answer to stopping another school shooting? *Dallas Observer*. Retrieved from: https://www.dallasobserver.com/news/dallas-isd-clear-backpack-requirement-questioned-by-education-experts-16800960.

Galicza, N. (2022, July 21). Palm Beach schools approve security system, panic buttons. *South Florida Sun-Sentinel*. Retrieved from: https://www.govtech.com/education/k-12/palm-beach-schools-approve-security-system-panic-buttons.

Giordano, G. (2022). *Parents and school violence: Answers that reveal essential steps for improving schools*. Lanham, MD: Rowman & Littlefield Education.

Governor Ron DeSantis signs HB 1421, *Improving School Safety in Florida*. (2022, June 7). Flgov.com. Retrieved from: https://www.flgov.com/2022/06/07/governor-ron-desantis-signs-hb-1421-improving-school-safety-in-florida.

Mayer, M. J., & Jimerson S. R. (2019). *School safety and violence prevention: Science. Practice, policy*. Washington, D.C.: American Psychological Association.

Perrodin, D. P. (2019). *School of errors: Rethinking school safety in America*. Lanham, MD: Rowman & Littlefield Education.

Piggott, J. (2023, November 13). City council discusses school safety, literacy, superintendent search in joint meeting with Duval school board. News4jax.com. Retrieved from: https://www.news4jax.com/news/local/2023/11/13/live-city-council-to-discuss-school-safety-literacy-superintendent-search-in-joint-meeting-with-duval-school-board.

Shapiro, E., Whitcraft, T., Winsor, M., & Zaki, Z. (2023, February 14). Parkland school shooting 5 years later: Remembering the 17 victims. Abcnews.go.com. Retrieved from: https://abcnews.go.com/US/teacher-coach14-year-freshman-florida-high-school-massacre/story?id=53092879.

U.S. National Threat Assessment Center. (2019). *School safety program*. Washington, DC: Author.

References for *Safeguarding Children at School—Enthusiasts*

Drummond, C. (2023, July 7). A CCSD school requires clear backpacks for students. News3lv.com. Retrieved from: https://news3lv.com/news/local/a-ccsd-school-requires-clear-backpacks-for-students.

Giordano, G. (2023). *Parents and Marginalized students: Answers that reveal essential steps for improving schools*. Lanham, MD: Rowman & Littlefield Education.

Habib, N. (2023, July 28). Newport News requires clear backpacks for all students. *Virginia Pilot*. Retrieved from: https://www.pilotonline.com/2023/07/28/newport-news-requires-clear-backpacks-for-all-students.

Jackson, K., & Franks, M. (2023, July 6). Lexington City Schools clear backpack policy. Wfmynews2.com. Retrieved from: https://www.wfmynews2.com/article/news/local/lexington-city-schools-clear-backpack-policy-to-enhance-school-safety/83-c13ac59a-a85b-4fb4-a721-769969b13d62.

Leach, O. (2023, August 2). School security changes involve new clear backpack rules for 2 North Texas districts. Cbsnews.com. Retrieved from: https://www.cbsnews.com/texas/news/school-security-changes-new-clear-backpack-rules-2-north-texas-districts.

Parker, D. (2023, August 30). Dorchester Co. Public Schools to get clear backpacks to ensure school safety. Wmdt.com. Retrieved from: https://www.wmdt.com/2023/08/dorchester-co-public-schools-to-get-clear-backpacks-to-ensure-school-safety.

References for *Safeguarding Children at School—Skeptics*

Harrell, G. (2022, June 28). Outrage causes Alachua County school district to reverse clear bag mandate within 24 hours. *Gainesville Sun*. Retrieved from: https://www.gainesville.com/story/news/2022/06/28/alachua-county-reverses-clear-bookbag-mandate-middle-high-schools/7759867001.

Miller, K. (2023, May 10). These schools are requiring clear backpacks as "security"—Here's what parents need to know. Yahoo.com. Retrieved from: https://www.yahoo.com/lifestyle/schools-requiring-clear-backpacks-security-155954688.html.

Payne, K. (2023, June 13). After rowdy town hall, Broward school board tilts against clear backpacks. Wlrn.org. Retrieved from: https://www.wlrn.org/education/2023-06-13/clear-backpacks-school-safety-broward-town-hall.

Sabovic, S., & Gothner, C. (2023, June 12). "This is a circus": Broward school board members get strong pushback over clear backpack plan. Retrieved from: https://www.local10.com/news/local/2023/06/12/broward-school-district-holds-town-hall-on-clear-backpacks.

Vigil, J. (2023, July 10). CCSD not requiring clear backpacks this school year. Retrieved from: https://www.fox5vegas.com/2023/07/11/ccsd-not-requiring-clear-backpacks-this-school-year.

Wolf, M. (2023, February 13). School security expert weighs in on effectiveness of clear backpacks. Retrieved from: https://www.wavy.com/news/local-news/school-security-expert-weighs-in-on-effectiveness-of-clear-backpacks.

REFERENCES FOR CHAPTER 10

References for *Chapter 10 Epigraphs*

De Cardenas, V. (2023, August 3). School voucher program expected to help 350k Florida students. Cbs12.com. Retrieved from: https://cbs12.com/news/local/school-voucher-program-helps-350000-students-florida-governor-ron-desantis-andrew-spar-florida-education-associaton-august-3-2023.

Dundon, D. (2023, April 9). Letter to the Editor: Florida, the "cultural desert". *Florida Times-Union*. Retrieved from: https://jacksonville-fl.newsmemory.com/?publink=191eceec1_134ab2d.

McKillip, M. (2023, February 2). HB1 Universal voucher program would cost billions. Education Law Center. Retrieved from: https://edlawcenter.org/news/

archives/school-funding-national/hb1-universal-voucher-program-would-cost-billions.html#:~:text=Even%20under%20conservative%20estimates%2C%20Florida,million%20in%202021%2D22).

Maxwell, S. (2023, June 2). The voucher school cash grab is on: Look for rising tuition prices. *Orlando Sentinel*. Retrieved from: https://www.orlandosentinel.com/2023/06/02/florida-vouchers-tuition-hikes-maxwell-look-for-rising-tuition-prices-commentary.

Passidomo, K.—*quoted by* Call, J. (2023, March 13). House prepares to debate vouchers: School choice plan would be biggest in US. *Florida Times-Union*. Retrieved from: https://jacksonville-fl.newsmemory.com/?publink=186a86852_134aacd.

Spar, A.—*quoted by* Izaguirre, A. (2023, March 27). DeSantis signs bill expanding school voucher program. Apnews.com. Retrieved from: https://apnews.com/article/desantis-florida-vouchers-school-d777ba50ce2c78d4f9de786826bf7253.

References for *Managing Yields at Airlines—Introduction*

Bouwer, J., Dichter, A., Krishnan, V., & Saxon, S. (2022, June 28). The six secrets of profitable airlines. Mckinsey.com. Retrieved from: https://www.mckinsey.com/industries/travel-logistics-and-infrastructure/our-insights/the-six-secrets-of-profitable-airlines.

Haqqi, T. (2023, June 12). 16 least profitable industries in the US. Yahoo.com. Retrieved from: https://finance.yahoo.com/news/16-least-profitable-industries-us-211749345.html.

Haqqi, T. (2023, June 13). Top 20 most profitable airlines in the world. Yahoo.com. Retrieved from: https://finance.yahoo.com/news/top-20-most-profitable-airlines-141424802.html#:~:text=According%20to%20the%20International%20Air,in%20the%20same%20time%20period.

Phillips, R. L. (2021). *Pricing and revenue optimization* (Second ed.). PaloAlto, CA: Stanford Business Books.

Shy, O. (2008). *How to price: A guide to pricing techniques and yield management*. Cambridge, UK: Cambridge University Press.

Vinod, B. (2022). *Evolution of yield management in the airline industry: Origins to the last frontier*. New York: Springer

What is yield management? (2023). Revfine.com. Retrieved from: https://www.revfine.com/what-is-yield-management.

Yield management in the airline industry. (2023). Ts.com. Retrieved from: https://www.tts.com/blog/yield-management-in-the-airline-industry.

References for *Managing Yields at Airlines—Enthusiasts*

Airline profitability outlook strengthens. (2023, June 5). Iata.org. Retrieved from: https://www.iata.org/en/pressroom/2023-releases/2023-06-05-01/#:~:text=Airline%20industry%20net%20profits%20are,%244.7%20billion%20(December%202022).

Plucinska, J., Shah, A., & Hepher, T. (2023, June 5). Global airlines more than double 2023 profit outlook. Reuters.com. Retrieved from: https://www.reuters.com

/business/aerospace-defense/global-airlines-more-than-double-2023-profit-outlook-2023-06-05.

Torry, H. (2023, March 12). Bowling for $418: Surge pricing creeps into restaurants, movies, gym class. *Wall Street Journal*. Retrieved from: https://www.wsj.com/articles/surge-pricing-creeps-into-restaurants-movies-gym-class-bowling-e9c4a395.

Whelan, R., & Passy, J. (2022, August 27). Disney's new pricing magic: More profit from fewer park visitors. *Wall Street Journal*. Retrieved from: https://www.wsj.com/articles/disneys-new-pricing-magic-more-profit-from-fewer-park-visitors-11661572819.

References for *Managing Yields at Airlines—Skeptics*

Holzhauer, B. (2023, May 25). Airline ticket prices are up 25%, outpacing inflation—Here are the ways you can still save. Cnbc.com. Retrieved from:https://www.cnbc.com/select/airline-ticket-prices-are-up-25-percent-why-and-how-to-save.

Kotoky, A. (2022, June 6). Why are airline tickets so expensive? Bloomberg.com. Retrieved from: https://www.bloomberg.com/news/articles/2022-06-06/sky-high-airfares-are-the-latest-headache-for-globetrotters#xj4y7vzkg.

Olson, G. (2023, April 19). Why are flights so expensive right now? Thriftytraveler.com. Retrieved from: https://thriftytraveler.com/guides/travel/why-are-flights-so-expensive-right-now.

Reed, T. (2023, July 17). American Airlines promises improved contract after United pilots unveil deal. Forbes.com. Retrieved from https://www.forbes.com/sites/tedreed/2023/07/17/american-pilots-say-united-pilots-got-a-better-deal/?sh=7c00a9f36603.

Schlappig, B. (2023, July 22). United Airlines pilots getting huge raises worth $10 billion. Onemileatatime.com. Retrieved from: https://onemileatatime.com/news/united-airlines-pilots-contract.

References for *Managing Yields at Schools—Introduction*

Bierman, N. (2023, April 21). Texas school voucher fight is a test of the power of "anti-woke" rhetoric. *Los Angeles Times*. Retrieved from: https://www.latimes.com/politics/story/2023-04-21/texas-school-voucher-fight-woke-abbott.

Bush, J. (2023, February 3). School choice is sweeping the nation from Florida to Utah. *Wall Street Journal*. Retrieved from: https://www.wsj.com/articles/school-choice-is-sweeping-the-nation-from-florida-to-utah-jeb-bush-education-learning-students-children-parents-11675435984.

Call, J. (2023, February 23). School choice bill advances in Senate: Proposal would expand scholarship eligibility. *Florida Times-Union*. Retrieved from: https://jacksonville-fl.newsmemory.com/?publink=101c6dd19_134aa73.

Durrani, A. (2023, April 14). What school choice is and how it works. Usnews.com. Retrieved from: https://www.usnews.com/education/k12/articles/what-school-choice-is-and-how-it-works.

House OKs bill to require public, charter schools to share tax funds. (2023, April 28). *Florida Times-Union*. Retrieved from: https://jacksonville-fl.newsmemory.com/?publink=3584c5c01_134ab40.

Jackson, A. (2015, August 7). We fact-checked Jeb Bush's claim that he launched America's first-ever statewide voucher program. Businessinsider.com. Retrieved from: https://www.businessinsider.com/did-jeb-bush-pass-the-first-school-voucher-program-in-the-nation-2015-8.

Lakeland Mom. (2023). 6 scholarship programs that can help you pay for private school, reading help, and special needs services in Florida. Lakelandmom.com. Retrieved from: lakelandmom.com. https://lakelandmom.com/florida-scholarship-programs.

Pandemic, culture wars revive "school choice" policy push. (2023, January 27). Journalrecord.com. Retrieved from: https://journalrecord.com/2023/01/27/pandemic-culture-wars-revive-school-choice-policy-push.

Passidomo, K. (2023, March 27). Historic school choice, parental empowerment legislation signed into law. Florida Senate. Retrieved from: https://flsenate.gov/Media/PressRelease/Show/4430.

Wall Street Journal Editorial Board. (2023, July 20). The post-pandemic teaching loss. *Wall Street Journal*. Retrieved from: https://www.wsj.com/articles/center-on-reinventing-public-education-report-teachers-education-pandemic-learning-loss-a28e7e7e?mod=hp_opin_pos_4#cxrecs_s.

References for *Managing Yields at Schools—Enthusiasts*

Cortez, M. (2024, March 5). Applications for Utah's inaugural K-12 voucher program have already eclipsed number of available scholarships. *Deseret News*. Retrieved from: https://www.deseret.com/utah/2024/03/05/utah-voucher-scholarship-fits-all-legislature.

DeAngelis, C. (2022, December 16). The little red schoolhouse could do with a little competition. *Wall Street Journal*. Retrieved from: https://www.wsj.com/articles/school-competition-savings-account-rural-district-private-choice-charter-florida-teachers-union-achievement-education-gap-11671218190.

Goñi-Lessan, A. (2023, March 18). Voucher 18 March 2023 bill moving quickly to approval: Advocates for public schools "fear the worst." *Florida Times-Union*. Retrieved from: https://jacksonville-fl.newsmemory.com/?publink=1bf6cb894_134aad2.

Goñi-Lessan, A. (2023, July 30). Demand rising for vouchers: New law creates record number of applications. *Florida Times-Union*. Retrieved from: https://jacksonville-fl.newsmemory.com/?publink=1c3e7d118_134ac6e.

Jimenez, K. (2023, February 2). School choice remains popular following COVID closures. Yahoo.com. Retrieved from: https://autos.yahoo.com/autos/school-choice-still-parents-minds-100004641.html.

Lavertu, S., & Tran, L. (2022, September 28). For-profit charter schools: An evaluation of their spending and outcomes. Fordham Institute. Retrieved from: https://fordhaminstitute.org/national/research/for-profit-charter-schools-evaluation

-spending-outcomes#:~:text=%5B3%5D%20Only%2012%20percent%20of,Florida%2C%20Michigan%2C%20and%20Ohio.
Sullivan, K. (2019, January 16). Are charter schools for profit? National Alliance for Public Charter Schools. Retrieved from: https://www.publiccharters.org/latest-news/2019/01/16/are-charter-schools-profit.
Wall Street Journal Editorial Board. (2023a, January 5). Florida's education model spreads. *Wall Street Journal.* Retrieved from: https://www.wsj.com/articles/floridas-education-model-spreads-11672962041.
Wall Street Journal Editorial Board. (2023b, January 22). Iowa's school choice comeback. *Wall Street Journal.* Retrieved from: https://www.wsj.com/articles/iowas-school-choice-comeback-kim-reynolds-education-savings-accounts-bill-11674338524.
Wall Street Journal Editorial Board. (2023c, January 27). The school choice drive accelerates. *Wall Street Journal.* Retrieved from: https://www.wsj.com/articles/utah-school-choice-bill-iowa-education-savings-accounts-kim-reynolds-spencer-cox-11674860799?mod=hp_opin_pos_6#cxrecs_s.
Wall Street Journal Editorial Board. (2023d, April 2). Georgia's school choice setback. *Wall Street Journal.* Retrieved from: https://www.wsj.com/articles/georgia-school-choice-esa-bill-house-republicans-vote-brian-kemp-1627ebd7.
Wall Street Journal Editorial Board.(2023e, May 26). The Illinois scholarship scandal. *Wall Street Journal.* Retrieved from: https://www.wsj.com/articles/illinois-democrats-invest-in-kids-scholarship-program-school-choice-emanuel-chris-welch-don-harmon-teachers-unions-9b5b3933.
Wall Street Journal Editorial Board. (2023f, July 13). The teachers union chokepoint against charter schools. *Wall Street Journal.* Retrieved from: https://www.wsj.com/articles/united-federation-of-teachers-lawsuit-new-york-success-academy-co-location-charters-lyle-frank-fa8c6f02.
Wall Street Journal Editorial Board. (2023g, July 16). More dollars follow Ohio students. *Wall Street Journal.* Retrieved from: https://www.wsj.com/articles/ohio-school-choice-vouchers-charter-schools-mike-dewine-383f5eb3.

References for *Managing Yields at Schools—Skeptics*

Cowen, J. (2023, April 19). How school voucher programs hurt students. *Time.* Retrieved from: https://time.com/6272666/school-voucher-programs-hurt-students.
Erney, P. (2023, April 9). Former educator: DeSantis' impact on education as dangerous as dreaded citrus disease. *Florida Times-Union.* Retrieved from: https://www.jacksonville.com/story/opinion/columns/guest/2023/04/09/florida-governors-impact-on-education-as-dangerous-as-citrus-canker/70088044007.
Riley, J. L. (2022, December 13). Charter schools' success makes them a political target. *Wall Street Journal.* Retrieved from: https://www.wsj.com/articles/charter-schools-success-makes-them-a-political-target-supreme-court-dress-code-lawsuit-education-aclu-teachers-unions-11670968061.
Wall Street Journal Editorial Board. (2021, July 23). Congress beats up charter schools. *Wall Street Journal.* Retrieved from:https://www.wsj.com/articles/congress

-democrats-house-bill-rosa-delauro-charter-schools-11627075560?mod=hp_opin_pos_3.

Wall Street Journal Editorial Board. (2023a, March 24). Tallahassee expands its ESA options, but a vote will be close in Atlanta. *Wall Street Journal.* Retrieved from: https://www.wsj.com/articles/florida-education-savings-accounts-georgia-school-choice-ron-desantis-brian-kemp-8f8c689a?mod=hp_opin_pos_6#cxrecs_s.

Wall Street Journal Editorial Board. (2023b, July 6). Josh Shapiro's school choice sellout. *Wall Street Journal.* Retrieved from: https://www.wsj.com/articles/josh-shapiro-school-choice-vouchers-veto-matthew-bradford-kim-ward-joe-pittman-pennsylvania-6707d3b9.

Wall Street Journal Editorial Board. (2023c, August 2). The teachers union counterattack. *Wall Street Journal.* Retrieved from: https://www.wsj.com/articles/nebraska-teachers-union-support-our-schools-school-choice-scholarships-nevada-joe-lombardo-1e8450ef.

REFERENCES FOR CHAPTER 11

References for *Chapter 11 Epigraphs*

Block, J.—*quoted in* Court to reconsider Connecticut's transgender athlete policy. (2023, February 14). Nbcnews.com. Retrieved from: https://www.nbcnews.com/nbc-out/out-news/court-reconsider-connecticuts-transgender-athlete-policy-rcna70681.

Collins, M. (2023, September 29). Why male athletes who identify as transgender should not compete in women's sports. Adflegal.org. Retrieved from: https://adflegal.org/article/why-male-athletes-who-identify-transgender-should-not-compete-womens-sports.

Kiefer, C.—*quoted in* Court to reconsider Connecticut's transgender athlete policy. (2023, February 14). Nbcnews.com. Retrieved from: https://www.nbcnews.com/nbc-out/out-news/court-reconsider-connecticuts-transgender-athlete-policy-rcna70681.

Modrovsky, L. (2022, May 12). Transgender athletes—Participation, equity and competition. *National Federation of State High School Associations.* Retrieved from: https://www.nfhs.org/articles/transgender-athletes-participation-equity-and-competition.

Schlott, R. (2023, June 1). "Fastest girl in Connecticut" Chelsea Mitchell suing state after losing to trans athletes. *New York Post.* Retrieved from: https://nypost.com/2023/05/31/runner-chelsea-mitchell-who-lost-to-trans-athletes-this-is-about-fairness.

Yearwood, A.—*quoted by* Dwyer, D. (2019, June 20). "I am a girl and I am a runner": Transgender athletes respond to the discrimination complaint in Connecticut. Boston.com. Retrieved from: https://www.boston.com/news/high-school-sports/2019/06/20/connecticut-high-school-track-transgender-athletes-respond-discrimination-complaint.

References for *Adult Rowing—Introduction*

Davis, C. (2023, February 4). USRowing's new gender-identity policy sparks controversy. Rowingnews.com. Retrieved from: https://www.rowingnews.com/2023/02/04/usrowings-new-gender-identity-policy-sparks-controversy/.

Sales, D. (2023, May 12). Now trans clash engulfs women's rowing as coach calls for the sport to follow World Athletics in banning biological males from competing in events—amid claims umpires at regattas cannot question gender of competitors. Dailymail.com. Retrieved from: https://www.dailymail.co.uk/news/article-12076891/Now-trans-clash-engulfs-womens-rowing-coach-calls-sport-follow-World-Athletics.html.

Sport timeline: How did we get here? (2022, July 12). Fairplayforwomen.com. Retrieved from: https://fairplayforwomen.com/sport-timeline-how-did-we-get-here.

USRowing. (2023). About us. Usrowing.org. Retrieved from: https://usrowing.org/sports/2016/5/19/805_132107059777909513.aspx?id=5.

USRowing. (2023). *Local Organizational Committee [LOC] Guidance Manual.* Usrowing.org. Retrieved from: *https://usrowing.org/documents/2023/2/15/Rules_Of_Rowing_2023_FINAL_PDF.pdf.*

USRowing. (2023). *Referee Procedures Manual.* Usrowing.org. Retrieved from: *https://usrowing.org/documents/2016/6/2//Referee_Training_Manual.pdf?id=68.*

USRowing. (2023). *Rules of Rowing.* Usrowing.org. Retrieved from: *https://usrowing.org/documents/2023/2/15/Rules_Of_Rowing_2023_FINAL_PDF.pdf.*

References for *Adult Rowing—Enthusiasts*

Transgender Rowers Association (tra.united). (2023, September). Author. Instagram.com. Retrieved from: https://www.instagram.com/tra.united/?hl=en.

USRowing. (2023, February 21). Statement on updates to world rowing's gender eligibility standards. Usrowing.org. Retrieved from: https://usrowing.org/news/2023/2/21/general-statement-on-updates-to-world-rowings-gender-eligibility-standards.aspx.

World rowing adopts tighter rules for transgender women athletes. (2023, March 15). Worldrowing.com. Retrieved from: https://worldrowing.com/2023/03/15/world-rowing-adopts-tighter-rules-for-transgender-women-athletes.

References for *Adult Rowing—Skeptics*

How transgender inclusion leads to female exclusion. (2022, April 14). Fairplayforwomen.com. Retrieved from: https://fairplayforwomen.com/transgender-inclusion-is-already-harming-uk-females-in-sport.

Ingle, S. (2022, October 5). British Rowing chief urges World Rowing to change its transgender policy. *Guardian.* Retrieved from: https://www.theguardian.com/sport/2022/oct/05/british-rowing-chief-urges-world-rowing-to-change-its-transgender-policy.

O'Connor, M. I. (2023, February 2). Sex difference—USRowing transgender policy. Rowingnews.com. Retrieved from: https://www.rowingnews.com/wp-content/uploads/2023/02/Sex-Difference-USRowing-Transgender-Policy-1.22.2023-with-references-49.pdf.

O'Connor, M. I., Simpson, A., Brown, C., Palchikoff, J., McClain, V., & Spratlen P. (2023, February 2). USRowing destroying fairness for females: Sex drives performance. Newsweek.com. Retrieved from: https://www.newsweek.com/usrowing-denies-fairness-female-athletes-opinion-1777151.

Progress report on the fight to restore fairness in female sport. (2022, December 27). Fairplayforwomen.com. Retrieved from: https://fairplayforwomen.com/a-progress-report-on-the-fight-to-restore-fairness-in-female-sport.

Rowing policies make no sense. (2022, December 28). Fairplayforwomen.com. Retrieved from: https://fairplayforwomen.com/rowing-policies-make-no-sense.

Smith, K. (2023, February 9). Female rowers object to US transgender policy. Binary.org. Retrieved from: https://www.binary.org.au/female_rowers_object_to_us_transgender_policy.

Woodyatt, A. (2023, February 4). UK rowing body bans transgender women from competing in women's events. Cnn.com. Retrieved from: https://www.cnn.com/2023/08/04/sport/transgender-women-british-rowing-intl-scli-spt-gbr/index.html.

References for *High School Track—Introduction*

Barnes, K. (2023, August 24). Transgender athlete laws by state: Legislation, science, more. ESPN.com. Retrieved from: https://www.espn.com/espn/story/_/id/38209262/transgender-athlete-laws-state-legislation-science.

Biden, J. (2021). Executive orders on diversity, equity, inclusion and accessibility. U.S. Office of Civil Rights. Retrieved from: https://www.commerce.gov/cr/programs-and-services/executive-orders-diversity-equity-inclusion-and-accessibility.

Connecticut General Statute. § 46a-64 (2023, July 1). Discriminatory public accommodations practices prohibited. Casetext.com. Retrieved from: https://casetext.com/statute/general-statutes-of-connecticut/title-46a-human-rights/chapter-814c-human-rights-and-opportunities/part-ii-discriminatory-practices/section-46a-64-formerly-sec-53-35-discriminatory-public-accommodations-practices-prohibited-penalty.

Giordano, G. (2023). *Parents and marginalized students: Essential steps for parents to improve schools.* Lanham, MD: Rowman & Littlefield

Iowa High School Athletic Association. (2022, August 17). IHSAA Handbook 2022—23. Author. Retrieved from: https://www.iahsaa.org/handbook.

National Federation of State High School Associations. (2023). Track & field rules book 2024. Author. Retrieved from: https://www.nfhs.com/p-1398-2024-track-field-rules-book.aspx.

References for *High School Track—Enthusiasts*

Ortega, R. P. (2023, April 4). World Athletics banned transgender women from competing— Does science support the rule? Science.org. Retrieved from: https://www.science.org/content/article/world-athletics-banned-transgender-women-competing-does-science-support-rule.

Petrovic, P. (2023, October 6). Wisconsin's transgender bill hearings were full of misinformation: Here are the facts.Wisconsinwatch.org. Retrieved from: https://wisconsinwatch.org/2023/10/wisconsin-transgender-bill-hearings-misinformation.

U.S. Department of Education. (2023, April 6). Fact Sheet: U.S. Department of Education's proposed change to its Title IX regulations on students' eligibility for athletic teams. Author. Retrieved from: https://www.ed.gov/news/press-releases/fact-sheet-us-department-educations-proposed-change-its-title-ix-regulations-students-eligibility-athletic-teams.

References for *High School Track—Skeptics*

Block, M. (2022, June 29). Americans are deeply divided on transgender rights, a poll shows. Npr.org. Retrieved from: https://www.npr.org/2022/06/29/1107484965/transgender-athletes-trans-rights-gender-transition-poll.

Barnes, K. (2021, September 1). Young transgender athletes caught in middle of states' debates. Espn.com. Retrieved from: https://www.espn.com/espn/story/_/id/32115820/young-transgender-athletes-caught-middle-states-debates.

Camera, L. (2023, June 13). More Americans say transgender athletes should only play for teams that match gender at birth. Usnews.com. Retrieved from: https://www.usnews.com/news/national-news/articles/2023-06-13/more-americans-say-transgender-athletes-should-only-play-for-teams-that-match-gender-at-birth.

Court to reconsider Connecticut's transgender athlete policy. (2023, February 14). Nbcnews.com. Retrieved from: https://www.nbcnews.com/nbc-out/out-news/court-reconsider-connecticuts-transgender-athlete-policy-rcna70681.

Kim, J. (2023, March 24). Transgender track and field athletes can't compete in women's international events. Npr.org. Retrieved from: https://www.npr.org/2023/03/24/1165795462/transgender-track-and-field-athletes-cant-compete-in-womens-international-events.

Kornick, L. (2023, October 5). Outrage over high school trans runner rising to 4th in girls' division after placing 172nd in boys'. *New York Post*. Retrieved from: https://nypost.com/2023/10/05/outrage-over-high-school-trans-runner-rising-to-4th-in-girls-division-after-placing-172nd-in-the-boys.

Pollina, R. (2023, May 22). High school track star appears to give "thumbs-down" after she's pushed out of state champs by transgender competitor: "Cheated". *New York Post*. Retrieved from: https://nypost.com/2023/05/22/transgender-athlete-claims-2nd-place-in-calif-high-school-track-meet.

Ta, L. (2022, October 18). Iowa school districts in limbo on handling transgender sports ban. Axios.com. Retrieved from: https://www.axios.com/local/des-moines/2022/10/18/iowa-school-districts-limbo-handling-transgender-sports-ban.

Transgender bathroom ruling hints at athlete issue. (2023, January 5). *Florida Times-Union*. Retrieved from: https://jacksonville-fl-app.newsmemory.com/?publink=1f1adbc92_134a9fd.

Tyler, M., Katzenberger, B., & Nguyen, T. (2023, October 12). Wisconsin Assembly passes transgender sports restrictions, gender-affirming care ban. *USA TODAY*. Retrieved from: https://www.usatoday.com/story/news/nation/2023/10/12/wisconsin-assembly-passes-transgender-bans/71161009007.

REFERENCES FOR CHAPTER 12

References for *Chapter 12 Epigraphs*

Collaborative for Academic, Social, and Emotional Learning. (2023). Fundamentals of SEL. Author. Retrieved from: https://casel.org/fundamentals-of-sel.

DeSantis, R. (2022, April 18). Twitter Post. Twitter.com. Retrieved from: https://twitter.com/GovRonDeSantis/status/1516183546968297482?

Goldstein, D., & Saul, S. (2022, April 28). A Look inside the textbooks that Florida rejected. *New York Times*. Retrieved from: https://www.nytimes.com/2022/04/22/us/florida-rejected-textbooks.html.

Rufo, C.—*quoted by* Goldstein, D., & Saul, S. (2022, April 28). A look inside the textbooks that Florida rejected. *New York Times*. Retrieved from: https://www.nytimes.com/2022/04/22/us/florida-rejected-textbooks.html.

Yettick, H. (2018, September 28). Demand for Social-Emotional Learning products and services is high and expected to grow. *Education Week*. Retrieved from: https://marketbrief.edweek.org/exclusive-data/sel.

References for *Neutralizing Fat Shame—Introduction*

Healthy life bariatrics. (2023). Weight loss medications—How they work, how much they cost & how to find them cheaper. Author. Retrieved from: https://healthylifebariatrics.com/weight-loss-medication-cost.

Jones, A. (2023, May 27). N.Y.C. Mayor signs ordinance outlawing discrimination based on body size—Including weight, height. Indiatimes.com. Retrieved from: https://timesofindia.indiatimes.com/life-style/parenting/web-stories/cartoon-characters-that-teach-us-body-positivity/photostory/96709953.cms.

Shin, R. (2023, July 9). Ozempic isn't alone: A whole class of "revolutionary" weight-loss drugs is on the market—But only for the wealthy. Fortune.com. Retrieved from: https://fortune.com/well/2023/07/09/ozempic-isnt-alone-a-whole-class-of-revolutionary-weight-loss-drugs-is-on-the-market-but-only-for-the-wealthy.

McKay, B. (2023, August 14). Ozempic settles the obesity debate: It's biology over willpower. *Wall Street Journal*. Retrieved from: https://www.wsj.com/articles/weight-loss-drugs-obesity-e4bb2173.

Winkler, R., & O'Brien, S. A. (2023, August 16). How dozens of websites sell knock-off drugs, no prescription required. *Wall Street Journal*. Retrieved from: https://www.wsj.com/health/healthcare/ozempic-mounjaro-no-prescription-websites-726b3928.

References for *Neutralizing Fat Shame—Enthusiasts*

Abrams, Z. (2022, March 1). The burden of weight stigma. American Psychological Association. Retrieved from: https://www.apa.org/monitor/2022/03/news-weight-stigma.

Cartoon characters that teach us body positivity. (2023, January 26). *Times of India*. Retrieved from: //timesofindia.indiatimes.com/life-style/parenting/web-stories/cartoon-characters-that-teach-us-body-positivity/photostory/96709953.cms.

Melody Fulton, M., & Srinivasan, V. N. (2023, March 13). Obesity, stigma and discrimination. National Institute of Health. Retrieved from: https://www.ncbi.nlm.nih.gov/books/NBK554571.

Reed, B. (2023, March 10). The Whale is not a masterpiece—It's a joyless, harmful fantasy of fat squalor. *Guardian*. Retrieved from: https://www.theguardian.com/film/2023/mar/10/lindy-west-on-the-whale.

Schocket, R. (2021, Mar 20). 19 times fat characters were portrayed super, super offensively. Buzzfeed.com. Retrieved from: https://www.buzzfeed.com/ryanschocket2/antifat-portrayal-fat-characters-tv-movies.

Series and films are changing the way fat women are seen on the big (and small) screen. (2019, July 31). The-unedit.com. Retrieved from: https://www.the-unedit.com/posts/2019/7/31/these-series-and-films-are-changing-the-way-fat-women-are-seen-on-the-big-and-small-screen.

Yu, A. (2022, April 11). The unspoken weight-discrimination problem at work. Bbc.com. Retrieved from: https://www.bbc.com/worklife/article/20220411-the-unspoken-weight-discrimination-problem-at-work.

References for *Neutralizing Fat Shame—Skeptics*

Horovitz, B. (2012, October 4). Advertisers put obese people in the spotlight. *USA TODAY*. Retrieved from: https://www.usatoday.com/story/money/business/2012/10/04/obesity-overweight-ads-blue-cross-nike-subway/1600869

Mazziotta, J. (2015, December 14). Study claims plus-size models in advertising may contribute to obesity and make women more self-conscious. *People*. Retrieved from: https://people.com/health/plus-size-models-in-advertising-may-make-women-even-more-self-conscious.

Partington, L. (2023, January 5). The backlash to Gatorade featuring a plus-size yoga instructor in their new advert proves fatphobia is still very much alive and well. *Glamour*. Retrieved from: https://www.glamourmagazine.co.uk/article/jessamyn-stanley-gatorade-advert-fatphobia.

Verhoeven, B. (2023, February 10). *The Whale* producer on criticism of the film: "We just want to be honest and truthful". *Hollywood Reporter*. Retrieved from: https://www.hollywoodreporter.com/movies/movie-features/the-whale-producer-film-criticism-brendan-fraser-1235319749.

Zilber, A. (2022, August 29). Abercrombie image sparks tweetstorm over "normalizing" obesity. *New York Post*. Retrieved from: https://nypost.com/2022/08/29/abercrombie-deletes-ad-after-fury-over-normalizing-obesity.

References for *Neutralizing Math Shame—Introduction*

Anderson, Z., & Brugal, S. (2021, December 14). Moms for Liberty. *Florida Times-Union*. Retrieved from: https://jacksonville-fl-app.newsmemory.com/?publink=2e37437bb_1346032.

Gross, T. (2022, April 28). How social-emotional learning became a target for Ron DeSantis and conservatives. Npr.org. Retrieved from: https://www.npr.org/2022/04/28/1095042273/ron-desantis-florida-textbooks-social-emotional-learning.

Hoffman, J. (2015, August 25). Math anxiety—A reporter knows the subject all too well. *New York Times*. Retrieved from: https://www.nytimes.com/2015/08/25/insider/math-anxiety-a-reporter-knows-the-subject-all-too-well.html.

Proulx, N., & Schulten, K. (2019, January 23). Empathy and resilience, responsibility and self-care: Resources for social and emotional learning from *The New York Times*. *New York Times*. Retrieved from: https://www.nytimes.com/2019/01/23/learning/empathy-and-resilience-responsibility-and-self-care-resources-for-social-and-emotional-learning-from-the-new-york-times.html.

Resanovich, M. (2020, May 12). SEL and math: A perfect partnership during COVID-19 school closures and beyond. Nwea.org. Retrieved from: https://www.nwea.org/blog/2020/sel-and-math-a-perfect-partnership.

Solochek, J. S. (2022, May 29). Florida embraced social-emotional learning after Parkland—Not any more. *Tampa Bay Times*. Retrieved from: https://www.tampabay.com/news/education/2022/05/29/florida-embraced-social-emotional-learning-after-parkland-not-any-more/?itm_source=parsely-api.

Wilson, S. (2015). Using critical incident technique to investigate pre-service teacher mathematics anxiety. In: Beswick, K., Muir, T., & Wells, J. (eds)., *Climbing mountains, building bridges: Proceedings of the 39th Conference of the International Group for the Psychology of Mathematics Education*. Hobart, AU.

References for *Neutralizing Math Shame—Enthusiasts*

California State Board of Education. (2023, July 12). California approves revised math framework as a step forward for equity and excellence [News Release]. https://www.cde.ca.gov/nr/ne/yr23/yr23rel54.asp.

Camera, L. (2015, September 30). Low-income students shortchanged on math curriculum. Usnews.com. Retrieved from: https://www.usnews.com/news/articles/2015/09/30/low-income-students-shortchanged-on-math-curriculum.

How school leaders can support Social-Emotional Learning (and retain teachers, too). (2022, June 14). *Education Week*. Retrieved from: https://www.edweek.org/sponsor/teachers-pay-teachers/how-school-leaders-can-support-social-emotional-learning-and-retain-teachers-too.

Inside Mathematics. (2014). Integrating social and emotional learning and the *Common Core State Standards for Mathematics*. Insidemathematics.org. Retrieved from: https://www.insidemathematics.org/sites/default/files/assets/common-core

-resources/social-emotional-learning/a__integrating_sel_and_ccssm_making_the_case.pdf.

Richards, E. (2020, February 28). Math scores stink in America. *USA TODAY.* Retrieved from: https://www.usatoday.com/story/news/education/2020/02/28/math-scores-high-school-lessons-freakonomics-pisa-algebra-geometry/4835742002.

Wong, A. (2023, March 27). Educational model wanted students "to be nice": That's controversial in Florida now under DeSantis. *USA TODAY.* Retrieved from: https://www.usatoday.com/story/news/education/2023/03/27/desantis-administrations-war-woke-targets-sel-florida/11414547002/

References for *Neutralizing Math Shame—Skeptics*

Anderson, M. (2022, September 26). How social-emotional learning became a frontline in the battle against CRT. National Public Radio. Retrieved from: https://www.npr.org/2022/09/26/1124082878/how-social-emotional-learning-became-a-frontline-in-the-battle-against-crt.

Blume, H., & Watanabe, T. (2023, July 13). California approves math overhaul to help struggling students—But will it hurt whiz kids? *Los Angeles Times.* Retrieved from: https://www.latimes.com/california/story/2023-07-12/california-math-overhaul-focuses-on-equity-amid-low-test-scores.

Bottum, F. (2023, August 18). California's weapons of math destruction. *Wall Street Journal.* Retrieved from: https://www.wsj.com/articles/californias-weapons-of-math-destruction-learning-k-12-education-curriculum-students-teachers-instructions-policy-d6f18070.

Florida Department of Education. (2020, February 7). Governor Desantis eliminates Common Core [News Release]. Author. Retrieved from: https://www.fldoe.org/newsroom/latest-news/governor-desantis-eliminates-common-core.stml#:~:text=(Benchmarks%20for%20Excellent%20Student%20Thinking,officially%20eradicated%20from%20Florida%20classrooms.

Goldstein, D., & Saul, S. (2022, April 28). A look inside the textbooks that Florida rejected. *New York Times.* Retrieved from: https://www.nytimes.com/2022/04/22/us/florida-rejected-textbooks.html.

Parents Defending Education. (2023). Social and Emotional Learning. Defendinged.org. Retrieved from: https://defendinged.org/sel.

Salaman, J. (2022, February 17). Whatever you do, experts say, "Do not call it social and emotional learning". *Hechinger Report.* Retrieved from: https://hechingerreport.org/jargon-may-have-turned-parents-against-social-and-emotional-learning.

Sandalow, M. (2023, August 4). Critics call California's new math curriculum "woke math". *San Francisco Examiner.* Retrieved from: https://www.sfexaminer.com/forum/critics-call-californias-new-mathematics-curriculum-woke/article_99a4c9ec-2fc8-11ee-a99b-5b7c6f96bda8.html.

Tyner, A. (2021, August). How to sell SEL: Parents and the politics of Social-Emotional Learning. Fordham Institute. Retrieved from: https://sel.fordhaminstitute.org.

Varn, K. (2022, July 20). At *Moms for Liberty* summit in Florida, political strategy comes with a dose of conspiracy. *Tallahassee Democrat*. Retrieved from: https://www.tallahassee.com/story/news/2022/07/20/moms-liberty-summit-tampa-florida-reveals-political-strategy/10029097002/.

Index

Academic Skills Textbooks. *See* Skills-Based Textbooks
ACLU. *See* American Civil Liberties Union

ADF. *See* Alliance Defending Freedom
ads with overweight models, 124–26, 130–34
adult rowing: enthusiasts, 113–14; introduction, 112–13; questions, 120–21; skeptics, 114–15
aerial surveillance: enthusiasts, 3; introduction, 2–3; questions, 9; skeptics, 3–4
AI. *See* Artificial Intelligence
airline boarding: enthusiasts, 25; introduction, 24–25; policies, 24–26, 28–32; questions, 30–31; skeptics, 25–26
airline investors, 106–7
airlines that accept unaccompanied minors, 93
airlines that refuse unaccompanied minors, 92–93
airline ticket prices, 102–4, 106–9
ALA. *See* American Library Association
Alliance Defending Freedom, 111
American Civil Liberties Union, 111
American Conservative, 37
American Library Association, 1

Ann Arbor Public Schools, 79
AP. *See* Associated Press
Artificial Intelligence: for homework, 69; for reading instruction, 69; chatbots, 70, 75; in College, 70–72, 75–78; in K—12 Schools, 72–78
Artificial Intelligence at school: enthusiasts, 73; epigraphs, 69; introduction, 72; questions, 77; skeptics, 73–74
Artificial Intelligence in college: enthusiasts, 71; introduction, 70–71
Associated Press, 43
audiologists, 11–15
Auto Industry Logistics, 80–82, 85–89
auto logistics: enthusiasts, 81–82; introduction, 80–81; questions, 87–88; skeptics, 82

B.E.S.T. Standards in Mathematics. *See* Florida B.E.S.T. Standards in Mathematics *Bloski* Software Company
boarding fees by airlines, 25
book bans, 1, 6–7
This Book Is Gay, 5
Broward County School Safety Policies, 91, 95–96
Broward Teachers Union, 92
Bush, George W., 53–54

California Math Framework, 128–29
California State Board of Education, 49
CASEL. *See* Collaborative for Academic, Social, and Emotional Learning
CDC. *See* Centers for Disease Control and Prevention
Centers for Disease Control and Prevention, 11–15, 17–21
chatbots, 70–78
ChatGPT, 70–72, 75–78
Chicago Mayoral Election, 33
Chicago Public Schools, 95
Chicago School X-Ray Machines, 95
Chicago's Unionized Teachers: enthusiasts, 38–39; epigraphs, 33; introduction, 37–38; questions, 41–42; skeptics, 39
Chicago Teachers Union, 33, 37–41
Children's Internet Protection Act of 2000, 62–67
Child Safety at School, 94–100
Child Safety on Flights, 92–94, 97–100
Chromebooks, 74
CIAC. *See* Connecticut Interscholastic Athletic Conference
CIPA. *See* Children's Internet Protection Act of 2000
clear backpack policies, 94–100
clear backpacks. *See* clear backpack policies
Clear Backpacks Company, 91
Collaborative for Academic, Social, and Emotional Learning, 123
College Transgender Rowers Policies. *See* Transgender Rowers Policies
Connecticut Interscholastic Athletic Conference, 115–22
Consumer Reports, 44
COVID-19 Pandemic, ix-x, 43, 47–56, 80–82, 85–89, 102–3
CPS. *See* Chicago Public Schools
CSBE. *See* California State Board of Education
CTU. *See* Chicago Teachers Union
CurrentWare Software Company, 57

Dahl, Roahl, 8
DC Metro, 34–37, 39–41
DC Metrobus, 34–37, 39–41
DC's Commuters: Enthusiasts, 36–37; Introduction, 34–36; Questions, 41; Skeptics, 37
DeSantis, Ron, 123
diesel school buses, 82–89
Diesel Technology Forum, 79
Dr. Seuss, 6
dynamic pricing, 102–4
dynamic ticket pricing. *See* airline ticket prices

earned media, 37–38
Education Law Center, 101
Education Week, 123
Edutech Global Company, 69
Electric School Buses, 82–89
electronic surveillance technology, 98
ELL. *See* English Language Learners
English language learners, 73
epigraphs: parenting feuds, 23; preface, ix; school AI feuds, 69; school athletics feuds, 111; school bus feuds, 79; school funding feuds, 101; school library feuds, 1; school masking feuds, 11; social-emotional learning feuds, 123; student safety feuds, 91; teachers union feuds, 33; testing feuds, 43; web filter feuds, 57–58
equitable grading, 50–53
ergonomic technology. *See* Artificial intelligence
error-prone instructional chatbots, 76
ESBs. *See* electric school buses
e-textbooks, 61

fare evaders in DC, 35–36
fat shame, 124–26, 130–34
FCC. *See* Federal Communications Commission
FDA. *See* US Food and Drug Administration
FEA. *See* Florida Education Association

Federal Communications Commission, 53
fight for schools organization, ix
filtering films: enthusiasts, 59–60; introduction, 58–59; questions, 66; skeptics, 60
filtering websites: enthusiasts, 63; epigraphs, 57–58; introduction, 61–62; questions, 67; Skeptics, 63–64
Florida B.E.S.T. Standards in Mathematics, 129
Florida Commissioner of Education, 11
Florida Department of Education, 49
Florida Education Association, 101, 106
Florida Governor, 123
Florida Governor Ron DeSantis. *See* DeSantis, Ron
Florida School Starting Times, 84
Florida Senate, 101, 105
Florida's Private School Vouchers, 106–9
Florida State Board of Education, 49
for-profit schools, 38
Fox News, 37

Gender Queer, 5
Gone with the Wind, 59–60, 64–67
Google Chromebooks. *See* Chromebooks

HBO. *See* HBO Max
HBO Max, 58–60, 64–67
hearing aids: enthusiasts, 14; introduction, 12–13; questions, 20; skeptics, 14–15
HeFei Airscape Textile Trading Company, 91
high school track: enthusiasts, 117; epigraphs, 111; introduction, 115–17; questions, 121–22; skeptics, 117
Homework Helper Company, 69

In Loco Parentis. *See* In Loco Parentis Policy
In Loco Parentis Policy, 26–28

International Society for Technology in Education, 69
Iowa High School Athletic Association, 116
ISTE. *See* International Society for Technology in Education

Johnson, Brandon, 39

LAUSD. *See* Los Angeles Unified School District
Law School Admissions Test, 44–47, 51–56
Lightfoot, Lori, 38–39
Local Organizational Committee [LOC] Guidance Manual, 112
Los Angeles Unified School District, 43
LSAT. *See* Law School Admissions Test

managing yields at airlines: enthusiasts, 103; introduction, 102–3; questions, 108–9; skeptics, 103–4
managing yields at schools: enthusiasts, 105; epigraphs, 101; introduction, 104–5; questions, 109; skeptics, 105–6
Marjory Stoneman Douglas High School, 95
mathematical equity, 128
mathematical excellence, 128
math shame, 126–34
Math Textbook Committees, 127–28, 132
math textbooks, 127–28
math textbook sales agents, 127–28, 131
MAX. *See* HBO Max
Microsoft Corporation, 69
Minors on Flights. *See* Child Safety on Flights

National Center for Education Statistics, 43
National Coalition Against Censorship, 57
National Federation of State High School Associations, 111, 115

National School Safety and Security Services, 91
NCAC. *See* National Coalition Against Censorship
NCES. *See* National Center for Education Statistics
NCLB. *See* No Child Left Behind Act
neutralizing fat shame: enthusiasts, 125–26; introduction, 124–25; questions, 132–33; skeptics, 126
neutralizing math shame: enthusiasts, 128; epigraphs, 123; introduction, 126–27; questions, 133; skeptics, 129–30
New York City's Mayor, 125
New York Post Editorial Board, 43
New York State Board of Education, 49
NFSH. *See* National Federation of State High School Associations
No Child Left Behind Act of 2002, 53–54

Obama, Barack, 53–54
obesophobia, 125–26
Olympics, 112, 115
Open Access Internet Searches, 58, 65–67
OpenAI Firm, 70, 75
OTC Hearing Aids. *See* Over the Counter Hearing Aids
over-filtering school computers, 63–64
over the counter hearing aids, 11–15, 17–21

paid media, 37–38
parenting: enthusiasts, 27; epigraphs, 23; introduction, 26–27; questions, 31; skeptics, 28
Parents and Marginalized Students, ix
Parents and School Tech, ix
Parents and School Violence, ix
Parents and Textbooks, ix
PEN America, 1
Pennsylvania School Board, 23
Pew Research Center, 43

Private School Vouchers. *See* Florida's Private School Vouchers
Private Security Guards, 98
Prodigy Company, 69
profit yields, 102–3, 106–9

questions, 76–77; academic testing, 51–56; athletic regulations, 117–22; child safety, 97–100; ergonomic technology, 75–78; filtered information, 64–67; financial strategies, 106–9; health restrictions, 17–21; highly editorialized groups, 28–32; journalistic caricatures, 39–42; logistics, 85–89; social and emotional goals, 130–34; suddenly contentious issues, 7–10

Race to the Top Act of 2012, 53–54
racial bias: in California School Tests, 49; in films, 58–60, 64–67; in LSAT, 44–47, 51–56
Referee Procedures Manual, 112
RttT. *See* Race to the Top Act
Rules of Rowing, 112

safeguarding children at school: enthusiasts, 96; epigraphs, 91; introduction, 94–96; questions, 99; skeptics, 96
safeguarding children on planes: enthusiasts, 93; introduction, 92–93; questions, 98–99; skeptics, 93–94
SBA. *See* Standards-Based Assessment
scholastic surveillance: enthusiasts, 6–7; epigraphs, 1; introduction, 4–6; questions, 9–10; skeptics, 7
school budgets, 106–9
school bus logistics: enthusiasts, 85; epigraphs, 79; introduction, 82–84; questions, 88–89; skeptics, 85
school facemasks: enthusiasts, 16–17; epigraphs, 11; introduction, 15–16; questions, 20–21; skeptics, 17
school librarians, 4–10

school starting times. *See* Florida school starting times
school vouchers. *See* Florida's private school vouchers
school X-ray machines, 95, 101
Science Journal, 58
SEL. *See* Social Emotional Learning
SEL math textbooks, 127–32
SEL textbooks, 130–34
skeptic, 71–72
skills-based math textbooks, 127–34
sniffer dogs, 98
social emotional learning, 69, 116, 123
spy balloons, 2–4, 7–10
standards-based assessment, 50–53
student counselor confidentiality, 26–27
student information disclosure policies, 26–32

TCM. *See* Turner Classic Movies
testing college students: enthusiasts, 46; introduction, 44–45; Questions, 54–55; skeptics, 46–47
testing public school students: enthusiasts, 49–50; epigraphs, 43; introduction, 47–49; questions, 55; skeptics, 50–51
Thomasbuiltbuses Company, 79
Track & Field Rules Book, 115
traffic problems in DC, 34
Transgender Rowers Policies, 111–15, 117–22
Transportation Security Administration, 93
TSA. *See* Transportation Security Administration
Turner Classic Movies, 58–59

unaccompanied minor airline fees, 93, 98
under-filtering school computers, 63–64

Universal Service Administrative Company, 53
Universal Vouchers. *See* Florida's Private School Vouchers
USAC. *See* Universal Service Administrative Company
US Department of Transportation, 92–93
USDT. *See* US Department of Transportation
US Food and Drug Administration, 12
US National Security Leaders, 2–4, 7–11
US News College Rankings. See US News & World Report College Rankings
US News & World Report College Rankings, 44–47, 51–56
US Office of Education, 47–48
USRowing, 111–15, 117–22

Vermont Energy Investment Corporation, Vouchers. *See* Florida's Private School Vouchers

WA. *See* World Athletics
Wall Street Journal Editorial Board, ix, 3–4, 33, 37–41
Washington Metropolitan Area Transit Authority, 34–37, 39–41
weapon-detecting radar, 98
web filters, 57–58, 62–67
Weight-Discrimination Ordinances, 125
WMATA. *See* Washington Metropolitan Area Transit Authority
World Athletics, 116
World Cup, 112

X-Ray Machines. *See* School X-Ray Machines

zero-tolerance discipline, 26

About the Author

Gerard Giordano served recently as a professor at the University of North Florida. He has written five previous books about the impact that parents have on schools. He has published all of them with Rowman and Littlefield Education.

www.ingramcontent.com/pod-product-compliance
Lightning Source LLC
Chambersburg PA
CBHW020912020526
44114CB00039B/375